T0330157

Transforming Private Landlords

Transforming Private Landlords

Housing, Markets & Public Policy

Tony Crook

Professor of Housing Studies
University of Sheffield

Peter A. Kemp

Barnett Professor of Social Policy
University of Oxford

WILEY-BLACKWELL

A John Wiley & Sons, Ltd., Publication

Blackwell Publishing was acquired by John Wiley & Sons in February 2007. Blackwell's publishing programme has been merged with Wiley's global Scientific, Technical, and Medical business to form Wiley-Blackwell.

Registered Office
John Wiley & Sons Ltd, The Atrium, Southern Gate, Chichester, West Sussex, PO19 8SQ, United Kingdom

Editorial Office
9600 Garsington Road, Oxford, OX4 2DQ, United Kingdom
2121 State Avenue, Ames, Iowa 50014-8300, USA

For details of our global editorial offices, for customer services and for information about how to apply for permission to reuse the copyright material in this book please see our website at www.wiley.com/wiley-blackwell.

Library of Congress Cataloging-in-Publication Data

Crook, Tony, 1944–
  Transforming private landlords: housing, markets and public policy / Tony Crook and Peter A. Kemp.
    p.   cm. – (Real estate issues)
  Includes bibliographical references and index.
  ISBN 978-1-4051-8415-1 (hardback : alk. paper)   1. Rental housing–England.
2. Landlords–England.   3. Landlord and tenant–England.   I. Kemp, Peter, 1955–   II. Title.
  HD7288.85.G7C76 2011
  333.33′8–dc22

                                                        2010020466

A catalogue record for this book is available from the British Library.

Set in 10/13pt Trump Mediaeval by SPi Publisher Services, Pondicherry, India
Printed and bound in Malaysia by Vivar Printing Sdn Bhd

1   2011

Acknowledgements

Many research and other colleagues helped us with this work, including Isobel Anderson, Mark Bevan, Peter Bibby, Stuart Bowman, Ceri Bryant, Max Craglia, Ed Ferrari, Ken Gibb, John Henneberry, John Hughes, Nile Istephan, Graham Martin, David Rhodes, Julie Rugg and Cathy Sharp. We also benefited from important collaborations with colleagues then at Coopers & Lybrand (now PriceWaterhouseCoopers) especially John Hawksworth, Jim Robertson and Rosalind Rowe. The analysis and interpretation we offer in this book is of course ours alone, but the book would not have been possible without their major contributions to a large series of projects. We offer them our very grateful thanks. We also thank Jenny Crook, who compiled the list of references for this book.

We are very grateful to Mark Long of BDRC for letting us cite their private landlord survey data, to the Council of Mortgage Lenders for allowing us to reproduce their buy-to-let data, and to the Office of National Statistics for granting public access to government data on housing. Responsibility for the analysis of these data in this book rests solely with ourselves.

We were also fortunate to receive substantial funding for our work and we gratefully acknowledge the support received from the British Property Federation, the Department of the Environment, the Department of Environment Transport & the Regions, the Economic and Social Research Council, the Joseph Rowntree Foundation, The Rent Service, The Scottish Executive, Scottish Homes and the Scottish Government. The views we express in the book do not of course necessarily reflect the views of the government departments and other organisations that supported our work.

The findings from our research reported in the book come from interviews conducted with thousands of landlords in Britain. Without their willingness to participate in our research this book would not have been possible. We offer them our thanks.

Tony Crook & Peter A. Kemp
Sheffield and Oxford
March 2010

RICS Research Series Page

The Royal Institution of Chartered Surveyors is the mark of property professionalism worldwide, promoting best practice, regulation and consumer protection for business and the community. It is the home of property related knowledge and is an impartial advisor to governments and global organisations. It is committed to the promotion of research in support of the efficient and effective operation of land and property markets worldwide.

Real Estate Issues

Series Managing Editors

Stephen Brown	Head of Research, Royal Institution of Chartered Surveyors
John Henneberry	Department of Town & Regional Planning, University of Sheffield
K.W. Chau	Chair Professor, Department of Real Estate and Construction, The University of Hong Kong
Elaine Worzala	Professor, Director of the Accelerated MSRE, Edward St. John Department of Real Estate, Johns Hopkins University

Real Estate Issues is an international book series presenting the latest thinking into how real estate markets operate. The books have a strong theoretical basis – providing the underpinning for the development of new ideas.

The books are inclusive in nature, drawing both upon established techniques for real estate market analysis and on those from other academic disciplines as appropriate. The series embraces a comparative approach, allowing theory and practice to be put forward and tested for their applicability and relevance to the understanding of new situations. It does not seek to impose solutions, but rather provides a more effective means by which solutions can be found. It will not make any presumptions as to the importance of real estate markets but will uncover and present, through the clarity of the thinking, the real significance of the operation of real estate markets.

Books in the series

Greenfields, Brownfields & Housing Development
Adams & Watkins
978 0 632 0063871

Planning, Public Policy & Property Markets
Edited by Adams, Watkins & White
9781405124300

Housing & Welfare in Southern Europe
Allen, Barlow, Léal, Maloutas & Padovani
9781405103077

Markets and Institutions in Real Estate & Construction
Ball
978140510990

Building Cycles: Growth & Instability
Barras
9781405130011

Neighbourhood Renewal & Housing Markets
Edited by Beider
9781405134101

Mortgage Markets Worldwide
Ben-Shahar, Leung & Ong
9781405132107

The Cost of Land Use Decisions
Buitelaar
9781405151238

Transforming Private Landlords: Housing, Markets & Public Policy
Crook & Kemp
9781405184151

Urban Regeneration in Europe
Couch, Fraser & Percy
9780632058412

Urban Sprawl
Couch, Leontidou & Petschel-Held
9781405151238

Real Estate & the New Economy
Dixon, McAllister, Marston & Snow
9781405117784

Economics & Land Use Planning
Evans
9781405118613

Economics, Real Estate & the Supply of Land
Evans
9781405118620

Management of Privatised Housing: International Policies & Practice
Gruis, Tsenkova & Nieboer
9781405181884

Development & Developers
Guy & Henneberry
9780632058426

The Right to Buy
Jones & Murie
9781405131971

Housing Markets & Planning Policy
Jones & Watkins
9781405175203

Mass Appraisal Methods
Kauko & d'Amato
9781405180979

Economics of the Mortgage Market
Leece
9781405114615

Towers of Capital: Office Markets & International Financial Services
Lizieri
9781405156721

Making Housing More Affordable: The Role of Intermediate Tenures
Monk & Whitehead
9781405147149

Global Trends in Real Estate Finance
Newell & Sieracki
9781405151283

Housing Economics & Public Policy
O'Sullivan & Gibb
9780632064618

International Real Estate
Seabrooke, Kent & How
9781405103084

British Housebuilders
Wellings
9781405149181

Forthcoming

Urban Regeneration & Social Sustainability
Colantonio & Dixon
9781405194198

Urban Design in the Real Estate Development Process
Tiesdell & Adams
9781405192194

Real Estate Finance in the New Economic World
Tiwari & White
9781405158718

Contents

Preface

This book draws together much of the research on which we have collaborated for over two decades. We were both independently examining the operation of the private rented sector of the housing market well before we started working together in the mid 1980s. Before then, the sector's long-term decline was regarded as terminal, with no prospects of revival, and it was a part of the housing market that attracted little research. As a result, policy debates were substantially less well informed than other areas of policy. It was, in effect, an unfashionable area in which to be doing research, but despite this we were both fascinated with the ownership of the sector, the factors that shaped investment and disinvestment and how public policy influenced this. We completed PhDs in the field and continued to research and publish work on the subject.

As a consequence, when private renting became a more central part of policy debates on housing, we found ourselves in the fortunate position of being jointly commissioned to undertake a wide range of studies on the structure of the sector's ownership and how landlords responded to government initiatives after deregulation. We collaborated on a series of studies that examined how the structure of ownership changed after deregulation, as well as studies of the impact of specific policy initiatives. We also found ourselves regularly taking part in briefings and consultations with the relevant policy and practice communities in government, professional institutes and the sector's trade bodies.

We were thus in the privileged position of being able to closely observe the changing nature of contemporary landlordism during the remarkable renaissance in private renting's fortunes that occurred in the three decades after the deregulation of the sector in 1980. In this book we have drawn on our own work and that of others to provide a detailed account and interpretation of the transformation of private landlords over that period. We completed the book in early 2010 and it is from that point in time that we have looked back at the changes that have occurred.

Introduction

This book examines what has been a remarkable transformation in the fortunes of private landlordism over the last three decades in Britain. The private lettings market has turned around from being a sector in long-term decline to one which has experienced strong growth, particularly over the past decade. Since the turn of the century, billions of pounds' worth of residential housing-to-let has been acquired by private investors. Whereas in the past private landlords were relatively under-geared (Crook & Kemp, 1996a; Ball, 2006a), much of this new investment in the private rented sector has been facilitated by the provision of mortgage finance from banks and building societies. New loan products targeted at private landlords have emerged and account for a sizable share of the mortgage market. What is often now referred to as 'buy to let' regularly features in the property and personal finance pages of the newspapers (Kemp, 2004). From being almost a pariah in the 1970s, the private landlord has become, if not respected, then at least respectable once again.

Private landlords have always been important actors in housing provision, not just in Britain, but also in most other market economies. However, their contribution to housing supply declined considerably during the seven decades from the end of the First World War and especially after 1945. By the late 1970s, the private rented sector in Britain had declined to such an extent that some observers wondered whether the landlord might disappear altogether. Even if most commentators believed that the landlord's condition was not terminal, few of them thought the decline was retrievable (see Eversley, 1975; Stafford, 1976; Finnis, 1977). It was not just that letting accommodation was less profitable and more time-consuming than alternative investments; it was also that few people now wanted or needed to rent their home from a private landlord. By the late 1970s, the majority of households could afford to buy their home with a mortgage and most of the remainder wanted to rent their home from the local council, not from a private landlord. For new households, private renting had become, in effect, a 'waiting room' where they saved up for a deposit to buy their own home or accumulated sufficient 'points' to gain access to council housing (Kemp, 1988a).

Moreover, public perceptions of private landlords had deteriorated to such an extent that the leader of the Labour Party and future Prime Minister, Harold Wilson, could declare that 'rented housing is not a proper field for private profit' (cited in Cullingworth, 1979, p. 61). This view reflected the fact that private renting was an area of sharp disagreement between the two main political parties. Debates about the private rented sector had become highly polarised in the 1950s and 1960s (Kemp, 2004). Although, by the late 1970s, political debates on private renting had become more muted, that was in large measure because the sector was then such a small part of the housing market that relatively few votes were to be won or lost over it.

Nevertheless, politicians remained wary about introducing legislation that might affect the fortunes of the landlords and tenants who remained in the sector. Legislation on private renting focused on ameliorating poor physical conditions and abuses of tenancy legislation, while housing policy in the 1970s was instead focused on the two main tenures of owner-occupation and council housing. Moreover, public perceptions of the private landlord remained 'firmly associated with the image of "Rachmanism" or at best the rather seedy resident landlord Rigsby of the TV sitcom *'Rising Damp'* (Kemp & Rhodes, 1997; Kemp, 2004, p. 1). The poor conditions that were prevalent in much of the privately rented stock appeared to confirm the poor image that the private landlord had acquired. There was little, let alone up-to-date, research on private landlords and, perhaps as a result, negative media stories tended to dominate discourse about private landlordism. And although there were criticisms of the paternalist way that council housing was managed, in the 1970s good practice was seen to lie in the public sector rather than among private landlords.

Reviving the market

It is now a matter for the history books that the late 1970s and early 1980s witnessed the emergence of what the US academic Frances Fox Piven (1986) has aptly described as a 'revivalist romance' with markets: a belief that markets were efficient, responsive to market signals and gave consumers what they wanted, when they wanted it; while public providers were increasingly viewed as remote, bureaucratic, inefficient and paternalistic. In Britain the Conservative Party, under the leadership of Mrs Thatcher, returned to power in 1979, determined to 'roll back the state', release market forces and 'set the people free'. Although its programme evolved over time, it ultimately included cuts in social security benefits, legislation designed to undermine the power of the trades unions, privatisation of state assets, removal of exchange controls and deregulation of finance markets, including mortgage lending.

In housing policy, the first Thatcher government promoted new low-cost home ownership schemes, gave council tenants the right to buy their home at very substantial discounts from its market value, and curbed local authority capital spending, with the result that council house-building was drastically reduced. In addition, tentative steps were taken to reduce the regulation of private lettings in order to encourage new investment by private landlords (Crook, 1986b; Forrest & Murie, 1988; Malpass & Murie, 1999).

However, in practice, expanding home ownership and shrinking the supply of council housing were more important objectives for the first Thatcher government than reviving the private rented sector. This was perhaps not just a reflection of priorities but also of realities: after such a prolonged and substantial decline in private renting, it was perhaps unrealistic to expect a significant resurgence of investment by private landlords. In any case, the measures introduced in the 1980 Housing Act to help revive the private landlord sector were too limited to have a substantial impact on supply. Moreover, the shadow of the 1960s Rachman scandal (see Chapter 1) still hung over debates about the private rented sector, a fact which may account for the relatively modest steps towards deregulation taken by the Housing Act 1980 (Kemp, 1987a). It also helps explain why the 1980 Act introduced the 'approved landlord' scheme for organisations that wished to take advantage of the deregulation of rents on newly constructed or refurbished dwellings. In 1982 the government introduced capital allowances for these approved landlords in order to entice corporate investors back into the private rental market. The response to this incentive was weak and, in any case, the capital allowances were abolished after only two years (Kemp, 1988a).

It was not until 1988 – almost a decade after the Conservatives came to power – that Mrs Thatcher's (third) government felt able to introduce more complete deregulation in the private lettings market. By this time, a political consensus had emerged about the important role that the private rented sector could play in meeting certain housing needs, such as easy access accommodation for young and mobile households (Best *et al.*, 1992). This was in stark contrast to the partisan manner in which debates were conducted in the period from the 1950s to the 1970s. It largely reflected a shift by the Labour Party, but was one made possible by a more gradual and less doctrinaire approach to the private rented sector by the Conservatives than had been the case in the 1950s and 1960s.

Deregulation in the 1980s was intended to set the market free in order to secure an increase in the size of the sector and to modernise it. Until then, residential lettings had been dominated by small-scale and part-time landlords, a structure of housing provision that we characterised as a 'cottage industry' (Crook & Kemp, 2002). Conservative and New Labour governments during the period covered by this book believed that a more 'modern' form of landlordism based on larger corporate landlords would both create a more professionally run sector and have a better reputation than was then the case. These were thought to be essential preconditions for attracting tenants and potential funders into private renting. Deregulation was also part of a wider strategy by the Conservatives to reduce the role of local councils in the provision of rented housing and encourage the growth of alternative providers, including private landlords and housing associations.

Under the 1988 Housing Act, new private lettings were freed from rent regulation and security of tenure was substantially reduced (see Chapter 2). Not confident that these measures would generate a revival of investment by private landlords, in the 1988 Budget the Conservatives extended the Business Expansion Scheme (BES) to include, for a five-year period, new property companies providing housing to let on assured tenancies. The BES provided substantial tax breaks to individuals investing in companies set up under the scheme. As we explain in Chapter 5, the BES led to a significant, but ultimately short-lived, burst of investment in rented property.

Shortly after the passage of the 1988 Act and the introduction of the BES, the secular decline of the private rented sector came to an end. In fact, the number of rented homes began to increase, much to the surprise of government statisticians, who had assumed that the decline would continue (Down *et al.*, 1994). However, as we explain in Chapter 3, this modest revival was as much a response to the owner-occupied housing market slump and the economic recession of the early 1990s as it was to the policy innovations introduced in 1988/89 (Kemp, 2009). The nominal decline in house prices resulted in about a million homeowners having negative equity, whereby the outstanding value of their home was less than the amount of mortgage they owed to their lender (Forrest & Murie, 1994). This prompted some of the homeowners who needed to move to let their homes for the duration and rent somewhere else instead while they waited for house prices and property transactions to recover (Crook & Kemp, 1996b). Meanwhile, some of the households that might have entered the owner-occupied market as first-time buyers delayed doing so until house prices had ceased to fall. Hence, the housing slump increased both the supply of and the demand for private rented housing. This growth in the rental market provided a surge of new customers for the residential lettings and management industry.

Once the owner-occupied housing market recovery began, however, the growth of private renting faltered as 'property slump landlords' sold their former homes and bought somewhere else to live (Kemp, 2004). Faced with the prospect of a much reduced volume of business, the Association of Residential Letting Agents (ARLA) – the trade association representing much of the letting and management industry – teamed up with a panel of mortgage lenders to offer new loan products aimed at private landlords (Ball, 2006b). This initiative, which they cleverly labelled 'buy-to-let', offered mortgages at interest rates that were significantly lower than those that had previously been available to private landlords (Kemp, 2004), but required the properties bought with these loans to be managed by members of ARLA.

The buy-to-let (BTL) market rapidly expanded and soon other lenders began marketing mortgages under this label. The boom in BTL lending, which took off after the turn of the century, was facilitated by the deregulation of, and subsequent innovation in, mortgage finance, as well as by the worldwide glut of savings and lower interest rates resulting from global imbalances between creditor and debtor nations (Schwartz, 2009). It was further fuelled by the sharp rise in house prices, which continued in Britain until the autumn of 2007.

Meanwhile, following lobbying from the property industry, in 1996 the Conservative government under Prime Minister John Major introduced legislation aimed at encouraging financial institutions to invest in private lettings via a new tax vehicle known as Housing Investment Trusts (HITs). Again, this was part of a continuing attempt by policymakers to bring new, more professional and larger-scale investors into the sector. It was not just about expanding the sector, but also about transforming its ownership and management (Crook & Kemp, 2002). As we explain in Chapter 6, this initiative failed to deliver on its object, as not a single HIT was established.

A similar attempt by the Labour government to entice financial institutions into the rental market also seems to have failed. Following the example of the USA and elsewhere, Labour legislated for the introduction of Real Estate Investment Trusts (REITs). These were vehicles that were intended to make direct ownership of commercial and residential property tax-efficient for pension funds and other 'gross funds' that are not liable for tax on the income from their assets (Jones, 2007). Although many existing commercial property companies converted themselves into REITs, to date no residential property companies have done so and nor have any *de novo* residential REITs been established. We examine the reasons why not in Chapter 6.

By contrast, there has been a resurgence of small-scale investment in the sector by private individuals and couples, much of it funded by BTL mortgages and all of it undertaken without tax incentives or other subsidies. As we explain in Chapter 7, although BTL was initially fashioned by ARLA, its rapid growth was in fact part of a wider credit and property boom that occurred in many advanced economies. It was not simply a response by investors to the deregulation of the private rental market. Deregulation was introduced in 1989, but the BTL investment boom did not take off until a decade later, when the credit and property bubbles got into full swing in Britain (Kemp, 2009).

Although the BTL lending boom was brought to an abrupt end by the onset of the credit crunch in 2007/08 and the subsequent Great Recession, the market for these loans is slowly coming back to life. And although some BTL landlords had their fingers burned as a result of falling house prices and rising rent arrears, many more benefited from increasing rental yields, falling interest rates and rising demand for rental housing. With both new construction by social housing landlords and the availability of mortgage finance for sub-prime borrowers likely to be highly constrained in the post-credit-crunch era, much greater reliance will need to be placed on the private landlord to meet housing needs than has been the case for many years.

Organisation of the book

Based mainly on our own studies of private landlords, this book explores the transformation in the fortunes of private landlords in Britain since the late 1970s. In doing so, it examines the extent to which the structure of landlordism changed over that period. It also considers the impact of public policy initiatives that sought to revive the private landlord and to bring a new 'structure of housing provision' (Ball, 1986) into the private rented sector, involving property companies and financial institutions. Finally, it examines the origins and development of the BTL boom after the turn of the century.

The starting point for our narrative is government attempts both to revive the market in private renting and to create a new corporate structure of rental housing provision. We show how difficult it has been for Conservative and Labour governments alike to achieve these twin goals by public policy alone. Among other things, both the finance market and the small-scale structure of provision that dominated the existing sector were central to shaping the eventual outcomes. Deregulation was a necessary condition for reviving the private landlord because it created a legal framework that helped to give landlords and their funders confidence to invest. But it was not, by itself, a sufficient condition for achieving the desired policy outcomes. The fact that governments introduced an array of tax-based schemes – capital allowances for approved landlords, the BES, HITs and REITs – indicates that something more was certainly needed to bring property companies and financial institutions back into the residential lettings market. Nevertheless, despite the tax incentives that these schemes offered, all suffered from poor design. The fact that they all did so revealed a paucity of policy learning on the part of government.

In addition, we show that many of the actual and implied assumptions on which policy was based – for example, that landlords were fully informed, rational market actors – were unfounded, with important consequences for outcomes. What emerged was different from many of the policy intentions, not least the limited investment by financial institutions and residential property companies and the rapid growth in private individual landlords with small-scale letting portfolios. While there was modest growth in investment by private individuals following deregulation, it reflected in part the slump in the homeownership market and the recession of the early 1990s. Moreover, substantial growth did not occur until a decade after deregulation; that is, from the turn of the century, when market conditions were much more conducive to investment by private landlords. The boom continued, however, even after house prices had risen to historically high levels and rental yields had been eroded to uncompetitive levels.

Chapter 1 sets the scene for the book by looking at private landlordism in historical perspective. It begins by considering the provision of rental housing by private landlords in late nineteenth-century Britain and then charts the origins of the long decline in private renting during the twentieth century. It also examines the nature of private landlordism in the 1960s and 1970s, during which period the private rented sector reached its nadir, and sketches out the legacy inherited by the Thatcher government that came to power in 1979.

Chapter 2 explores in some detail the development of public policy on private renting since 1979. The Conservatives introduced a number of policy initiatives during their three terms of office. Rent and security of tenure deregulation proceeded in three steps, with modest changes in 1980 and rather more radical reform in 1988, followed by a relatively minor but significant amendment in 1996. The Labour government left the tenancy legislation unchanged, but introduced a number of measures aimed at tackling poor quality houses in multiple occupation and 'rogue' landlords. In addition to discussing these developments, the chapter also outlines the measures aimed at encouraging property companies and financial institutions back into the residential lettings business.

Chapter 3 presents an overview of the changing nature of the private rented sector over the three decades from 1979. It focuses particularly on the growth of the stock as well as the changes in property conditions over that period. In addition, it looks at the changing composition of the households that rented privately and the tenancies on which they rented their accommodation. It also considers rents, affordability and the role of means-tested rent allowances.

Chapter 4 presents an in-depth examination of the changing nature of private landlords over the period since 1979. It shows that, contrary to the aims of public policy, the ownership of rental housing became increasingly the province of private individuals, most of whom held very small letting portfolios. However, it also shows that private landlords became more investment oriented over this period, with fewer landlords letting accommodation for non-financial reasons.

Chapter 5 reviews the impact of the BES on the provision of rented housing. It looks at the types of residential property company set up under the BES and shows that the scheme was unexpectedly used by universities and housing associations seeking ways to provide new accommodation for their growing number of students and low-income tenants, respectively. It also shows that the scheme was used by building societies seeking to offload the housing stocks that they had repossessed during the housing slump and economic recession of the early 1990s. In addition, the chapter looks at the management costs and rates of return that BES rental housing companies achieved and considers whether these were competitive with alternative investments. Finally, the chapter examines the amount of money raised and the cost of the scheme in relation to the tax relief provided to people investing in the BES.

Chapter 6 reviews the two main initiatives introduced to encourage financial institutions to invest debt and equity into private rental housing: HITs and REITs. The first of these schemes was introduced by the Conservatives and the second by Labour. Both have (so far) failed to entice financial institutions to re-enter the private lettings business from which they withdrew in the 1950s and 1960s (Hamnett & Randolph, 1988). The chapter examines the background to the introduction of these two schemes and considers why they were not successful.

Chapter 7 examines the buy-to-let boom that began in the late 1990s and accelerated after the turn of the century. It looks at the scale of BTL lending before considering why the BTL investment boom occurred. One of the recurrent themes in press commentary on this boom was that some of the people investing in BTL were naive or amateur investors. The chapter therefore examines whether BTL landlords were any different from their predecessors. Finally, the chapter assesses the impact of the credit crunch and the Great Recession on BTL.

Chapter 8 concludes the book. It first summarises the main findings of the research and analysis presented in the previous chapters. Next, it sets out the key lessons for policy that can be derived from our analysis. It also emphasises the importance of a bipartisan approach to the sector. Finally, it considers the future prospects for private renting in the light of our findings. What is clear from our analysis is that the outlook for private landlords is now far more positive than it seemed to be in the late 1970s.

1

Private Landlords in Historical Perspective

Although this book is focused on the transformation of private landlordism over the last three decades, it is important to place that process in its historical perspective. The privately rented sector that existed in 1979 was a product of its history. The nature of private landlordism at that time was profoundly affected by the historical development of the sector over the previous century and especially since the First World War, when rent control and security of tenure legislation were first introduced. The aim of this chapter is therefore to provide an overview of that history and thereby to set the scene for the chapters that follow. Much of the material presented here draws on the historical research on the private rented sector conducted by Kemp (1982, 1984, 1987b, 2004).

The Victorian landlord

The nineteenth century was arguably a 'golden age' for private landlords (if not for their tenants). In that century, private landlords were in the ascendant and by far the dominant provider of housing. Although national data are not available, local studies suggest that about nine out of ten households in Britain rented their home from a private landlord, with almost all the remainder being owner-occupiers. Indeed, most landlords seem to have been tenants of other private landlords (Kemp, 1984).

The importance of private renting appears to have increased with industrialisation and rapid urban growth in the late eighteenth and the nineteenth centuries (Harloe, 1985). As people moved from the countryside to the towns in search of work and opportunity, they generally moved into

Transforming Private Landlords: Housing, markets & public policy, by Tony Crook & Peter A. Kemp   © 2011 Tony Crook & Peter A. Kemp

accommodation rented from private landlords. In the nineteenth century, the great majority of newly built villas and rows of terraced housing were bought by investors seeking an income from letting property, rather than by people wanting somewhere for their own occupation. Thus, the house-builders' prime market – whether they were constructing middle-class sub-urbs or working-class slums (Dyos & Reeder, 1973) – was the investor in housing to let (Kemp, 1982).

Even in rural Britain, where the prevalence of owner occupation appears to have been greater than in the towns and cities, the majority of households rented their home. Very often, the rural tenant's landlord was also their employer, especially if they worked on a farm or for one of great landed estates. Indeed, tied accommodation, often let rent-free or for a low rent, was a pervasive feature of the countryside. Likewise, many of the servants that were such a ubiquitous feature in the life of middle- and upper-income households in urban and rural Britain lived in their employer's house. Hence households with live-in servants were not just employers but also landlords (Kemp, 2004).

Thus, in the nineteenth century private renting was by far the most com-mon form of housing tenure and the private landlord was a ubiquitous feature of the housing market (Kemp, 1982). Although most people could not afford to buy their own home, many wealthy people and other households that had the financial means to buy chose to rent their accommodation instead. Owner occupation did not have the financial attractions that it subsequently acquired, such as rising real house prices. And although mortgage interest payments could be offset against taxable liabilities, relatively few people paid income tax before the First World War. Where owner occupation did exist on a signifi-cant scale it was mainly confined to the more expensive parts of the housing market. There were also pockets of owner occupation among the labour aris-tocracy (skilled workers in well-paid employment), especially in small towns that were dominated by one firm or industry and where there was a large amount of company housing (Kemp, 1982). Nevertheless, some of these working-class owner-occupiers were also landlords (Kemp, 1987b).

Private rental housing was a popular investment prior to the First World War for households with savings to invest. Estate duty returns indicate that, at the turn of the century, one sixth of all personal wealth was held in the form of dwelling houses. It was second only to stocks and shares as a form of personal wealth. The ownership of rented houses was spread across all levels of wealth ownership, but was particularly important for those owning relatively small amounts of capital. House letting was popular in part because the available range of investment outlets was quite limited. But it was also attractive because the returns were competitive with the alterna-tives that did exist (Kemp, 1982). The income from rental housing, while not spectacular, was steady and dependable (Damer, 1976), important attributes in an era when few people has access to an old-age pension or insurance against the death of the family breadwinner.

Historical research suggests that private landlordism was a mainly small-scale business (Kemp, 1982), as it still is today. For example, in Liverpool in 1849, the average portfolio ranged from 3.0 to 9.6 dwelling houses across the 16 wards of the city (Treble, 1971). Daunton (1977) found that between 70 and 90% of the landlords in the various suburbs of Cardiff in 1884 owned fewer than six houses to let and the average holding per landlord was only 4.2 dwellings. In some localities, however, large landlords could play a major role. Thus, in the Newcastle-upon-Tyne suburb of Benwell in 1880, landlords with more than 50 dwellings accounted for only 3% of owners but 27% of the stock of dwellings (Benwell CDP, 1978). Landlord portfolios may have been larger in the Scottish cities, where much of the population lived in tenements. In Glasgow in 1900, for example, the average holding was 3.6 tenement properties, which represented about 22 flats (Morgan & Daunton, 1983).

Most Victorian private landlords borrowed money when investing in housing to let (Cairncross, 1953; Kemp, 1982). The main sources of mortgages in the housing market prior to 1914 were not building societies or banks, but private individuals and trust funds such as marriage settlements and bequests (Offer, 1981). Private mortgages offered the lender a regular flow of income without any of the costs or management hassles associated with property ownership. Estate duty statistics show that private mortgages on house property and business premises accounted for 6.8% of all personal wealth held in the UK (Kemp, 1982).

Borrowing enabled landlords to gear up their investment and obtain a higher return on the equity they had invested than would otherwise have been possible. Building societies and even insurance companies also provided loan finance to private landlords in the nineteenth century (Kemp, 1982). Private and building society mortgages were invariably made on a fixed-rate basis. But whereas building society mortgages involved annual payments of both principal and interest, private mortgages involved interest-only payments, the principal being repaid either at the end of the term or if the loan was recalled. Hence, landlords could obtain a higher rate of return by borrowing money privately than by getting a loan from a building society (Nevitt, 1966).

In the half century up to 1914, investment in new housing went in long waves of around 25 years, with a boom in house-building being followed by a slump. Hence, late nineteenth-century housing markets were subject to cyclical fluctuations, with periodic gluts and shortages (Saul, 1962). These cyclical fluctuations affected the amount of rent that could be charged by the owners of houses to let, particularly on new dwellings (Weber, 1960). The last house-building boom in the nineteenth century peaked in the late

1890s and early 1900s. Like its predecessors, it was then followed by a slump, but this time on an unprecedented scale. Between 1903 and 1914 house-building fell by as much as 70%. By the outbreak of the First World War, the output of new houses had fallen to a level that had not been seen for 60 years. From 1914 until the end of the twentieth century, house building for the private rental sector – apart from a short-lived resurgence in the 1930s – was negligible (Kemp, 2004).

The First World War and beyond

In December 1915, in response to rent strikes on Clydeside and elsewhere, rent controls were introduced for the first time in Britain. The tenant unrest was a response to rent increases imposed by landlords taking advantage of the acute local shortages of accommodation as manpower shifted to areas of munitions production. The government was forced to respond when the rent strikes threatened to extend into industrial action, thereby potentially endangering the war effort (Dickens, 1978; Byrne & Damer, 1980; Melling, 1980). Most other countries involved in the hostilities introduced rent controls during the war (Kemp, 1984; Harloe, 1985).

As its title suggests, the Rent and Mortgage Interest (War Restrictions) Act 1915 controlled not just rents, but also mortgage interest rates. Because repayment mortgages with loan terms of ten years or more were excluded from control, it was private lenders rather than building societies that were affected by the restriction on mortgage interest rates. The rateable value limits in the legislation restricted rent control to dwellings that, broadly speaking, were occupied by working class tenants (Kemp, 1984).

The 1915 Act was originally conceived as a temporary measure made necessary by the war and was due to expire six months after the cessation of hostilities. But by the end of the war, the housing shortage was far worse than it had been in 1915 (Bowley, 1945), which made it politically difficult to let the Act expire. Moreover, concerns had been raised during and immediately after the war about 'landlord profiteering' on middle-class properties, newspaper accounts of which damaged the image of private landlords (Kemp, 1984). Hence, rent control on existing dwellings was not only extended in duration, but also widened in scope in 1919 and again in 1920. However, newly constructed properties were exempt from all rent controls from 1919 to 1939 (Kemp, 2004).

In 1919 the Government also introduced Exchequer subsidies for local authority housing (Wilding, 1973; Merrett, 1979; Swenarton, 1981). It was realised that not only would there be very considerable excess demand for accommodation at the end of the war, but building costs would also be abnormally high, yet could be expected to fall after a few years. This seemed

to imply that, irrespective of the long-term prospects for a return of investment into rented housing, in the short term investors would hold off from
purchasing new house property until after building costs and house prices
had fallen, for otherwise they would have suffered a capital loss. Hence, in
turn, builders would be very unlikely to construct houses, since their traditional customer, the private landlord, would probably not buy them (Kemp,
1984). In these circumstances and in view of the likely social unrest that the
housing shortage would generate, the Government accepted the need to provide some kind of subsidy to house building until 'normality' had returned
(Wilding, 1973; Merrett, 1979; Swenarton, 1981).

During the 1920s, the building industry recovered from the slump into
which it had entered during the late 1900s, a recession much exacerbated by
the war. A prime cause of the initial slump was the downturn in the attractiveness of house-letting as an investment. The recovery of house-building
during the 1920s, however, was based not on private rental but on owner
occupation and local authority housing, two tenures that had been of considerably less importance before 1914. This recovery was greatly stimulated
by the provision of Exchequer subsidies to new local authority housing and
to private builders, as provided by the Housing Acts of 1923 and 1924
(Bowley, 1945; Merrett, 1979, 1982).

Following the publication of a report by the Onslow Committee into the
Rent Acts, the Conservative Government took steps towards decontrolling
the *existing* supply of rental housing. The 1923 Rent Act provided for decontrol on vacant possession, thereby transferring the basis of rent control from
the dwelling to the tenant. The Act also made provision for decontrol by class
of house as from 1925 when the position was to be reassessed in the light of
house-building progress (itself to be aided by Government subsidies).

But even after the return to some kind of 'normality' in 1923, when the
immediate effects of the post-war boom and slump had been felt and building costs had stopped falling from their 1920 peak, the prospects for investment in *new* private rental housing were poor (Kemp, 1984, 2004). Interest
rates and building costs were still at higher levels than they had been before
the war. Meanwhile, the wages of people in full-time work wages had not
kept up with the rise in the cost of living. Moreover, during the depressed
1920s, short-time working was common and unemployment at a very high
level (Bowley, 1947). Hence, the average working-class tenant would have
had difficulty affording the economic rent of a new dwelling. Those who
could afford the cost of new private housing tended to become owner occupiers rather than remain in the rented sector. In any case, the builders' traditional market – the private investor – was no longer prepared to buy new
rental housing (Kemp, 1984).

Existing private landlords not only had rent controls to contend with,
but also faced competition from the new, subsidised local authority rental

sector. Indeed, 98% of all new 'working class' dwellings produced in England and Wales between 1919 and 1931 were built for local authorities and only 2% for private owners. Moreover, the new local authority housing – built to higher standards and let at subsidised rents – tended to be let to clerks, teachers and better off working-class households in steady employment (Bowley, 1945). The rents of the new council houses, even with the subsidy, were simply too high for low paid or unemployed households to afford. Hence, the poorest households continued to rent their homes from private landlords.

After the First World War, people with money to invest were presented an increasing array of outlets for their savings, many of which were more attractive than housing to let. Moreover, compared with rental housing these new investments were more liquid, less 'lumpy', involved far fewer management problems and promised higher rates of return (Kemp, 1984). Thus, there was a marked growth in the number of joint-stock companies listed on the stock exchange after the war (Thomas, 1978), which made it easier for small-scale savers to invest in shares. Interest rates were much higher in the 1920s than they had been prior to the war. This not only reduced the profitability of geared investment in rental housing, but also increased the returns from money-lending investments such as Government bonds and building society share and deposit accounts (Kemp, 1984).

Thus, after the First World War a combination of rent controls, the investment environment and the tarnished image of investment in housing to let, helped ensure that a revival of new building for private rental did not occur in the 1920s (Kemp, 2004). When the building industry did eventually get back on its feet, from 1923 onwards, the recovery was not based on private renting, but on local authority housing and owner occupation. This recovery of house building was greatly stimulated by the reintroduction of Exchequer subsidies for local authority and private housing in the Housing Acts of 1923 and 1924 (the subsidies introduced in 1919 had been axed in 1921 as part of cuts in public spending). Whereas the 1923 Act passed by Chamberlain favoured the private sector, the 1924 Act passed by Wheatley favoured local authority house building (Merrett, 1979; Holmans, 1987).

The recovery of the private housing sector in the 1920s was based on owner occupation (Merrett, 1982; Ball, 1983). Much of the growth of owner occupation in the new housing market was the result of necessity. But home ownership also had important advantages in the 1920s. Whilst private renting was a reasonably attractive proposition for middle class households prior to 1914, the uncertainties and shortages of the war and early post-war years quickly highlighted its disadvantages. Buying one's home was thus a means of ensuring stability and security (Kemp, 1984). Moreover, the building societies had plenty of money after the First World War (Cleary, 1965). Of course, this increase in owner occupation would not have been possible had not there been an important increase in people's ability to buy (Cleary, 1965; Merrett, 1982; Ball, 1983). This was a product of increasing job security, the growth of 'white collar' employment and rising real incomes for those in work between the wars (Pollard, 1969).

Thus in the inter-war years there was a major shift in social attitudes towards owner occupation (Cleary, 1965; Jackson, 1973). This shift was reinforced during the 1930s, when there was a massive private house-building boom, based largely on owner occupation (Richardson & Aldcroft, 1968). Low house prices and generous lending terms meant that an increasing number of households could, for the first time, afford to buy rather than rent their own home (Ball, 1983). Hence growing numbers of better-off households left the private rental market and became homeowners. The fact that the vast majority of those purchasing in the 1930s were first-time buyers therefore meant that they did not have to sell their existing home in order to buy a new one (Merrett, 1982); they merely had to give their landlord notice to quit.

However, the conditions that made it possible for so many people to become owner-occupiers also helped make investment in private rental housing more attractive (Kemp, 2004). As well as low interest rates and building costs, working class rents increased during the 1930s, making rental yields relatively attractive. As a result, there was a notable revival of new private rental house building in the 1930s. In total, over 350000 new dwellings were built for private letting in the five and a half years from September 1933 to March 1939, together with a substantial but unknown number of more expensive ones (Kemp, 1984).

Many of the investors in this new rental housing were private individuals. However, an important and to some extent novel feature of this return of investment in private rental housing was that much of it was by newly-formed property companies. These new property companies were different from the typical Victorian private landlords, who tended to be individuals. Moreover, this new form of landlord tended to involve a larger scale of operations, had access to a different form of capital financing and could be expected to be more economically rational in outlook (Kemp, 1984). The big insurance companies and pension funds were also keen investors in blocks of flats, especially in London and the south-east (Kemp, 1984; Hamnett & Randolph, 1988).

Post-war decline

The Second World War marked an important turning point for the privately rented sector in Britain. It brought to an abrupt halt the 'Indian summer' in building for private rental that had commenced in the early 1930s (Kemp,

2004). Just a few days after war was declared, rent controls were extended to virtually all rented housing, with rents frozen at their September 1939 level. After the war, the sector declined rapidly, both in relative and in absolute size. In 1938 the privately rented sector accounted for 6.6 million dwellings or 58% of the housing stock in England and Wales, but by 1975 it contained only 2.9 million dwellings and represented only 16% of the stock (Holmans, 1987). A similar decline occurred in Scotland. During this period, therefore, private renting in Britain was transformed from being the most common tenure to being a relatively small and residual part of the housing market.

The housing shortage after the war and the election of a Labour government in 1945 were important reasons for the lack of new construction for private renting. One consequence of the post-war housing scarcity was that blanket rent controls remained in place on existing and new dwellings after hostilities had ended. The failure to exempt new dwellings from rent controls made it almost inevitable that little construction for private rental would be undertaken in the post-war years (Kemp, 2004). Moreover, under the immediate post-war system of building licences, local authorities were expected to provide 80% of new construction (Merrett, 1979). Given the existence of rent controls on new private homes, the lack of subsidies for new rental housing and the limited permission to build, it was hardly surprising that the private sector focused its output on the market for owner occupation rather than housing to let (Kemp, 2004).

When the Conservatives returned to office in 1951, the housing shortage was still very substantial and hence so was the political imperative both to maintain rent controls on the existing stock of privately rented dwellings and to increase the output of new houses. The Conservatives at this time were more concerned with reaching the target of 300 000 new homes per annum that they had promised in the 1951 election campaign than by whom the houses were built (Holmans, 1987). With private housing construction gradually recovering as building controls were removed, it was difficult to argue a case for the extension of subsidies to the private landlord (Kemp, 2004).

Meanwhile, private sector rents were frozen at their September 1939 level, which in many cases was the August 1914 level plus 40%. The result was that private rents fell in real terms as house prices, earnings and retail prices all increased following the war. The consumer price index increased by 105% between 1939 and 1951 and the price of building maintenance trebled (Holmans, 1987). Frozen rents and rising property values meant that rental yields fell substantially. With a significant gap opening up between tenanted and vacant-possession house prices, many landlords took whatever opportunities arose to sell up and invest elsewhere. The continuing housing shortage, combined with an increasing appetite for owner occupation and growing numbers of households able to afford to buy, meant that landlords had a ready market for their properties (Hamnett & Randolph, 1988). Between

1939 and 1953, an estimated half a million dwellings were sold by private landlords to owner-occupiers in England and Wales. A further 1.2 million were sold in the period from 1953 to 1961 (Holmans, 1987).

While the new Conservative government sought and succeeded in raising housing output to 300 000 a year by 1953, it also began to focus attention on the condition of the existing stock of (mostly privately rented) houses, much of which was seriously substandard. The Conservatives' 1953 White Paper 'Housing – the Next Steps' viewed the problem of substandard housing as one of the privately rented sector (Merrett, 1982). Apart from the age of the stock – 30% of which was at least a century old – the white paper identified post-war restrictions on building works and materials, and especially rent controls, as the two causes of the physical deterioration in the condition of private dwellings since the war (Kemp, 2004).

The structure of rents in the privately rented sector was described in the White Paper as 'hopelessly illogical', with, for example, different rents being charged for identical houses in the same street. In addition, many rents were insufficient to enable landlords to maintain their houses in adequate repair. Since the housing shortage was still sufficiently severe to prevent rents from being completely decontrolled, 'The main question resolves itself, therefore, into the most equitable way of allowing such increases in the rents of privately-owned houses as will enable the landlord to keep the house in good repair' (MHLG, 1953, p. 7).

The subsequent House Repairs and Rents Act 1954 permitted limited increases in the rents of dwellings which had been let before September 1939 and which had been maintained or put into a good state of repair (Doling & Davies, 1984). The size of the permitted increase varied according to the extent to which the landlord was responsible for repairs and decoration. The aim was to give landlords an incentive to increase their expenditure on repair and maintenance. In addition, rent control was lifted from newly constructed and converted dwellings (Kemp, 2004).

From the mid-1950s the Conservative government began a new drive towards the replacement of the slums (Merrett, 1979). This new approach involved the large-scale clearance of mainly privately rented terraced housing, much of it built to low standards in the nineteenth century and suffering from inadequate maintenance expenditure because of the low rents produced by decades of crude rent controls. The cleared stock was replaced by new council housing, built to modern standards and with the help of substantial subsidies from the Exchequer, which made it much more attractive for tenant households than privately rented accommodation. This process further hastened the decline in the privately rented sector.

Although rents on new construction had been decontrolled in 1954, there is little evidence that this led to a resurgence of building for private rental. The demand for new private housing was focused on the owner-occupied market. Decades of rent control in the private sector and large subsidies for council housing had created a low-rent environment that was not easily shed. The unwillingness of the Conservatives to provide subsidies to private landlords in the way that other west European countries had done reflected the political controversy that surrounded the privately rented sector from the mid-1950s onwards. This period witnessed a growing polarisation in political debates on the privately rented sector (Kemp, 2004). These debates were often marked by the use of stereotypical images of both landlords and tenants (Cullingworth, 1979).

This polarisation between Labour and the Conservatives in relation to private renting was exhibited most clearly in the debates surrounding the passage of the 1957 Rent Act. This highly controversial legislation included three main steps towards rent decontrol. First, all private dwellings with a rateable value of over £40 in London and £30 elsewhere were automatically freed from rent control. Second, dwellings below these limits that became vacant were decontrolled. Third, landlords were allowed to increase the rents of dwellings that remained subject to controls, although the tenant could object to this if the property was in disrepair (Cullingworth, 1979).

The impact of the 1957 Rent Act was much less dramatic than many commentators had anticipated (Cullingworth, 1979). A study funded by the Joseph Rowntree Memorial Trust found that many landlords increased their rents (some by a considerable amount) but others did not, even though they were allowed to do so under the legislation (Donnison *et al.*, 1961). Nor did rent decontrol bring a halt to disinvestment by landlords. Rather, landlords continued to get out of the sector by selling to owner-occupiers, including their own sitting tenants. Thus, the 1957 Rent Act failed to halt the decline of the privately rented sector (Kemp, 1987a).

From the early 1960s the Conservatives began to encourage the development of cost-rent housing societies. Initially it was hoped that this initiative would stimulate the return of investment in new privately rented housing. But when that failed, the societies were instead encouraged as an alternative to the privately rented sector. The development of this 'third arm' of housing provision (that is, in addition to owner occupation and council housing) was seen by the Conservatives as being especially important to counter the growing monopoly of council housing as the privately rented sector shrank and municipal housing increased through new building (Cullingworth, 1979; Malpass, 2000). The option of providing subsidies to enable the private sector to build new housing to let seems not to have been given serious consideration. This was perhaps hardly surprising given the political controversy surrounding the 1957 Rent Act and the subsequent Rachman scandal in the early 1960s (Kemp, 2004).

By the early 1960s, the housing shortage in pressure areas such as inner London had become acute, especially at the bottom end of the market.

With controlled rents well below market levels, creeping decontrol (that is, decontrol on vacant possession) gave landlords an incentive to remove their sitting tenants by whatever means they could, in order to charge a higher rent (Kemp, 1987a). Because of the gap between sitting tenant and vacant-possession house values – although this was not due to the 1957 Act – they also had an incentive to get rid of their tenants and sell their properties in the owner-occupied housing market (see Hamnett & Randolph, 1988).

Around this time, stories began to appear in the local papers in London about intimidation of tenants, evictions and homelessness, some of which implicated the West London landlord Peter Rachman. The issue gained notoriety when it became linked to the Profumo scandal in 1963 via a call girl who was associated with both Rachman and the Conservative defence minister. For a couple of weeks, the public was fed a daily dose of stories about the violence and intimidation that Rachman was said to have used against his tenants (Banting, 1979). This publicity confirmed and strength-ened the negative image with which private landlordism had come to be associated in Britain (Kemp, 1987a).

The Rachman scandal forced the Conservative government to set up the Milner Holland Committee to investigate the problems of housing in London (Banting, 1979). The committee's report, which was published in 1965, con-cluded that there was an acute shortage of rented housing in London. The surveys commissioned by the committee found that, although most tenants were satisfied with the way their landlords treated them, landlord abuse was too common to be treated as an isolated problem. The committee also dem-onstrated that, because of the tax and housing subsidy arrangements then in place, an identical house would cost a household less to buy with a mort-gage or to rent it from a local authority than it would to rent it from a private landlord (Milner Holland Committee, 1965).

From control to regulation

The Labour Party, which came to power in 1964, pledged to reintroduce security of tenure for private tenants. Later the same year it passed a tempo-rary measure, the Prevention of Eviction Act, in order to fulfil that promise (Banting, 1979). The Rent Act 1965 incorporated the security of tenure pro-visions of the 1964 Act and introduced 'regulated tenancies' and 'Fair Rents' assessed by independent rent officers. Labour's new system of rent regula-tion was an attempt to provide a fair balance between the interests of land-lords and tenants. It aimed to restore tenants' security of tenure while providing landlords with regular rent increases (Donnison, 1967). The expec-tation was that rents would largely be set by the market, but that where landlord and tenant disagreed, either or both could refer the rent to the new Rent Officer service. Rent regulation was a significant departure from the previous, rather crude, system of rent control that had prevailed in Britain up until 1965 (Kemp, 2004).

Surprisingly, the 1965 Rent Act extended rent regulation to include new construction, thereby making it highly likely that little new private housing to rent would be produced (Kemp, 2004). In fact, house building in the 1960s and 1970s was largely confined to local authorities and the market for owner occupation. Both Labour and Conservative governments supported major local authority house-building programmes from the Second World War through to the 1970s (Merrett, 1979). With the aid of subsidies from the Exchequer and from rate payers, local authorities were able to offer their tenants housing that was cheaper, more modern, built to higher standards, and – in practice if not in law – gave stronger security of tenure than that provided by private landlords (Kemp, 2004).

In the 1950s and 1960s, full employment and rising real incomes made it possible for an increasing number of households to enter the owner-occupied sector (Ball, 1983; Merrett, 1982). Although economic growth faltered in 1970s, increased participation in the labour market by married women helped to increase the ability of moderate-income households to buy their home on a mortgage (Holmans, 1987). Moreover, the attractions of owner occupation for households that could afford to buy increased in the 1960s and 1970s, in part as a result of government policies, which further helped to shift demand away from private renting and towards owner occupation (Whitehead, 1979; Holmans, 1987).

During the 1960s the fiscal treatment of owner occupation changed from one of relative indifference to active support (Holmans, 1987). One such measure was the abolition of taxation on imputed rental income on owner-occupied (but not on privately let) properties in 1963. Another was the intro-duction by the Labour government of the option mortgage scheme in 1967, which gave non-tax-paying households a subsidy equivalent to that provided to taxpayers by mortgage interest tax relief. And when tax relief on the inter-est payments on consumer loans was abolished, it was kept in place on mortgages (although a £30000 limit was introduced by the Labour govern-ment in 1974). These tax concessions became gradually more important as an increasing proportion of working people became liable to pay income tax during this period (Kemp, 1997).

The attractions of owner occupation over private renting were further enhanced by the rising trend of inflation in the 1960s and its acceleration after 1973. Inflation eroded the real value of mortgage repayments and out-standing debt, thereby allowing households to borrow larger multiples of their income than might otherwise have been feasible, safe in the knowl-edge that a few years' of inflation would reduce the real value of the repayments and outstanding debt to more manageable proportions. Moreover, for much of the 1970s the level of retail price inflation was greater than nominal interest rates, with the result that in real terms interest rates were negative (Merrett, 1982; Ball, 1983).

The high rates of inflation prevalent during the 1970s sharply reduced the rental yield on accommodation let on regulated tenancies with a Fair Rent. Since rents fell in real terms during the 1970s while vacant possession house values increased, landlords had a strong incentive to sell to owner-occupiers and invest their money elsewhere, rather than re-let when a property became vacant (Holmans, 1987). Although private landlords could make capital gains from rising property values, the Rent Acts gave tenants relatively strong security of tenure, which made it difficult for landlords to repossess their properties. Moreover, because of the gap between vacant possession and tenanted investment values, it was economically rational for landlords to realise their investment by selling when the property became vacant and putting the proceeds in more-profitable and less-risky investments (Doling & Davies, 1984; Hamnett & Randolph, 1988).

The gap between vacant possession and tenanted investment values created a space for property dealers to make large profits by purchasing tenanted property, 'encouraging' the tenant to leave and selling at vacant possession values (Hamnett & Randolph, 1988). In some cases, developers were able to obtain improvement grants to improve run-down privately rented houses, which they then sold at a substantial profit to owner-occupiers (Williams, 1976). In this way, local authorities, perhaps unwittingly, subsidised developers to gentrify inner-city neighbourhoods and to accelerate the decline of private renting and the growth of owner occupation (Crook & Bryant, 1982; Crook & Martin, 1988).

By the early 1970s, owner occupation had become the mainstream tenure to which a majority of households aspired (Whitehead, 1979; Holmans, 1987), while council housing had become the largest rental tenure. In contrast, private renting was now a minority sector and one that was continuing to shrink. It had also become much less central to policy debates (Kemp, 2004). The Conservative government under Prime Minister Edward Heath failed to address most of the problems facing the privately rented sector. Although the incoming Labour government under Harold Wilson introduced several changes to rent regulation in 1974, these affected only a small part of the sector. The 1974 Rent Act excluded lettings made by resident landlords from the regulated tenancy framework. It also extended rent regulation to include furnished accommodation, a part of the sector that had previously been left uncontrolled. This change was deemed to be necessary because some landlords were seeking to avoid rent regulation by letting their accommodation with a minimal amount of furniture included in the letting (Maclennan, 1978). This was just one of a number of means by which landlords hoped to avoid or evade the rent restriction and security of tenure provisions of the Rent Acts. Others such devices included letting property with breakfast, pretend 'holiday lettings' and non-exclusive occupation contracts (Kemp, 1988a).

Labour's Housing Act 1974 included several measures that affected the privately rented sector (Kemp, 2004). It introduced housing action areas (HAAs), which were intended to achieve rapid improvement in housing conditions in areas characterised by poor physical and social conditions. HAAs had more generous improvement grants than non-designated areas and local authorities had enhanced powers of compulsory purchase, which were used where landlords and owner-occupiers were unable or unwilling to improve their properties within the designated area (Cullingworth, 1979; Thomas, 1986). In Scotland, where HAAs took a different form from England and Wales, the Housing Corporation (which funded and regulated associations) was especially active in promoting the establishment of housing associations to take over from reluctant or recalcitrant owners and improve properties. This resulted in a significant transfer of inner-city private rental dwellings to housing associations within HAAs, especially in inner Glasgow (Kemp, 1979; Maclennan, 1985).

In the mid-1970s, the Labour government carried out a review of the Rent Acts, but it was concerned mainly with rationalising the existing system of controls rather than with a fundamental appraisal of the role of the sector in the modern housing market (Cullingworth, 1979). Indeed, the 1977 Rent Act consolidated the legislation that was already in place and introduced no major innovations (Stafford & Doling, 1981). By the time that Labour left office in 1979 the private rented sector had declined to 2.3 million dwellings or 11% of the housing stock in Britain. The rate of decline during the 1970s was approximately 80000 dwellings per annum. All the evidence seemed to suggest that the sector would continue to shrink in size for the foreseeable future.

Private landlordism in the 1960s and 1970s

The lack of new construction, and the loss of existing homes from the sector, meant that the number of private landlords decreased during the postwar years. By the 1960s, the sector was relatively moribund, with relatively little new investment. This had important consequences for the nature of private landlordism. For instance, as we shall see, it meant that most owners of housing to let had been landlords for a long-time and substantial numbers had inherited their properties rather purchased them.

However, prior to the 1980s there was relatively little information about the types of people and organisations that were landlords, the nature of their operations and their attitudes to lettings. This paucity of information, combined with the highly polarised political party attitudes to private renting, meant that policy debates about private landlordism tended to be based on myths and stereotypes. As the author of one of the earliest studies of private renting noted:

> Considering the controversy which has raged for so long over the private ownership of rented houses it is strange that no serious inquiry has been mounted of it. Much of the argument which has accompanied the passing of the Rent Act assumed that the typical private landlord was an 'economic man' owning houses which he regarded as a business investment. Yet there were no facts to support this idea, or the alternative ones of the bloated capitalist owner who (given the chance) would grind the faces of the poor, and the struggling widow trying to make ends meet with the meagre rent she drew from cottage property. (Cullingworth, 1963, p. 105)

Two years later, Greve was able to write that 'while the Government did not know much about private landlords, nor did anyone else' (Greve, 1965, p. 8). The evidence that Cullingworth, Greve and later researchers gathered showed how different the actual picture was compared to these caricatures and how much it contradicted 'what everyone knows' (Holmans, 1987, p. 438).

Types of landlord

Cullingworth rectified this ignorance in respect of Lancaster, a small town in north-west England. He found that all the private landlords in Lancaster were individuals and none were companies. He also found that 65% of them were 60 years or more in age and two-thirds were women. He commented that 'these figures are staggering and prompt the observation that the landlords of Lancaster are only slightly younger than the houses they own!' (Cullingworth, 1963, p. 107). However, Cullingworth admitted that Lancaster could not be regarded as representative of the picture nationally.

Fortunately, several other studies were carried out in the 1960s and 1970s that provided information on private landlords to supplement the insights gained from Lancaster. As Table 1.1 shows, these studies confirmed the importance of individual owners, whether measured as a proportion of all landlords or in relation to their share of lettings within the private rented sector. Companies accounted for at most a third of the stock of dwellings or of landlords, while 'other' types of landlord (who included a wide range of organisations, including charities, trusts and churches) owned only a much smaller share than companies. The evidence from successive *General Household Surveys* (which asked tenants about their landlords) suggests that

Table 1.1   Types of landlords

Landlord type	Lancaster 1960[a] (%)	England 1963[b] (%)	London 1964[c] (%)	England and Wales* 1976[d] (%)	England 1977[e] (%)	England 1978[f] (%)
Individual	100	69	51	55	65	64
Company	—	31	36	29	27	32
Other	—	—	13	16	8	4
Base	LL	LL	Le	Le	HH	HH

*Densely rented areas of England and Wales. LL, landlords; Le, lettings; HH, households.
Sources: [a] Cullingworth (1963); [b] Greve (1965); [c] Gray & Todd (1964); [d] Paley (1978); [e] DoE (1979); [f] Todd *et al.* (1982).

the proportion of the sector owned by companies had been in decline over the period covered by Table 1.1 (House of Commons Environment Committee, 1982a). Property companies were more likely to be owners of purpose-built flats than other dwellings (Todd *et al.*, 1982), a finding that reflected the significance of companies in the development and ownership of mansion and other blocks of flats specifically constructed for private rental in the 1930s (Kemp, 1984). Most of these rented flats were sold to owner-occupiers, especially in the 1960s and 1970s (Hamnett & Randolph, 1988).

These surveys also confirmed the continued general validity of Cullingworth's observations about the age and occupations of individual landlords, namely that the majority were elderly, with low incomes and only small rental incomes. Many were or had been skilled manual workers earning below average incomes. In the survey of landlords in densely rented areas of England in 1976, for example, 46% of individually owned lettings had landlords who were 60 years or more in age and 41% had owners who had retired from skilled manual jobs (Paley, 1978).

The fact that such a high proportion of privately rented dwellings was owned by elderly individual landlords reflected the fact that many of them had been inherited from relatives who had originally bought (or otherwise acquired) them as investments. In Lancaster in 1960, 70% of landlords had acquired their portfolio through inheritance. Greve's 1963 national study of landlords found that 49% of landlords owning fewer than 10 tenancies had inherited their properties. He also reported on the apparent lack of significant investment by private landlord (Greve, 1965).

Most landlords owned very small portfolios of property and, indeed, many had only one dwelling to let. However, some landlords had quite extensive holdings. For example, in Lancaster in 1960, although 61% of landlords owned just one dwelling each, they accounted for only 22% of the privately rented stock in the city. By contrast, although only 1% of landlords owned more than 20 houses, between them they owned 25% of

Table 1.2 Portfolio sizes

Size of portfolio (lettings)	Lancaster 1960[a] (%)	England 1963[b] (%)	London 1964[c] (%)	England and Wales* 1976[d] (%)
1	22	} 58	14	14
2–4	27		16	17
5–9	19		13	11
10–20	9	} 27	} 18	} 28
21–50				
51–99	} 25		7	6
100–499			12	8
500–999		} 15	5	7
1,000+			15	11
Base	LL	LL	Le	Le

*Densely rented areas. LL, landlords; Le, lettings.
Sources: [a] Cullingworth (1963); [b] Greve (1965); [c] Gray & Todd (1964); [d] Paley (1978).

the sector. Paley's 1976 survey of areas of England with high proportions of renting found that, while 42% of lettings had landlords with portfolios of fewer than ten dwellings, 26% had landlords with portfolios of more than 100 dwellings (Paley, 1978).

As all four surveys in Table 1.2 show, most private tenants in the 1960s and 1970s were renting their homes from landlords that had small portfolios. Interpolating the different-sized categories used in the surveys suggests that the majority of lettings were owned by private landlords with fewer than 21 lettings, while only a quarter were owned by those with portfolios of 100 or more dwellings. Not surprisingly, perhaps, privately rented properties let by companies were much more likely than those let by individuals to belong to large holdings. For example, in densely rented areas of England in 1976, 43% of company-owned lettings were parts of portfolios of 100 or more (Paley, 1978).

Length of ownership

In the 1960s and 1970s, most privately rented properties had been owned by their current landlord for many years. Indeed, in Lancaster in 1960 only 4% of all landlords had bought property for letting between 1948 and 1960. Moreover, the 19% who had become landlords for the first time since 1948 had all inherited their stock (Cullingworth, 1963). However, Greve's 1963 national study showed a different picture, with 27% of private lettings having been acquired in the previous five years, that is, since the Rent Act 1957. It had mainly been landlords with fewer than 100 properties, rather than landlords with larger portfolios, who had invested in the sector. Greve commented that, if there was to be a policy-induced increase in private rented housing it would have to come from these larger landlords with access to capital: 'It would not be possible to fashion a coherent and balanced policy for rented housing from the fragmented and haphazard activities of a few million private landlords' (Greve, 1965, p. 30).

Gray and Todd's 1963 study of landlords in Greater London found that 28% of lettings had landlords who had been letting for less than ten years, including 23% since the 1957 Rent Act. It was individuals more than company landlords who had invested in the sector. The lettings of 38% of the former, but only 22% of the latter had owners who had begun letting within the previous ten years. Gray and Todd also concluded that many of those new to landlordism were owners of a single property that they had converted to use as a house in multiple occupations (Gray & Todd, 1964). The latter finding may have reflected the high level of overcrowding in the capital and perhaps also the fact that (as noted above) furnished lettings were exempt from rent controls at that time.

Thus in the 1960s, although the private rented sector was declining at a relatively rapid rate, some investors were willing to counter the prevailing tide and enter the market. Paley's 1976 national study of private renting in densely rented areas showed that this trend continued into the next decade. Just under a quarter (23%) of all lettings within the private rented sector had been acquired between 1971 and 1976 (Paley, 1978). Most significantly, the survey revealed just how substantial were the holdings of those who had become landlords for the first time since the 1957 Rent Act. About half (53%) of all lettings had landlords who had first started letting within the previous 20 years. Furthermore, 18% were owned by those who had first become landlords within the previous six years. The latter included 23% of lettings owned by non-resident individuals and 17% of those owned by companies. Organisations such as non-charitable trusts and public bodies were much less likely to have first started letting within the previous six years (the landlords of 6 and 2% of such lettings respectively).

Paley's 1976 survey evidence also suggested that most of the new investment was by small-scale individual landlords. For example, 41% of lettings owned by small landlords (those with fewer than ten lettings) had landlords who first started letting in the previous six years, compared with 13 and 6% respectively of those owned by medium (10–99 lettings) and large (100 or more lettings) landlords. A final clue from this survey to the apparently positive climate for new investment in the 1970s is the fact that 39% of lettings were parts of portfolios that were either owned by landlords who first started letting in the previous six years (18%) or by landlords who has first started letting before then but had grown their portfolio in the previous six years (21%).

Attitudes to letting

The extent to which this new investment by landlords involved properties acquired with sitting tenants or with vacant possession is unknown. What is clear, however, is that, despite the continued decline of private letting, new landlords were entering the sector. Moreover, they were choosing to enter a market that was substantially regulated (and one in which private landlords generally had a tarnished reputation). Thus, while some owners were inheritors, others had actively chosen to become landlords. This raises the question of how private landlords viewed the business of letting residential property.

Paley's survey of landlords in densely rented areas of England and Wales in 1976 asked two questions about the sampled addresses to help discover their attitudes to letting: firstly what they thought an adequate rent should cover and secondly how they regarded the property. Table 1.3 shows that, with the exception of lettings by resident landlords and by public bodies, a large majority of lettings were regarded as financial investments. It also shows that many non-resident individual landlords, companies and non-charitable trusts regarded their lettings as investments with the return coming as a yield, based on current market value and not the original purchase price. Only in the case of public bodies were lettings substantially regarded for a special use, such as housing employees.

Not surprisingly, most resident landlords regarded their property as their home. Moreover, the majority of them were not looking for an investment return. Indeed, resident landlords appeared to be a rather special category of their own, letting out rooms to help cover their outgoings or to obtain companionship in sharing their home. They tended to let to retired single people

Table 1.3 How landlords regarded their property*

	Individual resident (%)	Individual non-resident (%)	Company (%)	Non-charitable trust (%)	Public body (%)	All (%)
Rent should cover:						
market value	18	53	70	59	37	52
purchase price	11	14	11	13	14	12
mortgage only	14	4	4	—	1	5
no return	57	29	15	28	48	30
Regarded as:						
home	92	9	1	—	—	18
investment	7	86	87	87	55	71
special use	—	3	10	7	38	9
else	1	2	2	6	7	2

*Densely rented areas in England and Wales.
Source: Paley (1978).

or young females. The general impression from surveys that included resident landlords is that they were a rather fluid group. Many let part of their home to help cover costs, but dropped out of this business when this was no longer needed.

Non-resident landlords mainly regarded their properties as investments (even if inherited) on which they were looking for a return. In most cases, they wanted the rent to provide a return on the market value of the property. However, it is not always clear from these surveys whether the investment returns that landlords sought were from rental income, capital appreciation or both. A rare example of evidence on this question comes from the research on Greater London's landlords in 1963, which showed that 63% of the rateable value units in the sample were regarded as investments. Property that had been bought as an investment was almost always thought of as an investment to provide income rather than as one to be sold for capital gain (Gray & Todd, 1964, pp. 341–342).

Hence, in a sector that – to paraphrase Holmans – 'everyone knew' was unprofitable there was, in fact, much evidence of active investment in the 1960s and 1970s. A qualitative study of landlords Edinburgh in the early 1970s asked the question: 'Why in a shrinking market and in a sector of the economy frequently depicted as very unprofitable [do] so many firms remain ... The answer lies in the fact that they never simply operate as landlords' (Elliott & McCrone, 1975, p. 553). What landlords did was to acquire blocks of properties and break them up to sell on to owner-occupiers, a finding that was strongly echoed in a later study of the flat break-up market in London (Hamnett & Randolph, 1988). As the authors commented, such enterprise readily commanded the skills of local entrepreneurs prepared to get their hands dirty. However, while some landlords were involved in property dealing, it is evident from the survey data from the 1960s and 1970s that many other landlords were seeking rental income rather than short-term capital gains.

Landlords' views on the legal framework

The 1976 survey of landlords letting property in densely rented areas in England and Wales found that only about half of all lettings had landlords who preferred to agree rents privately with their tenants (Paley, 1978). The remainder had owners who preferred to get a Fair Rent registered when letting accommodation. Moreover, in 88% of cases where a Fair Rent had been registered, the application had been made by the *landlord* and not by the tenant. However, these landlords sought to get Fair Rents registered not because they provided a satisfactory return, but because they enabled them to avoid disputes and disagreements with tenants about the rent that should be charged. What landlords disliked about the system was that, in their

Table 1.4 Perceived adequacy of rents on lettings by type of landlord in England and Wales in 1976

	Individual resident (%)	Individual non-resident (%)	Company (%)	Non-charitable trust (%)
Fair Rents:				
prefer to have rent registered	8	21	32	50
Fair Rent is adequate	9	12	11	20
Rent is adequate	65	30	31	22
Rent insufficient to cover repairs and give reasonable return	50	80	74	84
Lettings where landlord limited spending on repairs and improvement compared with what was needed	64	53	47	66

Source: Paley (1978).

view, Fair Rents were fixed too low, were reviewed too infrequently and increases were phased in over too long a period. As explained in the next chapter, these concerns were addressed by amendments to the Fair Rent system introduced in the 1980 Housing Act.

Landlords that charged tenants market rents did not necessarily earn competitive returns and nor were they always satisfied with the rents. Of course, adequacy depends to quite an extent on the items that landlords think rents should cover. Table 1.4 shows that, on a range of measures, few landlords of lettings in densely rented areas in 1976 were satisfied. Apart from resident landlords, fewer than a third of lettings had landlords who thought their rents (whether privately negotiated or Fair Rents) were adequate. Indeed, more than three-quarters thought rents were insufficient to cover repairs and give a reasonable return. Meanwhile, the landlords of upwards of a half of all lettings restricted what they spent on repairs. When asked what rents would need to be in order to give them an adequate return, the median increase (£3.60 a week) was almost double the rents then being charged (a median of £4.00 per week).

The evidence in Table 1.4 suggested that, not just registered Fair Rents, but also market rents made it difficult for landlords to achieve competitive returns and do necessary repairs. One strategy adopted by landlords for achieving adequate returns was to neglect repairs. Estimates on rates of return showed how low they were in the 1970s, except in certain niche sub-markets. Thus, estimates made in 1970 and 1975 used comparisons of registered rents with the median prices of second-hand houses sold with building society mortgages and took into account prospective increases in rents and costs (DoE, 1977, Vol. 3). This suggested that net income returns in 1975 were 6% outside London, which was not thought to be unattractive given that long-dated government gilts then yielded 9%. But by 1975 the net income return had fallen to 2% as a result of high house price and cost inflation. Repairs costs had risen 89%, but registered rents by only 40%. Dividends on ordinary shares were then averaging 6.5% so selling up and investing in equities appeared to be a much better investment prospect than residential letting.

Further evidence comes from a comparison made over the years 1970, 1973 and 1976 of the registered rents and the vacant-possession values of a sample of dwellings in England and Wales (House of Commons Environment Committee, 1982a). This confirmed that rental yields declined in the early 1970s, the mean falling from 8.0 to 4.4% between 1970 and 1973, although rising to 4.9% in 1976. The median was much lower than the mean (5.5, 3.1, and 3.7% for each of the years), which suggests that returns were skewed towards the lower end of the range.

Paley's 1976 survey examined landlords' attitudes to security of tenure. Four out of ten lettings had landlords who said the legislation affected their letting policies. In particular, they were reluctant to re-let properties that became vacant and, when they did re-let, it was typically to transient types of tenants. Some explained that they no longer put in furniture as a device to limit their tenants' security – rent regulation had been extended to furnished lettings in 1974 (see above) – and instead had started to let on 'non-exclusive licence agreements' or 'holiday' lettings as ways of trying to safeguard their ability to regain possession (Paley, 1978).

Plans to re-let or sell vacancies

Cullingworth (1963) found that 90% of landlords in Lancaster in 1960 would sell if they got vacant possession. However, as noted above, it is not clear that the situation in that town was representative of the country as a whole. In his national survey, Greve (1965) found that, over the period from 1960 to 1962, only 25% of landlords said they had sold all their vacancies, 8% had sold some and the remaining 67% had re-let all of their vacancies. Thus, the majority of properties that became vacant were re-let rather than sold.

Two surveys of London in the 1960s showed that the landlords of the great majority of sampled *furnished* lettings would re-let if their properties became vacant (Milner Holland Committee, 1965, Appendix V; Committee on the Rent Acts, 1971). To some extent these findings reflect the fact that, at the time, furnished lettings were not subject to rent control or rent regulation. Among *unfurnished* lettings in Greater London in 1963 that were not subject to control, 77% had landlords that would re-let if the property became vacant.

By 1969, however, there is evidence that the new system of rent registration had affected landlords' willingness to re-let unfurnished lettings because only 50% of these properties that had registered Fair Rents would be re-let. These findings were confirmed by a later study of central London, carried out in 1974/75, that showed that higher proportions of unfurnished lettings would be sold than the two previous surveys from the 1960s had shown, and also that, if whole buildings containing several furnished lettings became vacant, higher proportions of these would be sold (Whitehead, 1978).

The nationwide survey of lettings in densely rented areas in England and Wales in 1976 broadly confirmed the findings of the 1969 London survey. This distinguished between intentions if a sample letting became vacant 'tomorrow' and if the whole building did so (in cases where there was more than one letting in a building all owned by the same landlord). The survey did not, unfortunately, distinguish between unfurnished and furnished lettings, or their degree of protection. Only 54% of lettings would be re-let, a proportion that fell to 40% if landlords had vacant possession of the whole building (Paley, 1978).

The reasons landlords had for not re-letting are not hard to guess. The 1976 survey of lettings in the densely rented areas found that, among lettings that would not be re-let, 57% had landlords who said it was because the rent from the letting did not give an adequate income or economic return, and in 18% of cases it was because the return from investing elsewhere would give better value. Within this general picture, it is relevant to note that company landlords were the most concerned about financial issues. While many individual landlords were concerned about financial aspects of letting, more of them wanted to save themselves from the 'bother and fuss' of being a landlord (Paley, 1978).

Only 7% of lettings in 1976 were owned by landlords who expected their total holdings to increase in the next three years, 47% had landlords who expected no change in their holdings and 46% thought they would decrease. Those who expected to see their holdings decrease mainly said this was because it was no longer economic to let accommodation or because of government legislation (Paley, 1978).

Conclusions

By the time Labour lost office in 1979, private landlordism was a declining industry, a sector from which many more landlords were exiting than new ones entering. It was dominated by individuals rather than property companies and by small-scale operators rather than by landlords with large portfolios. The processes of centralisation and concentration in ownership that have characterised many other sectors of the economy had not occurred in private letting (Kemp, 1988a). Moreover, many owners of private rental housing were 'accidental landlords' in the sense of having inherited their properties rather than actively decided to invest in lettings. The fact that many of the properties inherited by landlords were occupied by tenants with strong security of tenure made it difficult for those who wanted to cash in on their new asset; hence some of them were not just accidental but also reluctant owners of housing to let. The Rent Acts had not just controlled the rents at which a significant proportion of properties were let, but had also, to a significant extent, ossified the ownership of the sector. Although new investors had entered the market, many others were getting out, and the overall position was one of net disinvestment.

Moreover, the Rachman scandal had further damaged the already tarnished image of the private landlord. This poor reputation almost certainly acted to deter potential landlords and made it more difficult politically to tackle the financial obstacles facing those who might otherwise have been willing to invest in housing to let. Finally, it also helped to highlight the attractions of owner occupation and council housing, two tenures that by the 1970s had come to dominate the housing market and that were the main focus of policy attention.

2

Government Policy Since 1979

Introduction

In this chapter we examine the fundamental change of stance taken by governments in Britain towards private rented housing over the last three decades and discuss the key instruments used to pursue this.[1] During this period, policy changed from suspending the operation of the market, mainly in the interests of existing tenants, towards facilitating the operation of the market to secure an increase in the supply and quality of dwellings for those seeking rented housing. This required a policy and market frameworks that would encourage and facilitate investment by existing and landlords.

The policy framework was implemented in January 1989 with the deregulation of rents and the introduction of more limited security for all new lettings. It replaced the control and regulation of rents and the statutory security of tenure that had covered the sector for most of the preceding 70 years (although existing tenancies continued to be protected). Deregulation was preceded by much debate about the sector's appropriate role and some limited and (in retrospect) tentative steps were made towards a market-based approach in 1980 as part of the Thatcher government's attempts to roll back the state in housing. Deregulation continued unchanged under the New Labour government that followed in 1997, although it placed more emphasis on dealing with poorly performing landlords and securing better management.

Transforming Private Landlords: Housing, markets & public policy, by Tony Crook & Peter A. Kemp © 2011 Tony Crook & Peter A. Kemp

Changing roles for private renting

Although rent control changed substantially in its detailed application between its initial introduction in 1915 and deregulation in 1980 and 1989, the aim was to protect existing private rented tenants from the consequences of housing shortages. Without control, it was assumed that rents would become unaffordable, tenants would run into arrears and thus risk eviction. Statutory security of tenure was an essential ingredient of rent control for otherwise landlords had every incentive to evict tenants to gain vacant possession.

In the 1980s a new discourse emerged favouring a new and pivotal role for the sector (for a review see, for example, Best *et al.*, 1992; see also Inquiry into British Housing, 1985) but with appropriate regulation (see for example Merrett, 1992; Pearce, 1983; and a speech by the then opposition housing spokesman to a lettings agents' conference, Soley, 1991). It recognised that owner occupation and social rented housing did not meet the needs of all households, especially those requiring flexibility in terms of jobs and personal circumstances. Ultimately such households would seek to own or to rent from councils (or housing associations) but in the meantime the major tenures did not meet their needs. If their long-term ambition was to own but they were not yet settled, they did not want to tie up capital and take out long-term mortgages. If they wanted to rent from a council or a housing association the shortages of such dwellings meant they were allocated according to criteria that did not include the need for short-term accommodation.

Gradually it was recognised that private renting's key attributes could provide major benefits for such households. It gave them flexibility so they could change housing quickly at little cost, they were not responsible for maintenance, and could usually find a wider range of dwelling types than in other tenures (e.g. shared accommodation), a wider range of contracts (shorter or longer leases), savings did not need to be tied up in ownership, and a well-functioning market could make homes available at short notice without waiting lists (Whitehead & Kleinman, 1986). In practice, the regulatory framework before 1980 prevented some flexibilities being available. For example, access was often hard because of shortages due to rent controls. Many prospective tenants needed substantial deposits and, sometimes, 'key money' to get hold of vacancies, as well as local knowledge about which current tenancies were likely to become vacant.

A more 'modern' sector with fewer regulations can thus provide a wide range of accommodation for households at early stages in their careers, including students, those switching jobs and needing short-term accommodation before they settle, and those needing somewhere to live as a result of changed personal circumstances, but without the social support provided by councils and housing associations. Flexibility can also improve the performance of the economy by enabling people to move to areas with labour shortages, and also by giving more housing choices to young households who would otherwise have to borrow heavily to buy their own homes. If they buy instead, their indebtedness can significantly influence consumer demand when interest rates change, and hence amplify business cycles (Muellbauer, 1990; Maclennan *et al.*, 1991). Hence macroeconomic (reducing the potentially inflationary effects of higher house prices created by an inflexible housing market), micro-economic (enabling people to move to jobs) and social welfare objectives (helping those in need) can be secured by having a vibrant private rented sector.

Policy objectives and barriers

This new approach was consistently accepted by both Conservative and New Labour governments in Britain and by devolved administrations (DoE, 1987; DETR, 2000a,b; ODPM, 2005; CLG, 2007a, 2008a; Scottish Government, 2007).[2] A consensus developed with only minor differences between governments of different persuasions. Their objectives were to increase the size of the market sector whilst also ensuring affordable rents, reasonable security and acceptable standards.

Three decades ago, before the major attempt by the Thatcher government in 1989 to revive the sector, its Minister of Housing argued that private renting had a significant role to play for the mobile, those wanting accommodation for a short period, those saving to buy, and those on low incomes who could see their income growing (Stanley, 1982). Just prior to the 1989 deregulation, the Thatcher government said it was a good option for people needing mobility and not wanting the ties of home ownership. It offered flexibility and responsiveness to market demand. It also helped better match labour supply and demand (DoE, 1987). In 2000 the New Labour government argued for a larger, better-quality and better-managed sector that would oil the wheels of the housing and labour markets (DETR, 2000a). In 2005 it stressed that the sector '... is a vital component of dynamic housing markets. It offers a flexible form of tenure to a wide variety of groups, contributing to greater labour mobility and supporting an efficient housing market' (ODPM, 2005, p. 34). A recent New Labour policy statement for England stressed how the sector offered flexibility, contributed to greater labour market mobility, was the tenure of choice for the young and had responded to increased student numbers (CLG, 2008a).

The difference between the Thatcher and the New Labour policies was the latter's greater emphasis on creating a better-managed sector whilst equally embracing the importance of nurturing a market framework. Although the initial emphasis was on younger households and others needing flexibility, there was a later desire to enable private landlords to house homeless people, supported by local authorities (nominating tenants and providing rent guarantees) and by housing associations and other not for profit organisations (the latter managing properties on behalf of landlords) (DoE, 1994; CLG, 2005; Scottish Government, 2007).

These new roles did not necessarily imply a larger sector because the old controlled and regulated sector continued to decline even as the new deregulated sector grew. It did, however, imply a change in the sector's ability to attract the kinds of landlords and funding that would provide higher quality accommodation while also giving competitive returns. Governments were thus keen not just to expand provision by existing landlords, but also to attract a new breed of landlords, especially corporate ones (as distinct from the individuals who had dominated supply in the past), with the institutional funding that would enable them to take a long-term view.

Because the sector did not provide landlords with competitive returns, consistent with acceptable risk and reputation, attracting new corporate interest was not going to be straightforward. Whilst it was possible to make good returns before deregulation, these tended to be restricted to three subsectors, two involving considerable reputation risk.

In the first subsector this involved 'dealing' in small rent-controlled properties occupied by elderly tenants, by buying them from long-standing landlords, renovating them with council grants and selling into the owner-occupied sector when the current tenants left – or died (see, for example, Cullingworth, 1963; Crook & Martin, 1988). The second subsector involved buying large vacant properties in run-down inner-city areas suitable for multiple-occupancy and letting them on licences in order to evade rent regulation and at standards breaching local authority physical and management codes (see Arden, 1983 on the legal issue of the use of licence agreements). Although good returns were possible, these were high-risk investments, because standards and rent regulation might be enforced, and hence they did not attract professionally qualified landlords but instead those prepared to operate on the margins of the law (Crook, 1991; Thomas & Hedges, 1986). Both instances enhanced negative images of landlords. In the third subsector, good returns could be made letting to companies outside the Rents Acts, providing short-term accommodation for professional people, an approach that involved fewer risks.

In all other subsectors, returns were simply uncompetitive with the alternative of securing vacant possession, selling properties into the owner-occupied sector and investing the proceeds in alternative ways (Nevitt, 1966; Doling & Davies, 1984). Buying new or existing vacant property and letting to mainstream tenants at acceptable standards did not give sufficient income return.[3] At best, net income returns were 3%, half that considered necessary by the British Property Federation (House of Commons Environment Committee, 1982a; Price Waterhouse, 1989). There were six principal reasons for this.

First, controls and regulation kept rents below market rates, but because most tenants were on low incomes it was unlikely that the market rents they could afford would give good returns. Even when property was let in the 'shadow' of the Rent Acts (on licences or on tenancies where landlords and tenants agreed the rents) good returns could only be made if the property was in poor condition, poorly managed and let at high occupancy rates. Evidence suggested that these quasi-market rents were only between 20 and 25% higher than the Fair Rents for comparable properties (House of Commons Environment Committee, 1982a). Without substantial subsidies, competitive returns would need a new set of tenants willing to paying the much higher rents that would make investment in decent property worthwhile. A House of Commons Committee referred to this as the central dilemma of any attempt to revive private renting because it was unlikely that competitive returns could be made without imposing hardship on tenants or a considerable rearrangement of subsidies (House of Commons Environment Committee, 1982b). Thus, although rent deregulation was a necessary condition for revival, it was not a sufficient condition because market rents alone would not yield competitive returns (Kemp, 1990; Crook, 1992a).

Second, taxation discriminated against residential letting. Depreciation was not tax-deductible (as it was for other businesses), discouraging new investment and the improvement of older housing (Nevitt, 1966; Hills, 1991). Councils and housing associations received capital subsidies on new investments. Although landlords could offset interest payments against their taxable income, as could owner-occupiers until the year 2000, they were also taxed on realised capital gains, unlike owner-occupiers (and when owner-occupiers received interest tax relief they paid no tax on their imputed income). Owner-occupiers' tax advantages were capitalised in higher house prices (compared to tenure-neutral tax arrangements).

Tax relief and rent control created two distinct prices for houses and placed landlords at a considerable disadvantage (Hamnett & Randolph, 1988). First was the price obtainable in the owner-occupied market and second was the considerably lower investment price worth paying to secure acceptable rental returns, based on the discounted net rental streams from controlled and regulated tenancies. This price gap encouraged existing landlords to sell when properties became vacant and discouraged others from buying vacant properties to let. The favourable tax treatment boosted demand for owner occupation because well-off households who could, in principle, afford the rents that would give landlords competitive returns were much better off buying instead. Indeed the real appreciation in house prices since the last war has helped owner-occupiers pay for the transactions costs of selling and buying homes out of capital gains rather than incomes or savings. This removed some of the relative attractiveness of renting compared with buying since it eased the costs to owner-occupiers of moving home.

Third, the sector's reputation was poor and had been in decline for many decades, with much negative publicity. All this would have to change if the sector was to attract not only new individual investors, but also the financial institutions that had the potential to bring substantial and long-term funds into the sector.

Fourth, the sector was a high-risk one for investors. There was the political risk that governments would change rent and other controls, putting long-term investments at risk. There was also the risk that local councils would enforce and tighten up physical and management codes and do so inconsistently. Risks such as these needed extra returns in compensation.

Fifth, were running costs. Little was known before deregulation about how much it cost to let private rented property. Costs include insurance, repairs, capital depreciation, including on fixtures and fittings, fees (if any) paid to managing agents, and interest payments. We now know from recent studies that these costs are considerable and take up, on average, a third of gross rental income (for example see Crook & Kemp, 1996a; Crook et al., 2000; Crook & Kemp, with Barnes & Ward, 2002). These reduce gross income returns (gross rental as a percentage of estimated capital value) considerably, giving much lower net income returns. In contrast, returns from letting commercial property are not reduced by these amounts because tenants bear them in full repairing and insuring leases.

The final barrier was liquidity. Before deregulation, there were almost no opportunities for indirect investments in residential lettings. There were almost no quoted residential property companies and even fewer property unit trusts in the residential sector. To make an investment it was thus necessary to buy property, inevitably less liquid than holding shares or even unit trusts because property transactions were time consuming and tenants' security of tenure reduced liquidity, making it difficult to sell properties as market opportunities changed. The only way to improve liquidity was to operate at the legal margins by evading the security provision of the Rent Acts. Thus, although total returns (real capital gains and net rents) could make residential letting attractive because of the long-term post-war real increases in house prices, these gains were, in practice, difficult to realise, especially as timing was often crucial to effective portfolio management. Hence low liquidity (plus the risks described above) meant higher returns were needed in compensation.

In our view creating a new, modern, private rented sector was not, therefore, going to be straightforward (Crook & Kemp, 1996b, 2002). There were two reasons why. First, investments had to give good total returns, consistent with risk, and be sufficiently liquid to allow the buying and selling of property to ensure good portfolio returns and to allow landlords to enter and exit the market as circumstances changed. There was no single 'hurdle' rate of return. Existing landlords might stay in the sector at a lower return than required by new investors for whom the investment was unfamiliar. Creating a more neutral tax treatment would also help.

The second reason was that after several decades of decline, anyone contemplating entering the market would need convincing that good returns could be made and that a change in government would not result in a return to control and regulation. Tenants would also need to be confident about several factors before the demand would exist to generate the returns needed by investors: the new legal framework, its enforcement against 'bad' landlords, and the existence of dwellings of a quality, and in the locations and on the contractual terms that met their needs.

It was in this context that a number of proposals were put forward in the 1980s for the kind of target rents or rates of return that would stem the decline of the sector or indeed attract new investment. The British Property Federation argued that rental returns of 9% gross (equivalent to 6% net) would maintain the sector at its then size, this yield taking account of future real increases in rents and capital values. It argued that a greater return than obtainable in commercial property was needed because of the higher risk of investing in residential lettings. Provided higher rents could be obtained, reducing security of tenure was not an issue, especially for larger institutional investors with long-term horizons. It might, however, be important for smaller-scale individual investors for whom capital gains were an important element of their return (House of Commons Environment Committee, 1982a). Other proposals came from the Committee of Inquiry into British Housing in its recommendations about ways to get 'responsible' private investment into the sector. Its basic idea was that rents should give an index-linked net return of 4%. Management and maintenance costs would be added to the rents that generated such net returns (Inquiry into British Housing, 1985). One of the weaknesses of this approach was that a single 'target' net rental return failed to take account of the very different risk and liquidity profiles of the many sub-sectors and also that in setting a long-run equilibrium rate of return it did not allow a market clearing rent to be realised, something that would be needed to draw in new investors to a fragile and novel product (Whitehead & Kleinman, 1988).

Reviving private renting: creating new model landlords

The Conservative governments also placed emphasis on the need for 'new model landlords' (Ridley, 1987). They thought these would be beacons for other potential landlords by demonstrating the renewed profitability of the sector. By running business responsibly they would also undermine and put bad landlords out of business. The objective was to modernise as well as to grow the sector by bringing in a different kind of business landlord: structured corporately and funded by long-term equity investments from pension and life funds. As one government minister colourfully put it, 'to use the good money to drive out the bad' (Patten, 1987). And as another put it, they would bring in the funds from mainstream institutions that were needed to grow the sector (Rifkind, 1988). As we shall see, the subsequent New Labour government fully supported this approach.

Historically, financial institutions had been substantial investors and owners of rental housing but by the eve of deregulation most had disinvested (Hamnett & Randolph, 1988). As a result, and as we have already seen in Chapter 1 (and will see again in Chapter 4), a large proportion of the sector was owned by individual landlords, often managing small portfolios in their spare time, with few having any professional or other qualifications in property and its management. Although few were deliberately operating outside the law, many were amateurs, unable to bring a professional approach. Even those who used managing agents did not necessarily offer better services. Because they had few lettings they could not realise economies of scale nor spread market risk by holding properties in a mix of locations and submarkets.

The governments thought that if larger scale landlords, funded by City institutions, seeking long-term returns and caring about their reputations, could be created, many of the problems of the sector would be solved: it would grow and be run professionally by managers who were adept at both housing and asset management. The larger size of these landlords would mean they would achieve economies of scale (helping both to improve returns and provide better services) and spread risk by operating in several markets. Having fewer and larger landlords would also make regulation easier and more effective.

1980: first steps towards deregulation

The initial steps taken in 1980 were, whilst tentative, part of the privatisation approach of the Thatcher government and paved the way for the full-blown deregulation of 1989.

Deregulation in 1989 built upon a number of 'experiments' taken in 1980 and later (Kemp, 1988b).[4] They were part of the Thatcher Government's drive to privatise housing, although 'setting the market free' paradoxically required renewed government subsidy and intervention (Crook, 1986a,b). The aims were to cut public spending, substitute private for public investment, and promote greater private ownership of housing by selling social rented housing to its tenants, either as individual owner occupiers or as collective owners through co-operative and other trusts. The government also reduced supply-side constraints on the private sector, modified the regulation of financial institutions with respect to mortgage lending, and made modest changes to private renting.

The Conservative government rejected the view, previously held by a broad spectrum of political positions, that housing had significant social value because good housing had positive externalities (for example providing better housing also reduced ill health) and provided an important means of redistribution in a society with significant income inequalities through the direct provision, or subsidy, of housing for low income people. Instead, it thought housing was primarily an individual good with limited social value and few externalities. Above a basic minimum, housing was a private good benefiting individuals alone and was something therefore for which individuals should pay, with subsidy restricted to ensuring that basic, justifiable, minimum standards were met. The state's job was to define this standard, to make sure existing and new housing complied, and to ensure the poor could afford it. The Conservative government believed that, by privatising existing social rented housing and increasing new private housing, it was increasing choice. Putting choice in the hands of consumers and not state-based producers promoted efficient provision in new supply and the management of existing stock because the market was more efficient in producing and allocating housing. Thus individuals' preferences were met at less cost in real resources than state provision and bureaucratic allocation.

There was, within this broad approach, a more specific belief in creating more owner occupation *per se*, because the government believed that specific benefits flowed to society as a whole, such as 'stability', when more households had an ownership stake. The housing privatisation thesis of the Thatcher government was broadly consistent with some of the rhetoric of the New Right. Its housing policies were intended to restrict the role of the state, reduce its alleged interference with and harm to the economy, reduce growth in money supply by restricting public expenditure on housing and thereby reduce inflation as well as the state's role (see Mishra, 1984).

But there were contradictions in the Conservative government's approach. The promotion of owner occupation required significant subsidies in both direct public expenditure and indirect tax expenditure. As a result, overall expenditure on housing rose rather than fell, although spending on social rented housing itself was reduced (Hills, 1991). The heavy emphasis on home ownership, allied to the deregulation of financial markets and the restricted supply of rented housing, contributed to the subsequent price booms and busts in the early 1990s and in the first decade of this century, with specific, although not wholly intended, consequences for private rented housing, as we shall see in later chapters.

Although full deregulation of private rented housing would have been consistent with the government's privatisation principles, it did not embark on this for another 10 years. Instead, in the 1980 Housing Act, it took a small number of steps or 'experiments'. The minister of housing argued that there was a big demand for short-term renting amongst those saving up to buy, those doing training and those whose incomes were low but who expected them to grow (Stanley, 1982). Private renting was ideal for them and changes were needed to enhance supply. No changes were made for existing regulated tenants, who kept their existing protection, and the measures to enhance new supply were small in scale and limited in impact (Crook, 1986b; Kemp, 1988b). There were three initiatives. The first increased liquidity and rental income for new lettings, the second provided tax incentives for new construction and the third made minor changes to the systems of Fair Rents and controlled tenancies.

First, a 'shorthold tenancy' (known as a 'short tenancy' in Scotland) was introduced. It could be used for new lettings of vacant property for one to five years, with a guaranteed right of repossession at the end. Initially rents had to be registered Fair Rents, but in 1982 this was restricted to London and then removed completely in 1987.

Second, 'assured tenancies' for newly built dwellings were introduced in England and Wales, the label providing 'assurance' to both tenants and landlords. This deregulated new construction for the first time since 1965 (Kemp, 1988b). Assured tenancies could be fixed-term or periodic and, although they allowed landlords to operate outside the Rent Acts and thereby charge market rents, they also enabled the continuation and renewal of tenancies, thus safeguarding tenants' interests, by using procedures similar to the renewal of commercial leases. The initiative was later extended to improving existing vacant dwellings. Landlords using assured tenancies needed government approval and had to be organisations and not individuals, the intention being that only reputable bodies could let outside the Rent Acts. To encourage assured tenancies the government allowed landlords to claim capital allowances against taxable income in 1982. Separate changes were made in 1986 to allow building societies to develop and own property themselves, thus enabling them to become landlords. New legislation in 1987 also allowed local councils to give grants of up to 30% of the cost of provision (subject to cost limits) to private landlords letting assured tenancies, at the same time as mixed public–private funding was introduced, allowing housing associations to let on assured tenancies (see Crook & Moroney, 1995; Kemp, 1988b).

Third, all remaining controlled tenancies were automatically converted into regulated tenancies. The Fair Rents regime was modified, phasing in rent increases over two instead of three years. Until then, phasing provisions meant that the rents paid were only 80% of the registered Fair Rent (Crook, 1986b).

All three initiatives had only a negligible impact on new supply. Few shortholds were created. Even fewer assured tenancies were created, although 188 bodies (mainly construction and property investment companies) were approved. Capital allowances created some interest, but very few units were built and assured tenancies let, the numbers estimated at just over 600 by 1986. Interest declined with the withdrawal of capital allowances in 1984, part of a Treasury reform of the corporation tax system that was made without consulting the Department of the Environment on possible housing policy impacts (House of Commons Environment Committee, 1984; Kemp, 1988b). If anything, changes to house improvement grants, combined with the faster phasing in of Fair Rent increases, had a far bigger impact on the existing stock, when a new breed of builder 'property-dealing' landlords started buying up tenanted property in improvement areas, renovating them with the aid of grants. This enabled them to earn large rent increases when the controlled tenancies were converted to registered ones after the improvements were completed and they could then patiently wait for vacant possession (Crook & Sharp, 1989).

The 1980 initiatives failed because they did not fully address the fundamental reasons for the lack of competitive returns, even though registered Fair Rents increased more between 1980 and 1985 than both the retail price and average earnings indices, compared with the previous five years. More significantly, however, the rents of 60–70% of new lettings in the early 1980s were not registered Fair Rents but were agreed between landlords and tenants (Crook, 1986b). Although struck in the shadow of the Rent Acts and hence not likely to be full market rents, they yielded returns that were far below the rents needed to generate new supply. Something more fundamental than these limited 1980 initiatives was therefore needed if a revival was to occur.

1989: 'full' deregulation: the overall approach

The approach adopted in 1989 and afterwards involved a combination of policies designed to create a market in private renting whilst also giving tenants assurances of reasonable security and that local councils would drive out the worst landlords. The principal legislation in England is the Housing Acts of 1988 and 2004. Policies evolved over the two decades after 1988 but can be grouped into the following statutory and other initiatives. They were designed to create a market, to provide information to help it work and to police it to ensure minimum standards of provision.

- Deregulation of rents and modified security of tenure to increase rents and improve liquidity, whilst affording tenants appropriate security and protection from harassment.
- Improving information for both landlords and tenants, including the accreditation of good landlords, important in a sector with limited, mainly voluntary, regulation and very large numbers of ill informed participants.
- New approaches to standards, to dealing with non-compliance to eliminate bad landlords and to better protecting tenants, including rent deposits.
- Tax incentives for individuals to 'kick start' the newly deregulated sector, to create new corporate landlords and to provide 'tax transparency' to attract financial institutions.

- Relevant contextual policies including helping homeless households, help for tenants to pay rents and urban planning policy.

In deregulating the sector much was assumed about existing landlords' ability and willingness to respond as rational market agents to changing price signals. As we shall see, this assumption was substantially unfounded.

Not all the initiatives came from government. Several came from the private sector, including a rent index to help with information costs and a buy-to-let initiative to help reduce the costs of debt funding. The range of schemes to regulate, register, accredit, licence and support landlords and their agents created a complex patchwork that depended upon the size of a property and its location (see Jones, 2009). This fostered uncertainty for landlords, especially those operating in more than one council area.

This 'full' deregulation was part of the Thatcher government's second stage in its project to privatise housing provision. Its first stage had focused on transferring ownership of the social rented sector to its tenants, plus removing constraints on private house builders and on the supply of mortgage finance (Booth & Crook, 1986). Private renting, although part of the privatisation agenda, had not been centre stage. In the second phase attention was turned to increasing the supply of private rented homes and on creating a commercially viable not-for-profit rented sector, outside the traditional council sector, for those needing long-term secure rented homes. Housing associations were used to supply new social rented housing, exposing them to market disciplines by requiring them to mix private funds with public grants for new provision, and freeing them to fix their own rents to enable them to cope with this discipline (Crook & Moroney, 1995). Local councils were restricted to strategic policy and an enabling, rather than a providing role. Initiatives were taken to transfer council-owned homes to other not-for-profit bodies. The rent allowance system was further reformed so that support for rent was related to the rent and tenants' needs, irrespective of their landlord, thus making it easier for tenants to move from one tenure to another since their entitlement to support became portable following a move to people or demand-side from producer or supply-side subsidies.

Deregulation of rents and more limited security

Deregulation was introduced in the Housing Act of 1988. It made it lawful to let at market rents and provided a much more predictable framework for regaining possession whilst also providing protection for tenants.

Since January 1989 all new tenancies have been subject to full market rents and more limited security. Greater liquidity was also achieved by enabling landlords to seek earlier possession through the courts, using more simplified and extended grounds. There were two kinds of tenancies. First, fixed-term assured shorthold tenancies, which were originally of a minimum six months in length, but with the possibility of extension. Second were assured tenancies, of indefinite length, which any landlord could use since it became no longer necessary to be an 'approved landlord'.[5] In Scotland, assured shortholds are known as 'short assured tenancies' but the legal framework is essentially similar to that in England and Wales.

Landlords were able to charge full market rents, with rent reviews set out in tenancy agreements and not specified by statute. The 1988 Act defined procedures to be used where periodic tenancy agreements were silent on these issues. Tenants could go to the Rent Assessment Committee if they wished to contest a landlord's proposed increase and the committee decided on a reasonable open market rent. Assured shorthold tenants could challenge the rent fixed at the beginning of a tenancy by asking the committee to review it. A lower rent was fixed only where an initial rent was significantly higher than for comparable local tenancies.

Assured shortholds enabled landlords to let their property for a short period only and to automatically get it back after six months without giving any grounds for possession, provided they gave two months' notice. If tenants refused to leave landlords could regain possession through an accelerated court process. In contrast, tenants of assured tenancies had the right to remain unless landlords could prove in court that they had grounds for possession. Landlords did not have an automatic right to possession when the tenancy ended even if the assured tenancy was originally let on a fixed term. Landlords could, however, seek possession on specific grounds such as non-payment of rent or other breaches of a tenancy agreement.

Until 1997 landlords could only lawfully create an assured shorthold tenancy if they followed specific procedures and served the correct forms on tenants. If they did not, and there was a dispute, the courts would assume that an assured tenancy had been created instead. This was a significant risk for landlords since it substantially reduced their liquidity – and many landlords made the mistake of not properly constituting their assured shortholds. Following an important modification in 1996, assured shortholds became the 'default' tenancy in 1997, that is the tenancy that would be assumed by the courts in the absence of documentation to the contrary. This meant that tenancies starting on or after 28 February 1997 were automatically assured shorthold tenancies unless special steps were taken to set up an assured tenancy. This 1996 measure significantly further reduced the risk of letting in the deregulated market. There was also no longer a minimum initial fixed term of six months for an assured shorthold, although landlords did not have the automatic right of possession during the first six months. When an assured shorthold tenancy came to the end of a fixed term, any replacement tenancy agreed was automatically on shorthold

Table 2.1   Steps towards deregulation

Before 1980	1980 Act	1988 Act	1996 Act
Regulated tenancies with agreed rents or registered Fair Rents	**Either** *regulated tenancies* with agreed rents or registered Fair Rents, **or** *shortholds* for 1–5 years with Fair Rents (until 1982 ex-London) **or** *assured tenancies* at market rents let by approved body	**Either** *assured tenancies* at market rents **or** (subject to being duly created) *assured shortholds* of a minimum 6 month term with guaranteed repossession at market rents	**Either** *assured shortholds* (no minimum fixed term) with guaranteed repossession after 6 months at market rents **or** (subject to being duly created) *assured tenancies* at market rents

terms (fixed term or periodic) unless the landlord chose to set up a replacement tenancy on an assured basis.

The 1996 Act also made it quicker and simpler to evict tenants in rent arrears or behaving antisocially. Some grounds for possession were mandatory and the courts had to grant possession if convinced the grounds existed. An example is two months' rent arrears where the rent was paid monthly. Others were discretionary and the courts granted an order if they thought it is reasonable to do so, such as persistent rent arrears or evidence of antisocial behaviour. Some were prior grounds, which had to be set out in tenancy agreements, such as the landlord requiring the house as his or her own principal residence.

To summarise the new regime, Table 2.1 sets out the key changes introduced by the 1980 and 1989 deregulations and the changes made in 1996.

The new regime thus remained largely unchanged since it had first been established in January 1989. The important changes introduced in 1997 actually improved the position for landlords with respect to liquidity, in the sense of making assured shortholds the default tenancy and speeding up repossession. Although this stability in the legal framework was significant to the modernisation of the sector and the attempts to attract long-term investment and new types of landlord. Political risk, that is the risk that incoming governments will change the policies of their predecessors on fundamental matters like rents and security of tenure, was significantly less than in the past. There was an explicit endorsement of the new framework by the incoming New Labour government very soon after taking up office in 1997. Ministers repeatedly stated that they were in favour of responsible private landlords and that they would not re-introduce rent controls (see, for example, Armstrong, 1997). This approach was subsequently and regularly restated in green and white papers. For example, in 2000 the Government stated that 'landlords can be assured that we intend no change in the present structure of assured and assured shorthold tenancies, which is working well. Nor is there any question of our re-introducing rent controls in the deregulated market' (DETR, 2000a, p. 44).

That is not to say that there have been no calls by housing lobby groups, by independent commentators, by individual MPs, and by parliamentary select committees to make changes. But their proposals were about fine-tuning, not reversions to the eras of controls and regulation (for examples, see Shelter, 2002, 2007; Law Commission, 2006, 2008; Bill *et al.*, 2008; House of Commons Committee on Communities and Local Government, 2008; Rugg & Rhodes, 2008). We return to these and other reviews in our concluding chapter.

Supporting and informing landlords

What New Labour did after coming to power in 1997 was to support and encourage good landlords, protecting them from tenants who misbehaved, and dealing with the minority of bad landlords. It did so because it recognised that bad tenants and landlords undermined attempts to improve the sector's image for potential investors and tenants. Thus it gave landlords 'encouragement, support and education rather than further heavy regulation' (DETR, 2000a, p. 45).

These were important initiatives because very large numbers of landlords provided accommodation to a very large number of tenants. Very few landlords had professional qualifications (see Chapter 4) and those using managing agents were using services then not regulated by statute (unlike estate agents) and not all managing agents were members of professional bodies or trade associations.[6] The emphasis was on voluntary and not statutory regulation, although the coverage of voluntary regulation was patchy (Carsberg, 2008; Jones, 2009).

After the 1989 deregulation a more proactive landlord and agent lobby appeared, including the National Landlords Association (also in Scotland) and the Association of Residential Lettings Agents (ARLA). Unlike professional bodies, not all of these trade associations disciplined members who failed to comply with codes of conduct. Nor did they all have redress mechanisms in place. Moreover, estimates suggested that only about half of all managing agents belonged to trade or professional associations (Crook & Kemp, 1996a; Law Commission, 2008; Jones, 2009). Managing agents were the group where there had been the least progress in establishing codes, disciplinary regimes for proven breaches and redress mechanisms for those affected.

There were several initiatives to help the market work better by informing landlords about their rights and obligations and providing them with benchmarking information on rents, capital values and yields. Local landlord forums and accreditation schemes were sponsored and organised by local authorities. They enabled councils and landlords to meet regularly to discuss matters of mutual concern. Increasingly, local authorities, landlords and, where appropriate, universities or colleges joined together to set up voluntary accreditation schemes (DETR, 2001a,b; Hughes & Houghton, 2007). Forums helped landlords to keep up to date with information and training schemes. Many provided landlords with one-stop shops for the many different services landlords needed from local authorities. Accreditation schemes enabled local councils to 'badge' landlords who matched or exceeded specific good practice about management and physical standards. Many were combined schemes, with an accreditation that covered a landlord and the landlord's portfolio. Some schemes involved landlords' self-certification but most involved formal inspection. Sometimes these were linked to insurance on preferential terms and provided access to councils' rent deposit or rent guarantee schemes, but the fundamental benefit for landlords was getting a 'badge' showing they were good landlords and being able to publicise this to potential tenants.

These schemes were important in an imperfect market where tenants found it hard to get information, making it difficult for them to reach judgements about how well a landlord performed before they took on tenancies. By 2001 there were 50 accreditation schemes in England and 40% of local authorities were running forums for their landlords (DETR, 2001b). A national accreditation network (ANUK) brought together organisations and professionals involved in accrediting landlords. In Scotland, a new Scotland-wide national accreditation scheme (Landlord Accreditation Scotland) was launched in 2008, part-funded by the Scottish Government, and developed from four local pilots. Members of this national scheme agreed to abide by a 'Core Standards for Accredited Landlords' code drawn up after the pilots. The national scheme was intended to replace new local schemes and offered economies of scale as well as a nationally recognised brand (Scottish Government, 2007).

The National Approved Lettings Scheme provided a single standard for letting agents (http://www.nlasheme.co.uk). It accredited lettings and management agents, guaranteed defined customer service standards to both landlords and tenants, had insurances to protect clients' money and a customer complaints procedure with independent redress. The scheme was supported by professional bodies in the sector: ARLA, NAEA and RICS. Agents benefited from having a single kitemark for tenants who were looking for the assurance of reputable management and customer service.

Because the market was imperfect, one important source of information was about rents and returns. In commercial property the Investment Property Databank (IPD) has long provided regular information on rents and yields for offices, shops and other commercial property, allowing asset managers in financial institutions to benchmark their performance and new acquisitions. Upon deregulation no such index existed for residential lettings, a barrier to getting City funding into the sector. An index for England was commissioned from the University of York by the Joseph Rowntree Foundation and the government department responsible for housing in England, supported by ARLA (Rhodes & Kemp, 2002). This index was later run by ARLA and funded by mortgage lenders. The IPD itself provided regular information after 2002 about returns from deregulated tenancies owned by large-scale investors (http://www.ipd.com). Mortgage lenders also produced regular information on rents and yields based on their buy-to-let loans (for example, Paragon, 2009). While more regular information about rents and returns emerged after deregulation than before, these indices were restricted to particular submarkets.

Standards, management and deposits

Government policy also addressed poor management and inadequate standards. For many reasons, despite deregulation, parts of the sector remained poorly managed and in poor condition. Market rents might not have justified the expenditure required to meet basic standards. Tenants may have worried about complaining for fear of being evicted. Many tenants did not stay for long and so might not have cared about structural problems that only impacted in the long run. Although the sector had voluntary codes of regulation and enforced them on members, as we have already seen only a minority of the sector was owned or managed by those signing up to them.

Licensing houses in multiple occupation

In England, houses in multiple occupation (HMOs) were defined in the Housing Act of 2004 as accommodation let to three or more tenants who formed two or more households and who shared kitchen, bathroom or WC. They could be an entire house or flat, or one that had been converted into bedsits, or one where a converted house had one or more flats that were not self-contained (CLG, 2007b).

Prior to deregulation, there were many debates about the best way to secure the health and safety of tenants in HMOs (Crook, 1989). Until 2006, local authorities had discretion about this. They had powers, but not duties, to register HMOs, to serve notices on their owners to ensure that locally determined standards were implemented and, as a last resort, to take over management themselves. Some of the worst housing conditions were in HMOs. Those wanting mandatory duties thought that local discretion meant HMOs were not given priority. Environmental health officers had many tasks and could be characterised as 'street-level bureaucrats' delegated the job of prioritising them (Lipsky, 1980). HMOs were particularly difficult to deal with. They were hard to locate and tenants tended not to complain for fear of being evicted. HMOs were thus neglected.

Two decades later, evidence suggested that reacting to complaints rather than strategically addressing the issues was still dominant. Research evidence from 2006 showed that only 46% of authorities in England had HMO strategies and only 22% had registration schemes. HMOs housed many vulnerable tenants whose situation qualified them for social rented housing but who were not getting re-housed because of long waiting lists. Many HMOs were owned by rogue landlords incapable of managing properly and sometimes operating outside of the law, others being described as 'naïve and informal', with no concept of how to manage properly (CLG, 2006, 2007b).

Although mandatory licensing of all HMOs was not required, it was introduced in 2006 for the larger, three-or-more-storey HMOs occupied by five or more people forming more than one separate household. These posed the greatest risks to tenants and confronted landlords with the biggest challenges. After 2006, licensed HMOs had to match occupancy, amenity, fire and other safety standards. Landlords or agents had to be 'fit and proper' to manage them. With respect to smaller HMOs, local authorities were given the discretion to establish additional licensing schemes if a significant proportion of these were being so poorly managed that the health and safety of tenants and the wider public was threatened. These additional schemes needed prior government approval (CLG, 2007b, 2009a).

Councils had a number of sanctions if landlords and agents failed to comply with licensing obligations, including securing repayment of all housing benefit (even if not paid direct to landlords) within the previous 12 months, fines of up to £20000, and the transfer of management to the local authority for up to five years. Even if not subject to licenses, HMO owners and managers were required to comply with defined management and standards and councils could step in with 12-month interim management orders or notices to reduce any overcrowding.

Mandatory licensing of all HMOs in Scotland was introduced in the year 2000. Properties occupied by three or more unrelated persons were defined as HMOs and anyone letting one, with limited exceptions, required a licence. Councils issued the licences and had to ensure that HMOs met all appropriate standards, including that landlord and agents were fit and proper persons (Currie, 2002; Scottish Government, 2004).

Pressure continued to licence all HMOs in England. There was also a growing concern about HMO concentrations in inner-city neighbourhoods, particularly those with many students, and also the consequences for lost community cohesion and community facilities, as well as the impact of disrepair and poor physical and management (ECOTEC, 2008). The New Labour government was lobbied to tighten up the definition of HMO for the purposes of planning control and, prior to the 2010 general election agreed to do so (CLG, 2010a). It also allowed councils to declare additional licensing schemes for small HMOs without prior government approval (CLG, 2010b).

Landlord registration and licensing

Whereas HMO licensing dealt with decent standards, landlord registration and selective licensing was targeted much more at dealing with the antisocial behaviour of both reprehensible landlords and marginalised tenants. There was not provision to register or licence all landlords in England but, since 2006, apart from limited exceptions, all private landlords in Scotland must be registered. The aim is to ensure that all landlords are fit and proper to let property. Registration is done by local councils using criteria to ensure registered landlords have not committed relevant offences, have not unlawfully discriminated, or contravened landlord and tenant law (Scottish Government, 2006).

In England, the New Labour government adopted a more selective approach. It focused on low-demand areas, manifested in above-average vacancy rates, low capital values, and poor physical conditions. These areas housed vulnerable households in privately rented property, many dependent on welfare payments and housing benefit, with evidence of persistent and pervasive antisocial behaviour (DETR, 2000a; House of Commons Select Committee on Transport, Local Government and the Regions, 2001). Landlords were buying up property and letting to vulnerable tenants whose behaviour disrupted the lives of the remaining and more long-standing residents. Tenants were often receiving housing benefit, but payments were made directly to the landlords, leaving them with little incentive to manage the property well since the rental stream was in effect guaranteed regardless of how badly they managed properties. There were suggestions that some of the purchasing was funded through money-laundering and that many migrants were being housed in these areas (CLG, 2007b; Sprigings, 2007).

In 2006 the New Labour government gave local authorities powers to introduce selective licensing of all private rented property in these low-demand areas (CLG, 2009a). A licence obliged landlords to be fit and proper persons and to provide specific standards and conditions. It was introduced to help local authorities tackle what were regarded as the worst problems in the private rented sector. Consultation was required with all affected parties, including landlords and tenants, before schemes were submitted for government approval (17 designations in 12 councils – mainly northern – had been approved by 2010), although the government announced in early 2010 that prior approval was no longer to be required (CLG, 2007b, 2010b).

There were repeated calls on the Government to introduce conditions on housing benefit, making payment to landlords conditional on keeping property up to standard or of being members of accreditation schemes. Although the option was discussed in the New Labour government's housing green paper of 2000 (DETR, 2000a), it was later rejected as being too complex to administer, with possible negative impacts on benefit recipients who might lose their homes if landlords simply withdrew from the market. An alternative approach was later adopted (see below) of placing more power in the hands of tenants by no longer paying benefit direct to landlords, thus in principle making it possible for tenants to bargain over rents with landlords and place pressure on them to improve conditions (DWP, 2002).

Repairs: standards, enforcement and incentives

Historically, physical conditions in private rented dwellings, rather than overall supply, were a key policy issue for governments. Conditions in private rented dwellings were the worst of all tenures, partly because of rent controls. Even when quasi-market rents were charged, these did not give landlords the returns needed to make repairs and improvements worthwhile. Strict commercial criteria did not always govern whether or not landlords made repairs. Some landlords were willing to invest more than was strictly needed because they adopted attitudes of stewardship towards their portfolios. But where landlords regarded their portfolios strictly in investment terms, they were more likely to own the properties in the worst conditions and spend significantly less than required (Crook *et al.*, 1998a, 2000). And despite the long-term decline in the overall demand for private renting, there were still pockets of excess demand, especially in major cities, with tenants willing to rent properties in poor condition.

The small scale and amateur nature of much ownership also militated against getting repairs done since landlords had neither the technical knowhow nor the resources needed, their small scale preventing them realising economies of scale in commissioning repairs. Moreover, there were also circumstances where both elderly low-income tenants and their longstanding, also often elderly landlords, with few financial assets had a mutual interest in deferring work that was needed, the tenants to avoid disturbance and rents increases, and the landlords to avoid the financial and organisational costs involved (Crook & Sharp, 1989).

Until deregulation in 1989, the approach taken by post-war governments was fourfold (Crook, 1989; Crook & Hughes, 2001). First, was the continuation of slum clearance, demolishing many private rented properties. Second, local authorities had (mainly) discretionary powers to enforce minimum standards. Third, and a significant change from earlier policy, incentives were introduced when grants for repairs as well as improvements were made available, as policy changed from redevelopment to improvement. Since landlords owned much of the poor stock in improvement areas, it was crucial that they had these incentives. Fourth, an additional emphasis was placed on buying out landlords who could not, or would not, do the works themselves. Significant loans and subsidies were devoted to enabling housing associations to acquire these properties (Maclennan, 1985). Indeed, local authorities tended to use their enforcement powers to persuade landlords to sell to housing associations rather than expecting them to do the work themselves (Crook & Sharp, 1989).

Evidence on the impact of these policies before deregulation suggested that *in situ* improvements by existing landlords were generally limited and that improvement was driven by three types of ownership change (Crook & Hughes, 2001). First, the transfer of better condition dwellings from the owner-occupied sector being acquired by new landlords entering the sector. Second, the transfer of the worst dwellings out of the sector, principally when housing associations acquired and renovated them. Third, the acquisition of tenanted dwellings by property dealers looking for capital appreciation, who acquired them at sitting tenant values, did the necessary remedial work, often with grant-aid, and then secured a vacant-possession sale after the existing tenants had moved.

Following deregulation in 1989, government policy towards conditions and achieving improvements by private landlords shifted significantly. The Conservative government considered that deregulation itself would secure the repairs and improvements needed. It would lead to higher rents and a more competitive market. Higher rents would make it more profitable to do the work, overall supply would increase and landlords would face more competition. It was thought that market rents would reflect the value of housing services provided and tenants would be willing to pay more for better quality, rewarding landlords who kept dwellings up to standard and penalising landlords with poorer properties. The latter would find it difficult to secure tenants and would thus have to bring them up to standard or go out of business. Meanwhile the hoped-for entry of new corporate landlords with large-scale portfolios would ensure that costs would fall as economies of scale were realised. Both the Thatcher and New Labour governments' views were that the prime responsibility for carrying out and financing repairs and improvements lay with landlords. Maintenance costs were part of the normal overhead of running a property letting business and landlords should not be subsidised for the costs of repairs (DoE, 1995). Hence deregulated rents should provide landlords with the means of doing regular maintenance work and of raising loans to deal with any backlog of capital repairs and improvements.

Hence, grants for private landlords were progressively withdrawn. Until 1996 grants were only mandatory when local councils took enforcement action. They also became 'deficit' grants, calculated on the extent to which costs could be funded through rent increases or increased capital values. In 1996 mandatory grants were wholly withdrawn (even when enforcement action was taken) and help was only available at the discretion of a local authority to help finance essential work in the continuing regulated sector and targeted at renewal areas, with the amount of grant also being at local authorities' discretion (DoE, 1996).

In 2003 these provisions were also withdrawn and replaced with a general power for local councils to provide assistance for housing renewal, within locally adopted strategies, based on partnership working including with private landlords. Assistance was to meet the needs of vulnerable households and to increase the supply of private rented accommodation. In determining loans or grant amounts, councils were required to take account of landlords' management track records and their rental income and could vary assistance if landlords belonged to local accreditation schemes or if an HMO was registered. They could also require assistance to be repaid if landlords subsequently sold up properties, in order to prevent public funds being used to support speculation (DETR, 2001c; ODPM, 2003a).

There was also a new approach to standards. A new risk-based Housing Health and Safety Rating system was introduced in 2006 in England and Wales. It replaced the previous fitness standard with its pass/fail approach. Local councils assessed the severity of health hazards, cold and damp in dwellings and the harm these could pose to occupants, and decided on appropriate action. If they found hazards and landlords did not then put things right, councils could take formal enforcement action. In the case of the most serious hazards they could do the work themselves and recover costs. Powers remained to prohibit the occupation or demand the demolition of dwellings (or clearance of several dwellings) if these were appropriate courses of action.

A new Repairing Standard was introduced in Scotland in 2007, setting out minimum repair and maintenance standards for private rented housing. The standard was to be enforced by a tenant complaining to the Private Rented Housing Panel (PRHP). The PRHP could take enforcement action to ensure that works were carried out (Scottish Government, 2008).

After 1998, landlords were also required to ensure that all gas appliances were maintained in good order. Although they were not obliged to do equivalent checks on electrical wiring and appliances, they would be liable if things went wrong.

Safeguarding tenancy deposits

There had been longstanding concerns about the potential abuse of tenants' deposits by landlords (for example see CAB, 1998; ODPM, 2002). Most tenants paid a deposit of approximately a month's rent at the beginning of a tenancy, providing landlords with funds to rectify damage or other breaches of tenancy agreements, including unpaid rent or utility bills that came to light when tenancies ended. If low-income tenants could not afford a deposit they could get help from local council rent or deposit guarantee schemes.

If there was nothing to rectify and no unpaid bills at the end of tenancies, tenants were entitled to have their deposit returned in full, but research showed that some landlords were holding onto deposits, despite no evidence of damage or unpaid bills. Partly this was because landlords and tenants often did not mutually agree the condition of the dwelling or its fittings and fixtures at the start of tenancies, and this was often the cause of disputes. Although landlords, on the whole, perceived there to be few problems in the handling of deposits, far more tenants did so.

To test models of protecting deposits, alternative schemes were piloted in 2000, including a custodial scheme (drawing on overseas experience) and a specifically constructed insurance-based scheme, for which there had been no experience to draw upon The evaluation confirmed that tenants' apprehensions about misuse by landlords were much greater than actual evidence of abuse but that a protection scheme would provide much reassurance to them. It concluded that more than one scheme was needed if deposit protection was to work (ODPM, 2002).

To ensure tenants were not out of pocket, all deposits paid by assured shorthold tenants had, after 2007, to be paid into a designated scheme in England and Wales. Three schemes were approved and within a year of operation 1.7 m deposits had been protected, worth £1600 m in total (Austin, 2010). One was a custodial deposit protection scheme where the deposit was handed over to the third party (a private company called Computershare) and the other two were insurance-based schemes where the deposit stayed with the landlords or their agents, but was protected by insurance backing, which also covered the possibility of the insolvency of landlords and agents. This was vital because managing agents were not regulated by statute and could hold client funds without any form of consumer protection, although those who were members of professional or trade bodies did have access, through that membership, to client-fund protection insurance. All three schemes had dispute-resolution mechanisms built into them. If landlords and tenants both agreed to use the service to resolve the dispute rather than go to court, they were both bound by its decision.

In Scotland in 2010, consideration was being given to setting up similar schemes and enabling legislation was passed to allow the Scottish Government to secure an improvement in deposit practice if it was minded to do so.

'New model landlords'

To achieve the specific objective of creating new model landlords, it was recognised that deregulation on its own was unlikely to be sufficient. Although it would allow landlords to let at market rents and with more limited security and would, in principle, lead to more competitive returns through higher rents and greater liquidity, it would take time for confidence to improve. In the short run there would be some unfamiliarity and risk about investing in the deregulated sector. Better returns might tempt more existing landlords to remain and new individual landlords to enter the market, but in order to speed up this process and especially to attract new corporate landlords and City funding, governments introduced a series of measures, including the Business Expansion Scheme (BES), the Housing Investment Trust scheme (HITs) and, more latterly, Real Estate Investment Trusts (REITs). In Scotland, for a limited period, grants to help stimulate market rented housing were introduced (Gibb *et al.*, 1998). Chapters 5 (BES) and 6 (HITs and REITs) describe these schemes in some detail and only brief descriptions are provided here.

The BES was introduced in 1988 to help kick-start the revival of private renting by attracting retail capital into the sector and to demonstrate to potential investors that private renting could, once again, provide competitive returns. To do this, the government adapted an existing mechanism, the BES, which had been set up in 1983 to stimulate venture capital investment in new companies. By extending an existing scheme the government was able to quickly provide tax incentives to those investing in the newly deregulated sector and underwrite investor risk. Chapter 5 shows that, whilst substantial funds were raised and many companies were formed, the long-run impact of the BES on private renting was much more limited.

The introduction of the HITs initiative was the second stage in the drive to get new capital into the deregulated sector and to create a more corporately owned sector. If the BES was about retail investment by individuals, the HITs scheme was aimed at getting wholesale, or institutional, funding into the sector. To do this the government announced in 1995 that it would enable the creation of HITs in order to provide a vehicle for financial institutions to invest in private renting (DoE, 1995). Many City institutions own commercial property as a key asset in their investment portfolio. Pension and life funds did not pay tax on their income from these directly owned assets, but they were not keen to own private rented property themselves. The alternative of indirect investment (such as buying shares in a residential property company) meant they would suffer tax losses. The HITs initiative was designed to encourage them to invest indirectly, but in a way that reduced their tax on such investments. The HITs legislation was passed in 1996. In Chapter 6 we describe the HIT scheme in more detail and explain why no HIT was formed.

Despite the difficulties of attracting major City funding into the sector and of creating new corporate landlords, New Labour nonetheless remained as committed to this as had been the previous Conservative government to its BES and HIT schemes. Indeed New Labour stressed its commitment to expanding the corporate sector and to fostering increased investment by major financial institutions (DETR, 2000a). However, although it said that it was willing to consider whether tax measures could help, it also stressed that it did not want to introduce tax breaks (i.e. tax subsidies) that would distort investment choices.

Instead New Labour adopted the recommendation in the Barker Report on Housing Supply to establish bespoke tax transparent investment vehicles like US Real Estate Investment Trusts (Barker, 2004). The attraction is that the REITs provide total tax transparency, paying no tax on their profits. Instead these are distributed to shareholders, who then pay tax according to their own tax liabilities. Hence a pension fund would pay none, putting tax liabilities for this indirect holding on the same basis as its direct property assets. Legislation in 2006 enabled REITs to be formed from January 2007 onwards for all property investment, not just residential. But like the previous HIT scheme, no residential REIT was formed and in Chapter 6 we explain in more detail the REIT structure adopted in Britain, the reasons for its lack of impact in attracting investment into residential REITs and the contrasting success of commercial REITs. We also discuss the continuing attempts to attract institutional investment to the sector despite the lack of success to date.

Other key policies

The policies we have described above were directly targeted at the private rented sector but there were three other important policies that had an important impact on the sector, although not all were targeted specifically at private renting.

Housing the homeless and the vulnerable

Although the sector's revival was principally designed to house those needing short-term accommodation and thus benefiting from the flexibility that the sector could provide, policy also sought to widen the sector's role, including housing homeless people. All the governments in Britain examined ways of enabling landlords to do this through the support of local councils and voluntary groups (e.g. DoE, 1995; CLG, 2005; Scottish Government 2007). There were a range of initiatives, including rent deposit guarantee schemes to help the homeless who had no funds to pay deposits, and private-sector leasing schemes whereby councils leased property from private landlords, undertook all the management, guaranteed the rent and returned the property to the landlords at the end of the lease in the same condition as at the beginning (Rhodes & Bevan, 1997; Rugg, 1997).

At the same time, the sector continued to house many vulnerable, but not necessarily homeless people, few of whom benefited from these support schemes, many living in the low-demand areas subject to selective licensing schemes. These policies and trends had important consequences for the regulation and reputation of the sector, and for investor confidence, matters to which we return in the final chapter.

Helping tenants to pay their rent

Since 1983, housing benefit, which provides income-related assistance with the rent for low-income tenants, has been the responsibility of the UK government but is administered by local councils. Before rents were deregulated in 1989, there was much concern that any move to market rents would produce a steep rise in housing benefit payments and that, in effect, deregulation would be underpinned by a government subsidy, especially at the bottom end of the market, where many low-income tenants depended on benefits. At the time, tenants on benefit had any rent increases fully reflected in higher benefits (provided their income did not change) and any rent reductions were fully offset by lower benefit. Hence tenants had no incentives to bargain with landlords over rents or to move into smaller accommodation if this helped improve their overall income.

To prevent this happening rent officers (responsible for the registration of Fair Rents in the regulated sector) were given a new role: to monitor market rents and to use this information to restrict benefit payments (Kemp, 1990). Local authorities (the bodies responsible for paying housing benefit) referred claims from those paying market rents to rent officers, who ruled on whether the rent was above a reasonable market rent for the locality or whether the accommodation was too large for claimants' reasonable needs. Local councils were free to pay benefit on the market rent (even if it was above this guidance from rent officers) but only received reimbursement from the central government department on the amount notified by rent officers after they had vetted the market rent.

In 1996 additional mechanisms were introduced to police benefit payments, for example rents in excess of local reference rents or single room rents (the latter for single, childless tenants under 25), but the principal objective was to prevent the creation of a market in private tenancies largely underpinned by government funding. In this way, a conflict was avoided between one government department keen to see an expansion of the private rented sector and another government department anxious to control public spending on housing benefit. The government introduced a backdoor method of regulating market rents but it also introduced risks for landlords since survey evidence showed that large proportions of tenants faced significant gaps between the rent they had agreed to pay their landlords and the amount covered by housing benefit (see Kemp, 1990, 2004).

In April 2008, following a pilot in 18 local authorities, a new form of housing benefit, known as the Local Housing Allowance, was introduced for new claimants and for existing claimants who move house. This new scheme involved a flat-rate allowance payable to claimants within broad rental market areas, of which there were about 150 in Britain. The reform had a range of goals, including that of seeking to encourage more shopping around by tenants (DWP, 2002). The allowance was normally paid to the claimant. However, if the claimant was vulnerable, unlikely to pay their rent or at least eight weeks in arrears, the allowance could be paid direct to their landlord. If the claimant could obtain accommodation the rent of which was less than the allowance, they could keep up to £15 per week of the difference. If the rent was higher than the allowance, they had to make up the difference out of their own pocket (DWP, 2009).

Urban planning policy

Throughout much of the period under discussion, urban policy in Britain favoured development in urban areas in attempts to stem decentralisation and to reverse the economic and social decline of inner-city areas. Spatial planning policy played a key role in facilitating this by limiting the release of land in greenfield areas and promoting the re-use of brownfield sites. Targets were set for the proportion of new residential development built on brownfield sites (In England at 60%) and, allied to grants for the amelioration of contaminated land in inner areas, urban policy fostered much high density, especially high rise, development of one and two bedroom flats in city-centre areas as well as the redevelopment of sites of large single-family houses in suburban areas into higher-density flats. In this way planning policy generated the supply of small dwellings in locations where there was strong demand from private tenants and where, as we shall see in Chapter 4, good rental and total returns could be made by investors. We shall also see in Chapter 7 how this development provided significant opportunities for buy-to-let investors.

Conclusions

We have now seen how policy has evolved over the last three decades to place private renting in a more pivotal position, in the belief that private provision of rented housing can secure important economic and social objectives, especially if the ownership of the sector is modernised. Deregulation was a necessary, but not a sufficient condition. The market also had to be created and nurtured and effectively policed, both to secure its reputation and to enable it to house a much wider range of types of household than had originally been envisaged. Moreover the market conditions had to be right to allow landlords to make competitive returns. In Chapter 4 we will show how landlords responded to these new opportunities but, before then, Chapter 3 shows how the market as a whole evolved over the period under review.

Notes

1. In the course of these three decades, aspects of domestic policy were assigned to the devolved administrations in Britain, specifically to the Scottish government and the Welsh Assembly government. This led to some divergence of policy within Britain and this divergence is referred to where appropriate. The legal framework within Scotland was always different, given the long-standing existence of its separate legal system as well as the practice of separate policymaking and legislation.
2. We review the most recent policy statements in the last chapter of this book.
3. Net income returns (or net rental yields) are defined as the rent after deducting management and other costs expressed as a percentage of the capital value that could be realised upon vacant possession (Crook & Kemp, with Barnes & Ward, 2002).
4. We use the term 'deregulation' to describe both rent deregulation and the changes to security of tenure that were introduced in 1980 and 1989.
5. Both assured shorthold and assured tenancies applied to all lettings made after January 1989 unless they were business or holiday lets, a tenancy of an agricultural holding or an educational institution, one let with either no rent or a very low or very high rent, or by resident landlords. Nor did they apply when a licence to occupy had been granted instead of a tenancy.
6. It is, however, important to note that those agents and landlords who are members of the Royal Institution of Chartered Surveyors (RICS), the Association of Residential Lettings Agents (ARLA), the Incorporated Society of Valuers and Auctioneers (ISVA), and the National Association of Estate Agents (NAEA) were required to operate to standards recognised by their organisations.

3

Private Renting Since 1979

By the time that the Conservative government led by Prime Minister Margaret Thatcher came to power in 1979, the private rental housing market was very different from what it had been immediately after the Second World War; it was not just private landlordism that had changed. The size and composition of the sector, as well as the main roles that it played in housing provision, differed significantly from what they were when most people rented their home from a private landlord. Moreover, the private rental housing market has continued to evolve over the three decades since 1979.

This chapter considers the ways in which private renting has developed since 1979. In doing so, it seeks to set out the wider context of the private rental housing market within which the changes in private landlordism have taken place. It first considers the stock of privately rented dwellings, focusing on changes in its size, composition and condition. Next, it looks at who rents from private landlords and how that has changed over the past three decades. It then examines the terms on which tenants rent their homes, looking particularly at tenancies, rent levels, and financial assistance from housing allowances. Finally, the chapter closes by assessing the extent to which tenant satisfaction and the image of private renting have changed over this period.

Reversal of fortunes

The private rental housing stock had declined continuously throughout the period from 1945 until Mrs Thatcher came to power (see Chapter 1). Yet, although many other advanced economies had also witnessed a decline in

Transforming Private Landlords: Housing, markets & public policy, by Tony Crook & Peter A. Kemp © 2011 Tony Crook & Peter A. Kemp

Table 3.1   Privately rented dwellings as a percentage of the total in Britain

1971 (%)	1981 (%)	1991 (%)	2001 (%)	2007 (%)
20	11	9	10	12

Source: Calculated from housing data at http://www.clg.gov.uk

the size of their private rental housing sectors over that period, the rate of decline was particularly sharp in Britain (Kemp, 1997). By 1981, the privately rented sector accounted for 2.35 million dwellings or only 11% of the total stock, compared with an estimated 3.50 million and 20% in 1971 (Table 3.1). The annual rate of decline over that decade averaged over 100000 dwellings, equivalent to about 3% of the 1971 stock each year.

Despite the measures to revive the sector included in the 1980 Housing Act (see Chapter 2), the number and proportion of homes rented from private landlords in Britain continued to shrink during the 1980s, albeit at a slower rate than previously. The fact that private renting continued to decline was hardly a surprise. After all, to many commentators, the sector had seemed to be in almost terminal decline; indeed, some thought that it might disappear altogether. While private renting was never likely to disappear completely, the question of just how small it might become was certainly a valid one to ask, given its precipitous decline since 1945.

The decline of private renting in Britain eventually came to a halt at the end of the 1980s, a development that caught government statisticians (Down *et al.*, 1994) and many other people by surprise. Perhaps even more unexpectedly, the number of privately rented dwellings actually began to increase, as did (albeit to a lesser extent) the share of the stock accounted for by this tenure. Indeed, the number of such homes rose from 1.99 million in 1991 to 3.24 million in 2007, an increase of 1.24 million or 63% in just 16 years. Over that period, the share of the total housing stock accounted for by privately rented dwellings increased from 9% to 12% (Table 3.1). Thus, the proportion of all dwellings that were owned by private landlords in Britain grew by a third between 1991 and 2007. While the sector still accounts for a relatively small share of the total housing stock, this growth represents a significant turning point after many decades of decline (Kemp, 2004).

Meanwhile, private landlords had also increased their share of the *rental* market, which rose from a quarter in both 1981 and 1991 to a third in 2001, and then to two-fifths by 2007 (Table 3.2). Private renting has once again become the largest rental tenure in Britain. This unexpected turnaround was largely due to the decline of council housing from 1980, which itself was a result of right-to-buy sales to sitting tenants, *en-bloc* transfers to (often

Table 3.2 Rental dwelling stock by tenure in Britain

Year	Privately rented (%)	Housing association (%)	Local authority (%)	Total (%)
1981	26	5	69	100
1991	26	9	65	100
2001	32	21	47	100
2007	41	28	31	100

Source: Calculated from housing data at http://www.clg.gov.uk

new) housing associations, and a virtual cessation of new building. Even so, it would not have happened without the resurgence of investment in private lettings. As a result, the growth in private renting has contributed to the 'de-municipalisation' of rental housing, an objective announced in the Conservative's 1987 housing white paper (DoE, 1987) and implicitly continued by New Labour after it was returned to office in 1997.

The initial revival of private renting took place just as both the Housing Act 1988 and the Business Expansion Scheme (see Chapter 2) came into affect. It might, therefore, be tempting to attribute this recovery to those two initiatives. Certainly, the deregulation of rents and changes to security of tenure that came into effect in January 1989 made it much more attractive to let accommodation privately. And the fact that the Labour Party made it clear that it would not reintroduce rent controls when it was returned to office undoubtedly helped to reduce the political risk associated with investment in the sector. Yet, despite deregulation, the yields on private lettings were still uncompetitive with alternative investments, taking into account relative liquidity and investment risk. Moreover, the 81 000 BES properties that were bought over the five-year life of the initiative (see Chapter 5) accounted for only a small share of the increased rental supply (Crook & Kemp, 1996b).

Although the 1988 Housing Act was a critical precursor and the BES an important stimulant and advertisement for investment in the sector, the recovery of private renting was also fostered by the housing slump that began at about the same time and continued into the early 1990s. During this period, in the face of rising unemployment and increased interest rates, mortgage arrears and possessions increased to record levels. Meanwhile, property transactions declined sharply, house prices fell in real as well as in nominal terms, and around a million home owners found themselves with negative equity (Forrest & Murie, 1994; Dorling & Cornford, 1995). One result of this slump was that some owner-occupiers who needed to move but were unable to sell their property opted to let their properties and rented somewhere else instead. Meanwhile, people who might have become first-time buyers delayed house purchase and rented their accommodation from a private landlord.

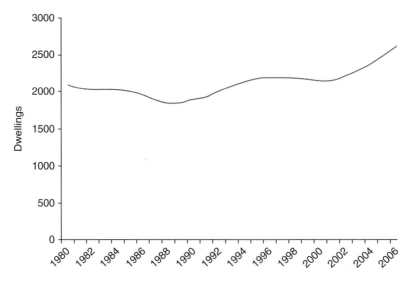

Figure 3.1   Number of private rental dwellings in England, 1980 to 2006 (000s).
Source: Housing data at http://www.clg.gov.uk

Hence, the housing market slump of the early 1990s increased both the demand for, and the supply of, privately rented accommodation. Crook *et al.* (1995) found that, in 1993/94, about one in ten of all privately rented addresses in Britain were owned by what they termed 'property slump landlords' who were unable or unwilling to sell because of the state of the owner-occupied housing market. Crook and Kemp (1996b) estimated that these landlords accounted for around half of the increase in lettings between 1988 and 1993.

Further circumstantial evidence for the important stimulus of the housing market slump to the growth of private renting is provided by the time-series data on the size of the housing stock shown in Figure 3.1. The growth of private renting did not occur in a smooth upward trajectory and nor did it occur in a uniform pattern across Great Britain. As Figure 3.1 indicates, in England, while the number of dwellings in the sector increased in the early 1990s, it fell back in the second half of the decade, before rising again after the turn of the century. The small decline in the number of privately rented dwellings in England in the mid-1990s occurred just as house prices and transactions were beginning to recover. By contrast, in Scotland, which did not experience the housing slump to anything like the same extent, the sector more or less flatlined for most of the 1990s and then increased sharply in the early 2000s, a pattern that was broadly replicated in Wales. Thus, the initial revival of private renting in the early 1990s was largely confined to England.[1]

However, in all three British nations, there was a marked upward growth in the size of the private rental sector after the turn of the century. Thus, between 2000 and 2007, the number of privately rented dwellings increased by 37% in England, 50% in Scotland and 15% in Wales. These substantial increases were associated with the buy-to-let investment boom and the wider housing-market bubble over this period, which were subsequently brought to an end by the onset of the global credit crunch in 2007. The buy-to-let boom is examined in Chapter 7.

Improving the stock

The lack of new construction during the four decades after the Second World War meant that the stock of privately rented dwellings became increasingly old. The impact of relatively inflexible forms of rent control, the low incomes of many private tenants and the seller's market that characterised private renting meant that the stock was not just ageing, but gradually decaying during this period of stock decline, as landlords had little economic incentive to repair or improve their properties (Kemp, 2004). As a result, privately rented housing was disproportionately in disrepair, lacking in standard amenities or unfit for human habitation. In 1978, for example, 12% of privately rented households in England had no bath or shower and 2% had no access to a flush WC (Dodd, 1990).

The condition of the privately rented dwelling stock varied by age and type of letting agreement. Not surprisingly, the worst conditions were among dwellings with controlled tenancies. In England in 1978, although nine out of ten resident landlord lettings and eight out of ten regulated lettings had all basic amenities – bath, inside toilet, wash basin and kitchen sink – this was true of only a third of controlled tenancies. Two-fifths of controlled tenancies did not have a bath and a third did not have a fixed wash basin (Todd *et al.*, 1982).

As successive house condition surveys in England, Wales and Scotland have shown, the privately rented sector contains a greater than average proportion of dwellings that are sub-standard. However, in recent years, the overall condition of the privately rented housing stock has improved. According to the English House Condition Survey, for example, the proportion of privately rented households living in dwellings that were below the statutory fitness standard declined from 25% in 1991 to 10% in 2001 (Table 3.3).

In England the government now uses an updated standard to assess the overall condition of the dwelling stock, which distinguishes between dwellings that are 'decent' and those that are 'non-decent'. According to the English House Condition Survey, in 2001 50.7% of privately rented dwellings were judged by surveyors to be non-decent, but by 2006 it had fallen to 40.4% (Table 3.4). This was a significant improvement in the condition of the privately rented stock,

Table 3.3   Percentage of households living in unfitness private rental dwellings

1991	24.7
1996	17.9
2001	10.3

Source: English House Condition Survey data cited in Kemp (2004) Table 6.7. Reproduced by permission of Chartered Institute of Housing. Kemp (2004), *Private renting in transition.* Chartered Institute of Housing, London.

Table 3.4   Percentage of non-decent private rental dwellings

2001	50.7
2006	40.4

Source: English House Condition Survey data at http://www.clg.gov.uk

though levels of non-decency remained higher than in the owner-occupied or social housing sectors. At an estimated £8524 per dwelling, the median cost to make the privately rented properties decent was also higher than for non-decent dwellings in the social housing (£3899) or owner-occupied (£7218) sectors.

Although there has been some renovation activity within the privately rented housing sector, this does not appear to be the main reason why the overall condition of the stock has improved. Instead, among *existing* dwellings, there has been an outflow of poor condition properties from, and a flow of better condition properties into, the privately rented sector (Crook *et al.*, 2000). In addition, much of the growth of private renting has involved *new* properties, particularly among buy-to-let investors. In 1988, over half (55%) of all privately rented lettings in England were in dwellings that were built before 1919, but by 2007/08 a third (32%) were that old. Meanwhile, over the same period, the proportion of lettings in dwellings constructed in 1965 or later increased from 11% to 34%. Overall, the proportion of privately rented dwellings constructed in 1985 or later trebled between 1993/94 and 2007/08, rising from 5% to 17% over that 14-year period (Table 3.5). The influx of new properties into the sector has resulted in a corresponding fall in the age of dwellings and an improvement in the overall condition of stock.

Deregulating lettings

When the Conservatives returned to office in 1979, private renting was still a largely regulated market. As Table 3.6 shows, a survey conducted in 1978 found that three-quarters of all lettings in that year were subject either to the old rent control regime or were regulated lettings. Most of

Table 3.5 Age of construction of privately rented dwellings in England (percentage lettings)

Date built	1993/94	2007/08
Pre-1919	47	32
1919 to 1944	25	20
1945 to 1964	11	15
1965 to 1984	12	17
1985 or later	5	17
Total	100	100

Sources: Carey (1995) Table A3.5; Survey of English Housing data at http://www.clg.gov.uk

Table 3.6 Type of letting in England, 1978

Type of letting	%
Controlled	7
Regulated	
registered rent	22
unregistered rent	46
Rent-free	12
Tied to business or job	6
Resident landlord	6
Others	1
Total	100

Source: Todd *et al.* (1982).

the remainder were either employment-related (a majority of which were rent-free) or lettings by resident landlords, which were not subject to rent regulation.[2] Although two-thirds of regulated tenancies did not have a registered rent, the amount charged was nonetheless set 'in the shadow of the Rent Act' (Maclennan, 1978) because the possibility existed that the tenant might refer it to the Rent Office Service for a regulated rent to be determined. In theory, this uncertainty surrounding unregistered, regulated tenancies increased investment risk for landlords letting such accommodation.

Rent regulation was still pervasive a decade later.[3] As Table 3.7 shows, in 1988 nearly three out of five lettings were regulated tenancies. The Housing Act 1980 had converted the remaining controlled lettings into regulated tenancies and introduced shorthold and assured tenancies (see Chapter 2). By 1988 these two new forms of tenancy accounted for 5% of lettings, almost all of which were shortholds. The majority of lettings classified as being 'not accessible to the general public' were tied to a job or business, including lettings to students by colleges. The 'no security'

Table 3.7   Type of letting in England in 1988 and 2007/08

Type of letting	1988	2007/08
	%	%
Assured	—	11
Assured shorthold	—	64
Regulated		
registered rent	26	2
unregistered rent	33	3
Not accessible to general public		
rent free	15	7
rent paid	13	7
Resident landlord	5	5
Pre-1989 shorthold and assured	5	—
No security	3	—
Other	—	1
Total	100	100

Sources: Dodd (1990) and housing data at http://www.clg.gov.uk

category includes holiday lettings, lettings with meals, and non-exclusive occupancy agreements, many of which were devices used by landlords to avoid the Rent Act (Kemp, 1988a).

If the Housing Act 1980 made relatively little difference to the extent to which the privately rented sector was subject to regulation, the same charge can not be made about the Housing Act 1988. Over the past two decades, the tenancy composition of the sector has radically changed, from one mainly comprising regulated lettings to one dominated by deregulated tenancies let at market rents. A similar development occurred in Scotland (Bailey, 1999) and in Wales. Whereas in 1978, three-quarters of lettings in England were subject to either rent control or rent regulation, by 2008 the same proportion was deregulated. This transformation in tenancies has meant that private renting is now much more explicitly affected by market forces than it had been in the 1970s and 1980s (Kemp, 2009).

As Figure 3.2 indicates, the growth in deregulated lettings has been concentrated in assured shorthold tenancies. Shortholds provide much weaker security of tenure for tenants than assured tenancies, but the evidence suggests that most moves within the private rental market are voluntary rather than because the landlord has asked the tenant to leave. Other things being equal, assured tenancies are more likely than shortholds to be let unfurnished, and are arguably more suitable for long-term renting, and yet the growth of private renting over the past two decades has been disproportionately in unfurnished tenancies. The number of private tenants renting unfurnished tenancies increased by 998 000 or 82% between 1988 and 2008, while furnished tenancies increased by 282 000 or 58% over the same period.

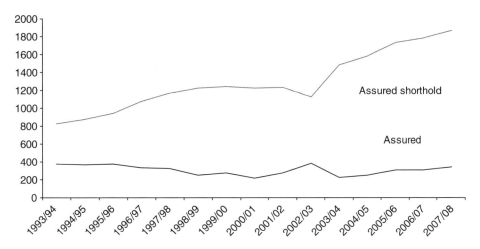

Figure 3.2   Assured and assured shorthold lettings in England (000s).
Source: Housing data at http://www.clg.gov.uk

Changing tenants

Over the past three decades, the characteristics of the people renting their homes from private landlords changed in many important ways. When Mrs Thatcher became prime minister in 1979 the role of the privately rented sector was very different from what it had been when it was the most common form of housing tenure. Instead of being the tenure in which most people lived for most of their lives, by 1979 private renting was a residual form of housing provision catering mainly for a limited number of housing market segments (Kemp, 2004). Bovaird *et al.*'s (1985) seminal article identified four main roles that the sector was performing at the time:

(1) a traditional role, housing what were by now elderly people who had rented from private landlords for all or most of their lives, stretching back to when it was the predominant form of housing provision;

(2) tied housing rented as part of a job (for example, in agriculture) or as part of a business (such as a flat rented with a shop);

(3) an easy-access role, providing accommodation on demand to mainly young and mobile households, many of whom would eventually move into owner-occupation;

(4) a residual role, housing low-income households who were not (at least for the time being) able or willing to gain access to council housing or housing association accommodation.

Table 3.8   Age of head of privately renting tenancies in England*

Year	Under 30 (%)	30 to 59 (%)	60 and over (%)	Total (%)
1978	27	38	36	100
1988	29	38	33	100
2005/06	38	51	11	100

*Head of household (1978 and 1988) or household reference person (2005/06).
Sources: Calculated from Todd *et al.* (1982) and housing data at http://www.clg.gov.uk

Table 3.9   Tenancy group composition in England

Year	1978 (%)	1988 (%)	2006/07 (%)
One adult aged 16 to 59	16	25	32
Two adults aged 16 to 59	18	15	24
Couple with dependent children	⎫	14	14
Lone parent with dependent children	⎬ 32	2	6
Multi-person group	⎭	11	12
One or two adults aged 60 and over	33	33	12
Total	100	100	100

Sources: Calculated from Todd *et al.* (1982) and housing data at http://www.clg.gov.uk

The relative importance of these four roles has changed considerably over the last three decades (Kemp, 2004). In particular, the traditional role has dramatically declined. The 1978 survey of private tenants in England found that elderly people were the largest single demographic group within the sector: people aged 60 or over accounted for more than a third of heads of privately rented households (Table 3.8). However, by 2005/06, this age group comprised little more than one in ten private tenants, a decline that reflected both the departure of older people from the sector (due to death or moves into alternative accommodation) and the influx of younger households.

Meanwhile, the easy access role has become more important, at least insofar as it involves young people. While heads of household aged under 30 were already over-represented in the privately rented sector in 1978, they were even more so in 2005/06. By the end of this period, young people under 30 years of age accounted for two-fifths of all private tenants. The proportion of middle-aged heads of privately rented tenancies also increased, rising from four out of ten in 1978 to five out of ten in 2005/06.

Table 3.9 shows that these trends in the age of private tenants are reflected in the household composition of the sector. Since 1978, the proportion of single people living alone has doubled and the proportion of childless couples has increased by a third over these three decades. Meanwhile, the proportion of tenancy groups that comprise either lone parents or couples with dependent

Table 3.10 Length of residence of head of tenancy group in England

Year	1978 (%)	1993/94 (%)	2007/08 (%)
Less than 1 year	21	39	40
1 but less than 3 years	19	21	30
3 but less than 5 years	8	8	10
5 but less than 10 years	13	8	9
10 years or more	39	24	11
Total	100	100	100

Sources: Todd *et al.* (1982), Green & Hansbro (1995) and housing data at http://www.clg.gov.uk

children has not changed, at least since 1988. The proportion of multi-person tenancy groups (which includes those living in flat shares and houses in multiple occupations) has also remained the same over at least the last two decades despite the increase in young people living in the privately rented sector. Hence, the growth of young people has involved a shift towards living in self-contained rather than in shared accommodation among this group.

The easy-access role provided by the sector is reflected in the relatively short length of residence of private tenants. Private tenants as a whole are much more mobile than people living in owner-occupation or social housing. The increase in younger tenants and decline in elderly ones has been an important reason why tenancy turnover has increased substantially over the past three decades. The proportion of heads of tenancy groups who have lived at their present address for less than a year doubled between 1978 and 1993/94 and then stabilised at about two-fifths. However, the proportion resident for more than one but less than three years stayed the same from 1978 to 1993/94, after which it increased by a half. The latter trend matches the trend in the 30–59 age group (see Table 3.10), which was stable between 1978 and 1988 but significantly increased after that. Meanwhile, there has been a sharp drop in the number of tenants living in their current address for five or more years, which fell from about one in two in 1978 to only one in five by 2007/08.

Part of the growth in younger tenants and in the easy-access role of the sector is accounted for by the increase in students in higher education. Students now account for about one in ten private tenants, which is three times their market share in 1988 (Kemp, 2004). As a result, student housing has become a sizable and distinct part of the rental housing market in university towns (Rugg *et al.*, 2002). The shift in higher education student support from grants to loans has also helped to boost the demand for private renting. Most newly graduated students now have substantial loans to repay, thereby reducing their ability to save up for house purchase and potentially delaying their entry into owner-occupation (Andrew, 2006).

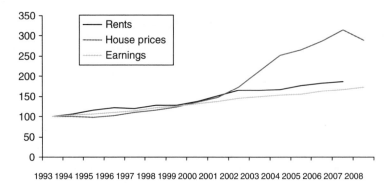

Figure 3.3   Average house prices, deregulated rents and earnings.
Sources: Halifax (house prices), Survey of English Housing (rents), Office of National Statistics (earnings).

Rental demand was also fuelled by the sharp, decade-long rise in house prices from the mid-1990s, which as Figure 3.3 shows, outstripped earnings growth and made owner-occupation less affordable to low- to medium-income households (Andrew, 2006). The increase in the average age at which people marry or have children has also helped to boost the number of people wishing to rent their home (Holmans, 1995; Ball, 2004). For these and other reasons, there has been a marked increase in the average age of first-time buyers and a corresponding increase in the proportion of adults under 35 years renting their home privately (Holmans, 1995).

Meanwhile, the growth in economic migrants to Britain, especially since the expansion of the European Union to include countries in Eastern Europe such as Poland, has added a new dimension to the easy-access role of private renting. Economic migrants from the EU are disproportionately young compared with the general population. Many of them do not initially have the resources to purchase their own home and some intend staying only temporarily; the great majority are also unlikely to gain access to social housing on their arrival. Hence, the private rental market is the main source of accommodation for newly arrived migrant workers (Thomas, 2006).

Only about a sixth of *working-age* private tenants was unemployed or otherwise economically inactive in 1978 and the figure has remained broadly the same since then. About three-quarters of working-age tenants at all three dates shown in Table 3.11 were working full-time or part-time in paid employment or self-employment, but because of the decline of retired people they accounted for a somewhat higher share of the total in 2005/06 than in 1978 or 1988.

The importance of the tied-housing role has declined very considerably (see Kemp, 2004 for a discussion of the reasons for this development). Thus, the proportion of private tenants reporting that their landlord was also their

Table 3.11   Economic status of head of tenancy group in England

Year	1978 (%)	1988 (%)	2005/06 (%)
Working full- or part-time	59	58	68
Unemployed	3	7	5
Retired	20	25	9
Full-time education	5	3	9
Other economically inactive	11	7	10
Total	100	100	100

Sources: Calculated from Todd *et al.* (1982) and housing data at http://www.clg.gov.uk

employer has fallen from fifth (22%) in 1978 and a quarter (25%) in 1988 to only one in 20 (4%) in 2005/06. Indeed, tied housing has declined to such an extent that it is no longer routinely distinguished in national statistics on the privately rented sector.

The residual role remains important in the sense that a significant proportion of private tenants have a low income and (according to the Survey of English Housing) many are either in receipt of housing benefit (29% in 2007/08), registered on social housing waiting lists, or do not expect to become owner-occupiers (40% in 2007/08). When asked what was the main reason why they did not expect to buy, the great majority of private tenants in the 2007/08 Survey of English Housing cited financial factors of one sort or another: 62% said they were unlikely ever to be able to afford it, 9% said they would not want to be in debt, 4% that they did not have a secure enough job and 2% that the cost of repairs and maintenance would be too high. Only 4% said they preferred the flexibility that renting offers.

Low-income tenants tend to live in the bottom end of the rental housing market, where problems of poor conditions and overcrowding are the most prevalent. Rising demand combined with shortage of social housing has meant that overcrowding has increased in both rental sectors. This is particularly the case in London, where the overcrowding rate is 12.7% in social housing and 9.8% in private renting, according to the Survey of English Housing.

Images of renting

When Mrs Thatcher became prime minister, private renting had a relatively poor reputation. The tenure was viewed by many as containing poor quality or even decrepit housing, often let at high rents on insecure conditions by unscrupulous if not criminal landlords. For those not trapped in the sector, private renting was to a large extent seen as a sort of 'waiting room' while the tenants saved up for a deposit to buy their own home or earned enough points to be allocated a tenancy by their local housing authority (Kemp, 1988a).

Over the past decade, however, public perceptions of renting privately have altered, becoming much less tainted with the largely negative images associated with living in this tenure in the late 1970s (Kemp, 2004, 2009). Moreover, the relationship between private renting and social housing has also altered in subtle but important ways. In the 1970s, council housing was the largest rental housing tenure and widely regarded as far more attractive for most tenants than private renting. However, in recent years, while the image of private renting has improved, that of council housing has deteriorated. Indeed, the most recent data from the Survey of English Housing indicates that private renters are more likely to be satisfied with their accommodation than either council or housing association tenants.[4]

Indeed, research has shown that there is a small but not insubstantial flow of tenants from social housing to private renting. In some cases, this reverse flow reflects push factors such as people leaving social housing as a result of relationship breakdown or rent arrears. But survey data suggests that it also reflects a desire to move into a better home or neighbourhood. Kemp and Keoghan (2001) argued that using private renting as an escape route from undesirable dwellings or neighbourhoods in social housing represents a small but significant new role for the sector. In Scotland, the evidence indicates that many tenants who have exited social housing for this reason hope ultimately to return if they are able to get somewhere better than they lived before (Gibb *et al.*, 1998).

Rents and housing benefit

The primary purpose of rent-controlling legislation has been to keep the rents that landlords charge to a level that is affordable to tenants. Until 1965, rent control took a relatively inflexible form, with rents held constant in nominal terms at a fixed date (see Chapter 1).[5] The result was that the real level of rents declined over time as their value was eroded by inflation; and hence they also failed to keep up with increases in earnings or house prices. Not only were rents relatively low, but they also varied in an inconsistent pattern between similar properties depending upon whether and when the property had been decontrolled and whether landlords had taken advantage of clauses in the Housing Repairs and Rents Act 1954 or the Rent Act 1957 to increase rents.[6]

The Rent Act 1965 introduced a more flexible form of rent control for the new regulated tenancies, which allowed landlords and tenants to negotiate the rent or, if they could not agree, to refer it to the new Rent Officer Service. It also provided for controlled tenancies to be converted over time into

Table 3.12 Tenancies paying more than one-fifth of net income in rent and rates[a]

	1978		1988 (%)
	Furnished (%)	Unfurnished (%)	
All tenancies[b]	45	24	54
Controlled	n/a	5	n/a
Regulated			
registered rent	—	35	76
non-registered rent	48	21	66
Resident landlord	30	32	66

[a] Before rent allowances and rate rebates; [b] households in 1978. Data are for tenancies paying rent and therefore exclude those that were rent-free.
Sources: Todd *et al.* (1982); Dodd (1990).

regulated ones. As Table 3.6 showed, by 1978 two-thirds (68%) of all tenancies in England were regulated, of which about a third had a registered rent and two-thirds did not. Only 7% of tenancies were controlled by that date.

The net result was that average rents varied by the type of tenancy and the date at which it had commenced. In 1978, the median rent (net of local rates) in England was £4.75 per week. In contrast, for controlled tenancies it was only £0.85 – that is, 18% of the median for all tenancies – while for regulated tenancies with a registered rent it was £4.67 and for those without a registered rent it was £5.81 per week. The median rent paid by people renting from resident landlords – lettings that ceased to be subject to rent restrictions in 1974 – was £5.68 (Todd *et al.*, 1982).

However, while rents were often relatively low in the private rental housing market, so too were incomes, and hence rent to income ratios could be high. This was especially so in furnished lettings, which until 1974 had not been subject to rent restrictions. As Table 3.12 shows, in 1978, 24% of unfurnished tenants were paying a fifth or more of their net income in rent and rates, compared with 45% of furnished tenants. Meanwhile, only 5% of tenants with controlled tenancies in England were paying more than one-fifth of their net income in rent and rates. By contrast, 35% of tenants with regulated tenancies and a registered rent were paying over that amount in rent and rates from their weekly income.

It appears, therefore, that the shift from controlled to regulated tenancies had facilitated a considerable uplift in rent levels and in rent-to-income ratios by 1978. A decade later, as Table 3.12 shows, rent-to-income ratios across the sector had increased considerably. Thus, by 1988 just over half of all private tenants, and 76% of regulated tenants with a registered rent, were paying more than a *fifth* of their net weekly income in rent and rates. The proportion of tenants living with resident landlords paying over that amount doubled over the decade from 1978 to 1988 (Table 3.12). Hence, although the measures contained in the 1980 Housing Act had relatively little apparent impact on the decline of the privately rented sector (Crook, 1986b; Kemp, 1988b) rent-to-income ratios rose considerably under that legislation. Moreover, considerable numbers of private tenants were paying substantial shares of their net income in rent and rates. In 1988, 34% of all private tenants, and 46% of regulated tenants with a registered rent, were paying more than a *third* of their income in rent and rates (Dodd, 1990). Thus, by the time that the rents of new lettings were deregulated by the Housing Act 1988 (see Chapter 2) it was no longer true that the sector was characterised by low rent-to-income ratios.

Figure 3.3 shows trends in deregulated (assured and assured shorthold) private rents, average house prices and earnings since 1993, which was approximately the point at which the so-called 'NICE' decade (of non-inflationary, continuous expansion) commenced. It thus covers the period from the end of the late 1980s/early 1990s recession to the onset of the recent global financial crisis. Following a deep slump, house prices increased from the mid-1990s and the rate of growth accelerated sharply from about the turn of the century, fuelled by the consumer credit boom.

The chart is particularly interesting for the light it sheds on rents in the deregulated private rental housing market. First, it shows that rents increased broadly in line with or slightly above average earnings, something that was not possible in the days when rents were restricted by the Rent Acts. Second, it suggests that market rents are in general more 'sticky' than house prices and less prone to cyclical fluctuations. This picture is partly a statistical artefact, in that the rents are for the *stock* of deregulated tenants as a whole, while the house price data are only for the *flow* of newly sold properties. However, the evidence from the recent housing slump suggests that, while house prices decreased across almost all housing markets, rents fell only in some localities; and also that house prices declined by much more than rents did. One consequence of this differential was that rental yields increased in the wake of the Great Recession of 2008/09, something that is discussed further in Chapter 7.

Although rent levels and rent-to-income ratios increased in real terms over the three decades being considered here, low-income tenants have been able to claim means-tested housing benefits in one form or another throughout the period.[7] The availability of housing benefit has arguably been one of the factors that enabled rents to increase at the bottom end of the rental market. Indeed, when the Thatcher Conservative government proposed deregulating private and social housing rents, it argued that housing benefit 'would take the strain' and thereby protect the poorest tenants from the full impact of the rent increases that were expected to result from the legislation. Nevertheless, four years later, in 1993/94, the first Survey of English Housing revealed that 26% of private tenants were paying a third or more of their net income on rent, even after housing benefit had been taken into account. Rent-to-income ratios were especially high for deregulated tenants, of whom about a third were paying a third or more of their net income in rent after housing benefit (Carey, 1995).

The number and proportion of private tenants receiving housing benefit fell from the mid-1990s until the onset of the credit crunch and consequent economic recession. Thus, in 1993/94, one in three private tenants in England was in receipt of housing benefit, but by 2006/07 only one in five was getting this help with their rent. This trend is likely to have reflected the falling unemployment and rising employment over that period, as well as the decline in the numbers of elderly tenants with the privately rented sector. Meanwhile, the amount of the rent covered by housing benefit fell over the same period (Rugg & Rhodes, 2008). In 1993/94, the mean weekly rent for private tenants receiving housing benefit was £58 and the mean benefit received was £51, a difference of £7. By 2006/07, the mean rent had risen to £104 and the mean benefit to £80, a difference of £24 per week. In proportionate terms, on these figures, housing benefit fell from an average of 88% to an average of 76% of the rent.

An important reason behind such shortfalls is the restrictions placed on the amount of rent eligible for housing benefit, which since 1996 have included local ceilings, the aim of which is to prevent benefit from being paid on rents that are deemed to be unreasonably expensive or on accommodation that is too large or too upmarket. In 2008, a new local housing allowance was introduced in place of housing benefit for private tenants, following a pilot scheme in 18 local authority areas. An important objective of that reform was to give housing benefit recipients in the private rental housing market a 'shopping incentive' when looking for accommodation and to encourage them to negotiate the rent with the prospective landlord (DWP, 2002).

Conclusions

Since 1979, the privately rented housing sector in Britain has undergone a major transformation (Kemp, 2009). At the beginning of this period, it was in the throes of what many believed was an inexorable process of decline. The stock of dwellings was for the most part very old and in poor condition relative to owner-occupation and council housing. Most people renting from private landlords did so from constraint rather than choice, and increasing numbers did so only temporarily or bypassed it altogether and moved directly into owner-occupation or council housing when they left home.

The initial measures introduced in the Housing Act 1980 to revive the sector failed to achieve that objective, although as we have seen, rent levels did increase. The more radical measures introduced in the Housing Act 1988 paved the way, but were by no means solely responsible, for the cessation of decline and the return of new investment in the sector. Economic, social and demographic factors were also important (see Chapter 7). The significant increase in renting privately was also predicated upon increased demand from tenants, particularly from young people unable or unwilling (in the short term) to buy their home, the expanding number of students in higher education, and the influx of migrant workers from Eastern Europe. For many of the new private tenants, living in the sector was made more attractive by the fact they were renting newly-built flats and houses, often in relatively attractive central city locations. But at the bottom end of the market, conditions could be rather less desirable and – because of the growing shortage of affordable rental accommodation – overcrowded, especially for those living in houses in multiple occupation. Thus, while many aspects of private renting had changed and got better, some aspects of private renting had not improved very much over the three decades since 1979.

Notes

1. As in England, after many years of decline, the private rented sector expanded in Northern Ireland from the turn of the decade. Yet, rent control never accounted for more than a small share of the stock in the province and deregulation did not precipitate the revival. This lends indirect support to our argument that rent deregulation was a necessary but not a sufficient factor behind the recovery of private renting in Britain.
2. For this purpose, employment-related includes lettings by higher education institutions.
3. The classification of lettings used in the 1988 survey does not map exactly onto those used in 1978 and hence the data are not strictly comparable.
4. However, analysis of the 1999 British Social Attitudes Survey has shown that a significantly smaller proportion of the public in Scotland would prefer to rent their home from private landlords than is the case in England or Wales, and a correspondingly higher proportion would prefer to rent from a local authority (Kemp, 2000).
5. Landlords were allowed in law to increase the rent to reflect increases in local rates (where they were paid with the rent) and from 1954 to increase the rent by a certain percentage if they had carried out major repairs or improvements.
6. Research carried out in the aftermath of the 1957 found that, while some landlords took advantage of the provision in the 1957 Act that allowed them to increase the rents of controlled tenancies, others did not (Donnison *et al.*, 1961).
7. Since the Second World War, means-tested income support benefits had included an amount to cover the claimant's rent. In the 1972, rent allowances for private tenants and rent rebates for council tenants, administered by local authorities, were introduced to help other low-income tenants afford their rent. The administration of the rent component of social security was given to local authorities in 1983, which they ran in tandem with the rent rebate and allowance system; and in 1988 the dual system of support was merged into a single housing benefit scheme. In 2008, following a two-year pilot, a new local housing allowance replaced housing benefit for private tenants (see Kemp, 2007).

4

Private Landlords in Contemporary Britain

Introduction

This chapter examines whether the small-scale industry we described in Chapter 1 has been transformed since the 1980 and 1989 deregulations. Have large corporate landlords grown? Are landlords more informed and acting more rationally and thus better managing risk? Have changes to the legal framework and to the wider economic and housing markets given landlords more confidence? Are landlords now getting competitive returns and doing necessary repairs? Do contemporary landlords have sufficient confidence to grow?

We look first at why individuals and organisations became landlords, their different types, portfolio sizes, and how they regarded their properties. We then look at how portfolios were managed, including by agents, policies on repairs, and landlords' reflections on the post-deregulation world. Finally we examine investment returns and whether landlords had plans to expand.

We look at the evidence for the three decades after 1980, concentrating mainly on the period after 1989. We draw very substantially from our own work (Crook & Martin, 1988; Kemp & Rhodes, 1994; Crook & Kemp, 1996a; Crook et al., 1998a, 2000; 2009) but also from official surveys. We concentrate on landlords as a whole. The subsequent three chapters deal with specific groups of landlords and their funding, including those established under the BES, the attempts to use the HIT and REITs initiatives to get City funding for corporate landlords, and the growth of buy-to-let landlords.

Transforming Private Landlords: Housing, markets & public policy, by Tony Crook & Peter A. Kemp © 2011 Tony Crook & Peter A. Kemp

The evidence

We can rely more than in Chapter 1 on national surveys of landlords. We can compare the findings for England with the previous 1976 national survey reviewed in Chapter 1. This is not possible for Scotland because there was no pre-deregulation survey, but we can compare one done shortly after deregulation with a much later one.

Finding landlords has always been difficult, especially identifying representative samples of landlords. There are no registers unambiguously listing all private rented addresses and their owners (or agents), although a near-comprehensive register in Scotland was compiled in 2006. Hence we have used a 'sieving' technique. Surveys were first done of dwellings across all tenures to identify those that were rented privately, with their occupants asked to provide information about their landlords and/or agents, providing the frame for subsequently sampling landlords and agents. These 'sieve' and follow-on surveys were usually tied to related surveys, including house condition surveys, enabling us to link information on sample dwellings with their tenants and landlords. This allowed us to examine links, for example between the location and condition of dwellings, landlords' motivations for owning them, with data on returns and landlords' plans for investing in repairs and improvements.

Other recent surveys have used evidence from the loan books of mortgage lenders, especially those in the buy-to-let market. Yet others have drawn on in-house information from managing agents' client portfolios. Whilst this information was partial it gave valuable insights into particular market segments and allowed whole portfolios to be examined.

It is important to emphasise that the findings discussed in this chapter come from surveys of the landlords of representative samples of lettings. In such surveys the owners of the largest compared with the smallest portfolios therefore have a greater chances of being sampled. This makes it possible to make statistically valid statements about the proportions of the stock owned by landlords with different characteristics and different policies. This is a particularly useful approach when trying to assess the possible impact of new policy initiatives.

Typologies of landlords

We adapted a classification developed in the early 1990s and based on qualitative research with private landlords in England. It is three-fold: business, organisational and sideline landlords (Thomas & Snape, 1995; for an alternative approach see Allen & McDowell, 1989).

It was based on landlords' initial routes into the sector, their reasons for letting, how they perceived their role and their future. By no means had all become landlords through deliberate investment decisions and not all thought of themselves as landlords. Some had inherited properties or property companies, others had bought a company that had property as part of its assets, yet others were individuals who let out their own homes when they moved jobs whilst some became landlords when they could not sell what had once been their family homes.

Business landlords were those for whom letting was their primary activity, although for some it might be a close secondary and related activity to an occupation or business such as estate agency or building contracting. Organisational (or institutional) landlords tended to be large scale and had often accumulated large portfolios for philanthropic or other not-for-profit reasons, for example because churches needed to house ministers of religion. They were not registered social landlords even though their motives were often charitable.

For sideline landlords, letting was wholly incidental to their business or occupation. They became landlords to achieve personal security such as a future or current home, to invest for income and capital growth (including for retirement), to help someone out, to house for employees, to let their own home whilst they relocated for work – or for a wide range of other essentially non-financial reasons. Some intended to be long-term landlords but others only intended to be involved in the letting market for a short time (whilst sons or daughters were away at university or until they were back from work overseas).

We have adapted this typology by splitting sideline landlords into those whose motives were primarily about investing and those whose reasons were primarily non-financial.

Landlords in the 1980s

In this section we look at three 1980s studies that give insights into specific market segments after the 1980 deregulation: landlords in inner Sheffield, HMO landlords in England and landlords of new lettings made between 1982 and 1984 throughout England.

Types of landlords and portfolio sizes

All three studies confirmed that small-scale individual landlords dominated the sector in the 1980s (Tables 4.1 and 4.2). The panel study of inner Sheffield between 1980 and 1985 confirmed that company ownership was very limited. Although ownership by companies was slightly higher amongst the new lettings made throughout England between 1982 and 1984, and also amongst HMOs in 1985, ownership by individuals still accounted for well over half. Others (including charities, trusts and churches) owned much less.

Table 4.1   Types of landlords in 1980s

Type of owner	Inner Sheffield 1980[a] (%)	Inner Sheffield 1985[b] (%)	England 1982/84 New lets[c] (%)	England 1985 houses in multiple occupation[d] (%)
Individual	75	81	59	81
Company	14	11	19	19
Other	11	8	22	–
Base	Le	Le	Le	D

Le, lettings; D, dwellings.
Sources: [a] Crook & Bryant (1982); [b] Crook & Martin (1988); [c] Todd & Foxon (1987); [d] Thomas & Hedges (1986).

Table 4.2   Portfolio sizes in 1980s

Size of portfolio (lettings/ dwellings)	Inner Sheffield 1980[a] (%)	Inner Sheffield 1985[b] (%)	England 1982/84 New lets[c] (%)	England 1985 Houses in multiple occupation[d] (%)
1		22	24	47
2–4	} 44	20		26
5–9		} 35	} 50	} 22
10–20	} 35			
21–50		} 17		
51–99				
100–499	} 21		} 26	} 5
500–999		} 6		
1,000+				
Base	Le	Le	Le	D

Le, lettings; D, dwellings.
Sources: [a] Crook & Bryant (1982); [b] Crook & Martin (1988); [c] Todd & Foxon (1987); [d] Thomas & Hedges (1986).

In Sheffield and in England as a whole, most lettings were owned by landlords with less than 21 lettings in all. Those with portfolios of 100 or more owned less than a quarter. HMOs were parts of very small portfolios with 73% being owned by landlords with fewer than five properties in all.

Reasons for becoming landlords

New landlords continued to enter the sector for the first time in the 1980s, for reasons that often included investment. For example, 30% of the new lettings made between 1982 and 1984 had landlords who had first acquired their properties within the previous five years. A significant number had been landlords' previous homes (Todd & Foxon, 1987), especially amongst HMOs, where the proportion was one in five (Thomas & Hedges, 1986).

Table 4.3 Landlords' reasons for first letting properties where a letting had been made between 1982 and 1984 in England

| | Individuals | | | | | | |
Reason	1 let (%)	>1 let (%)	<20 lets (%)	>20 lets (%)	Companies (%)	Institutions (%)	All (%)
Help with mortgage	18	25	20	—	8	—	11
Help with expenses	14	40	14	8	7	3	13
To provide an income	15	40	33	47	27	6	27
To get return on investment	17	58	32	67	48	4	36
To house employee	3	—	9	1	27	64	21
To make use of space	6	5	10	—	8	1	5
Something else (incl. helping someone out)	18	12	10	6	3	30	14

Landlords gave more than one reason so percentages are the percentage of lettings whose landlords gave that reason.
Source: Todd & Foxon (1987).

In inner Sheffield in 1985 over half the total stock had changed hands in the previous 15 years. The new owners were not longstanding landlords buying up from other landlords but new ones entering the business for the first time (Crook & Martin, 1988).

Why were new landlords continuing to enter this market, one still bound by regulations and restrictions, despite the deregulation of 1980? Getting an income and an investment return were the main reasons why landlords of new lettings made between 1982 and 1984 had first entered the market (Table 4.3). Investment motives were especially important for large individuals and companies. Personal circumstances were more important for small landlords, especially those with few lettings. The main reason for institutions (and some companies) was to house employees. In contrast HMO landlords often seemed to have drifted into rented property, examples being those who had bought large properties, found them too expensive to run and had then taken in tenants to help with costs (Thomas & Hedges, 1986).

In inner Sheffield, those seeking capital growth bought rent-controlled unfurnished property in the expectation of making capital gains upon securing vacant possession. Two-thirds of the purchases of unfurnished property made in the 1980s were for capital gains alone. In contrast, those seeking income returns tended to buy vacant property, let it furnished at high occupancy and on licence agreements (Crook & Bryant, 1982; Crook & Martin, 1988).

The local council's improvement and enforcement policy helped shape the Sheffield market. Property dealers looking for capital growth acquired unimproved property whose longstanding landlords did not want to do the work the council required. They then improved them with grants to high standards and later sold them with vacant possession when the sitting tenants died or were re-housed (Crook & Martin, 1988; Crook & Sharp, 1989). The expertise needed to make this type of investment was summed up by the Small Landlords Association: '.... supposing you are one of the speculator type landlords buying up tenanted property, you hardly look at the property, you are looking at the tenants, how long is the tenant going to live, has he any children, is there going to be a statutory succession' (House of Commons Environment Committee, 1982b, pp. 200–221).

Rates of return

In the 1980s, achieving vacant possession to make capital gains was critical to securing acceptable investment returns, unless landlords were prepared to take the risk of neglecting repairs and letting outside the Rent Acts, in which case good income returns could be made.

The Sheffield study compared returns with alternative investments and showed that, although nominal rental returns on unfurnished properties were not competitive, total returns were, particularly where acquisitions had been made at sitting tenant value. With furnished property, nominal rental returns were comparable with alternative investments, but unless capital appreciation was taken into account the net present value of a five-year investment was not as competitive as deposits in building societies or purchases of equities in about half the sample cases (Crook & Martin, 1988).

As we saw in Chapter 1, before 1980 few landlords were satisfied with their rents and returns, but a different picture emerged in the 1980s. By then, most new lettings did not have registered Fair Rents and most were let outside the Rent Acts. This partly explains why 74% of the landlords of lettings made between 1982 and 1984 said their rent was adequate. Even so, 47% also said their rent was inadequate to both do repairs and to get a reasonable return (Todd & Foxon, 1987).

Hence a strategy for getting adequate returns was to neglect repairs. For example, although HMO landlords thought returns were good or adequate they were not necessarily satisfied because they faced high maintenance costs and suffered a lot management stress (Thomas & Hedges, 1986). Most tried to screen out potential bad tenants. Others opted out, especially larger landlords, who considered all tenants bad, and maximised income by spending only an irreducible minimum. These strategies either reduced access for those not conforming to landlords' stereotypes of the desirable tenant or led to physical and other neglect of HMOs (see also Crook, 1989).

Table 4.4 Non-resident landlords' attitudes to letting in general

Statement	Agree (%)	No view (%)	Disagree (%)
Tenants generally look after accommodation	69	14	18
Tenants are generally good at paying the rent on time	68	19	14
Landlords find it better to let outside Rent Acts	55	37	8
Landlords find that wear and tear on property is quite small	45	12	43
Law allows landlords to charge a reasonable rent these days	39	30	32
It is hard for landlords to find out how they are affected by the law	37	27	37
Landlords spend a lot of time arranging new lets because tenants move so frequently	38	20	42
Landlords are adequately protected by law against tenants refusing to leave	17	23	60
Landlords only let if they can't sell	15	21	65
Landlords find it difficult to fill their vacancies	9	8	84

Source: Todd & Foxon (1987).

The legal framework and views on policy

The 1980 deregulation did not make a major difference to how landlords let their properties or to their overall confidence about letting in general.

By the 1980s the use of licences had become even more widespread, notwithstanding the introduction of shortholds in 1980, because shortholds then required Fair Rents to be registered. In 1982 a House of Commons committee declared that legal evasion put most recent lettings outside the Rents Acts and few benefited from Fair Rents. In their evidence landlords said they had no incentives to give tenants security or to charge Fair Rents (House of Commons Environment Committee, 1982a, p. 174 and p. 290). The 1982 to 1984 new lettings survey confirmed this. Most lettings had only limited protection and rents were privately agreed. Large individual and company landlords were more likely to use agreements with limited protection, including licences. Although over a quarter had landlords making some use of shorthold, 41% had landlords who had never heard of it, especially those with few lettings (Todd & Foxon, 1987). Most HMO landlords were unaware of shorthold and thought the law so biased towards tenants that they could not be evicted for rent arrears or serious misconduct (Thomas & Hedges, 1986).

In the 1980s, as Table 4.4 shows, landlords were finding it relatively easy to let accommodation (but better to let outside the Rent Acts), had tenants who paid rent on time and looked after accommodation (although wear and tear might be quite high). It was, however, still a sector where landlords did not think themselves adequately protected by the law, where a significant minority thought it hard to find out how the law affected them and that it did not allow them to charge a reasonable rent. It was individual landlords with a few lettings (fewer than 20) who tended more than others to have negative views.

Landlords before 1989: a summary

Landlordism was basically a small-scale, cottage industry with most lettings being owned by individuals, and not companies or organisations, mostly with small portfolios. But, despite the long-term decline of the sector, a significant proportion was owned by those who had only recently become landlords, much acquired through active purchasing, and not inheritance. Whilst some were positive about being landlords – and reasonably well informed – others were disgruntled. Only a small proportion had owners who thought the law allowed them to charge a reasonable rent and adequately protected them against tenants. Similarly a small proportion had landlords who thought rents were adequate or sufficient to cover repairs and give a return. Significant numbers of lettings had landlords who let in ways that limited tenants' protection.

Whilst it was possible to make good investment returns, this depended either on realising vacant possession to achieve the required capital gains or on neglecting repairs in order to get good returns from rents alone. Taking lettings as a whole, the landlords of the majority did not intend to re-let them when they became vacant, but when examining only the landlords of the most recent lettings, the majority of these were to be re-let (Todd & Foxon, 1987).

Landlords after 1989

We now turn to examine findings from the series of surveys conducted after deregulation. They show that the sector became even more of a cottage industry, with small-scale individual landlords dominating ownership. We start by looking at the evidence on landlords' motives for first becoming landlords.

Becoming landlords after 1989

As in the 1980s and earlier decades, people and organisations in England first became landlords for many reasons, often unrelated to investment strategies. A qualitative study of the early 1990s illustrated this great variety (Thomas & Snape, 1995).

Those thinking of becoming landlords in the 1990s included people needing to let out homes that they could not sell or who were having difficulty paying mortgages. For those who inherited property or worked away from home, letting gained them extra income or covered mortgages whilst keeping their own homes. Others who had inherited worried about leaving property empty. For all, assured shortholds gave them the flexibility to adapt by reducing risk. On the other hand, the need to extract capital from property, the lack of information about being landlords, plus the worries involved and the uncertainties about returns (and tax implications), all worked against becoming landlords.

Existing 1990s landlords had also first got into the market for family and occupational circumstances. For example, those currently in tied accommodation themselves had bought homes for retirement but let them out in the meantime, using the rent to pay their mortgages. Others had been temporarily relocated by their firms but wished to keep their homes for when they returned, letting them out meanwhile. Some had bought property to house extended family members but when this need had passed, kept the properties to make some extra money. Others had inherited properties that proved difficult to sell. A few had inherited family companies and felt they had to carry on businesses that had been the product of hard work by parents or grandparents. The early 1990s property slump also meant there were some who had decided to let out their own homes, which they had been unable to sell when moving jobs and where they needed income to fund their mortgages.

Others wanted to help those in need and had raised funds to buy property to let at low rents, accepting limited profits themselves. This also applied to some who acquired property to house employees at low rents. But many of the reasons for letting job-related accommodation (to have staff living close to work) no longer applied and instead they now provided perks, attracted higher-quality staff, or were let on the open market and not just to employees.

But there were also those who had become landlords for commercial reasons. Some had acquired property as part of their investment portfolio or pension scheme, the latter usually set up two decades before retirement. Some had retired early through ill-health or redundancy and used lump sums to generate income. Others had seen getting into property as something easy to do whilst still in full-time work. Often these latter landlords were in building or related professions. Echoing findings from case studies before deregulation (Rex & Moore, 1967; Crook & Martin, 1988), Thomas and Snape found that minority ethnic landlords saw property as a high status and reliable investment.

This wide variety also characterised the reasons for becoming became landlords in Scotland. Although many had first become landlords for similar personal and other non-financial reasons as their English counterparts, many of them had later continued (and expanded) as landlords for investment reasons (Crook *et al.*, 2009).

Types of landlords

We now turn to the large-scale surveys to see how ownership changed after deregulation, starting by looking at the different types of landlords. As Table 4.5 shows, there was not the increase in company ownership that governments had hoped to see. Instead, there was a rise in the proportion owned by individuals and couples, increasing in England from just over 60% in 1993 to just under 75% in 2006 while the ownership by companies and by other organisations (including charitable trusts, government departments and educational establishments) fell. The growth in the concentration of ownership amongst individuals and couples was even more pronounced in Scotland, where it rose from 47% to 84% between 1993 and 2008.

Moreover, not all the companies were in residential letting. In 1993, for example, only 58% were in property and only three-quarters of these were mainly in residential property. Overall, therefore, companies specialising in residential lettings owned only 8% of addresses in 1993. This picture had changed little by 2006 when only half the dwellings owned by companies had landlords for whom residential lettings were their main business, accounting for only 9% of all dwellings in the sector.

Furthermore very few private individual landlords let property as a full-time job or occupation. In England in 1993 only 14% of the addresses owned by individuals had full-time landlords, the rest being owned by those who were mainly in paid work or retired. Although this picture of individual landlords being mainly part-time did not change over the period, there were significant changes in the age and gender of landlords. In Scotland, for example, in 1992/93 only 19% of dwellings was owned by women, compared with

Table 4.5 Proportion of addresses owned by individuals, companies and other types of landlords

Type of landlord	England 1993	England 1998	England 2001	England 2003	England 2006	Scotland 92/93	Scotland 2008
Individual[a]	61	61	65	67	74	47	84
Partnerships	5	4	5	na	na	} 39	6
Company	20	22	13	17	16		8
Other	14	14	17	16[b]	10[b]	14	2
Sample base	Dw	Dw	Dw	Dw	Dw	Dw	Dw

[a] Includes couples; [b] includes partnerships; Dw, dwellings; na, not applicable.
Sources: Crook & Kemp (1996a); Crook *et al.* (2000); ODPM (2003b); ODPM (2006); CLG (2008b); Kemp & Rhodes (1994); Crook *et al.* (2009).

48% in 2008. In 1992/93 those 70 years or more in age owned 30%. By 2008 this was only 10% (for those 65 or older). In England in 1993, landlords were also more likely to be drawn from the black and minority ethnic communities (especially those with Indian and Pakistani backgrounds), with 9% of addresses owned by them. This was much less pronounced in Scotland where the proportion was only 2% in 1992/93.

Our first conclusion about landlordism in contemporary Britain is that two decades after deregulation it had become even more dominated by individual landlords, with only very small proportions, less than one in ten, owned by residential letting companies As we shall see in Chapter 7 this was partly a consequence of the buy-to-let phenomenon.

Portfolio size

Before deregulation, landlords' portfolios were small. Afterwards they became even smaller. This was not just because small-scale individual ownership increased, but also because company-owned portfolios also got smaller. So, far from the government aims of fostering large landlords being achieved, the opposite happened.

In England in 1993 just over a quarter of the sector was owned by landlords who had only one letting and only 9% had landlords with portfolios of 500 dwellings or more (Table 4.6). Not unexpectedly, corporate landlords had larger portfolios, with 22% of their stock being in portfolios of 500 lettings or more. By contrast 43% of the stock owned by individuals had landlords owning just one letting.

By 1998 portfolios sizes had become smaller and the median holding was only seven lettings. Significantly, landlords owning only deregulated lettings had smaller portfolios than others (80% were in portfolios of less than five lettings compared with 30% of those that were regulated). By 2001 the trend to smaller portfolios had become even more pronounced. This was partly due to the growth in the proportion of the stock owned by individuals, but the portfolios of company landlords also fell in size over the period. For example, in 1993, 30% of company-owned lettings were parts of portfolios of 250 or more properties. By 2001 this proportion had fallen to 21%.

Two decades after the 1989 deregulation, the figures for England in 2006 further confirmed the trend to smaller portfolios, with 58% of the sector owned by landlords with fewer that five dwellings in all, compared with 33% in 1993. Seventy-one per cent of dwellings owned by individuals were parts of portfolios of less than few and, most significantly for policy objectives, only 12% of lettings owned by companies were in portfolios of 250 or more.

The picture for Scotland was similar. Landlords with less than five dwellings in all increased their share of the total stock from 37% in 1992/93 to

Table 4.6   Proportion of addresses owned by landlords with different portfolio sizes

Number of dwellings	England 1993	England 1998	England 2001	England 2003	England 2006	Scotland 92/93	Scotland 2008
1	26	27	30	33	35	22	39
2–4	17	16	23	22	23	15	34
5–9	12	13	13	11	14	12	14
10–24	14	15	11	13	11	12	8
25–49	7	5	5	6	5	11	2
50–99	5	5	5	4	5	5	2
100–249	6	7	7	4	3	11	
250–499	3					4	
500–999	2	12	6	8	3	5	1
1000+	7					2	
Sample base	Dw	Dw	Dw	Dw	Dw	Dw	Dw

Dw, dwellings.
Sources: Crook & Kemp (1996a); Crook *et al.* (2000); ODPM (2003b); ODPM (2006); CLG (2008b); Kemp & Rhodes (1994); Crook *et al.* (2009).

73% in 2008. This reflected the very substantial increase in ownership by individuals with small portfolios, but also the reduction in portfolio size of all landlords, including company landlords. In 1992/93, 37% of dwellings owned by companies were parts of portfolios of 100 or more dwellings. This fell to 5% by 2008.

Percentage of income from lettings

The small size of portfolios is reflected in the small percentage of landlords' income derived from letting (either as percentages of personal income from all sources, including employment and pension income for individuals, or of total gross company income including rents).

Table 4.7 shows that in 2006, 59% of the sector in England had landlords who got less than a quarter of their income from rents, including 12% who got no income at all, including those who had let for a wide range of non-investment reasons. The picture in Scotland was broadly similar, with findings that reinforce the observation that a significant proportion of dwellings had landlords who drew none of their gross income from rents.

There were exceptions of course, especially where letting was landlords' main occupations or businesses and when sideline landlords had acquired for investment purposes. In 1998, for example, 73% and 25% respectively of the dwellings owned by business landlords and sideline investors had owners who got 51% or more of their income from rents, compared with only 8% of the dwellings owned by other sideline landlords.

Table 4.7 Proportion of landlords' income that comes from rents

Percentage	England 1993	England 1998	England 2001	England 2006	Scotland 1992/93	Scotland 2008
Nil	na	15	13	12	na	27
Up to 25	60[a]	35	45	47	73[a]	41
25–50	13	13	15	18	9	8
51–75	7	7	10	5	5	4
76–100	12	23	17	18	13	6
Don't know	8	6	na	na	na	14
Sample base	Dw	Dw	Dw	Dw	Dw	Dw

Dw, dwellings; [a] includes 'nil'.
Sources: Crook & Kemp (1996a); Crook *et al.* (2000); ODPM (2003b); CLG (2008b);
Kemp & Rhodes (1994); Crook *et al.* (2009).

When, why and how properties were acquired

There was much new investment after the 1989 deregulation. Although significant proportions of dwellings continued to be acquired for non-investment purposes, the proportions acquired as investments and acquired with loans increased. The sector was also remarkably under-geared in the period immediately after 1989 deregulation but this had changed significantly a decade later.

By 1993 a quarter of all lettings and a third of recent lettings had been acquired since the 1989 deregulation. Just under two-thirds had been acquired with cash or with loans, the rest through inheritance, gifts (especially institutions), or through acquiring the organisation that previously owned them. Of those that had been purchased, a fifth had originally been acquired as the landlords' own home. This was especially the case with new (those who had become landlords for the first time after January 1989) rather than continuing landlords. Of the remaining dwellings, nearly two-thirds of those that had been bought had been acquired to let and only a tenth to sell.

As Table 4.8 shows, although acquisitions for non-financial reasons continued to be important after deregulation, the proportion originally acquired for investment purposes increased. Only a minority of addresses in England in 1993 had been acquired solely as investments, more for capital growth than for rental income, and nearly half had been mainly acquired for other reasons: as somewhere to live, to house employees or to help other people. Nearly one in six (16%) had been acquired as an inheritance or as a gift, or in acquiring a firm or organisation that had been the previous owners.

By 1998 and 2001, greater proportions had first been acquired as investments but, as Table 4.8 also shows, many properties, as in past decades, were also acquired for many other purposes. The 2001 survey revealed that 26% had owners who had not intended to become landlords and had got into the business through inheritance or an inability to sell their home,

Table 4.8   Main reason (or reasons) for acquiring address

	England 1993 (%)	England 1998[a] (%)	England 2001 (%)	Scotland 1992/93[a] (%)
Investment: rent income	17	41	35	20
Investment: capital growth	20	36	14	21
To live in at some time	14	17	19	9
Other	33	39	29	43
Inherited/incidental to other transactions	16	6	3	58
Sample base	Dw	Dw	Dw	Dw

Dw, dwellings; [a] the percentages are for all reasons and do not sum to 100.
Sources: Crook & Kemp (1996a); Crook *et al.* (2000); ODPM (2003b); Kemp & Rhodes (1994).

13% had landlords who felt they played an important social role in providing accommodation, 11% provided a home for landlords' friends or relatives, and 12% had landlords who said it was because they enjoyed being in the business.

The evidence thus confirmed that since the 1989 deregulation, whilst an increasing proportion of addresses had landlords who set out to acquire property as investments, many others had owners who continued to come into the sector for a wide variety of other reasons, including some without initially intending to do so because of inheritance or not being able to sell a property in a depressed market.

As well as the increase in acquisitions for investment purposes, the greater use of loan finance was the other principal change after deregulation. A 1994 survey had shown how little borrowing landlords incurred when acquiring property (Crook *et al.*, 1998a). Two-thirds had been purchased but only 14% of these had any loans outstanding (and, of these, a third were the loans originally taken out when they were the landlords' own homes). In 1998, three-quarters of dwellings purchased since deregulation had no loans, confirming the degree of under-gearing and possibly explaining the small average size of landlords' portfolios since landlords' own equity had funded most acquisitions (Crook *et al.*, 2000).

However, in later years access to debt funding changed. In 2001 53% of properties that had been purchased had used loan finance, a reflection of the emergence of buy-to-let lending (ODPM, 2003b). In 2003, 72% of dwellings had originally been purchased (rather than inherited, built or acquired in some other way) and while 47% had relied on mortgage finance for the acquisition, this proportion rose to 64% for those who had acquired the property in the previous two years. If commercial and other loans are taken into account the proportion of acquisitions funded by mortgages and loans rose to 65% of all dwellings (ODPM, 2006). In part this greater reliance on debt funding also reflects the large proportion of private-sector lettings that were once landlords' own homes.

The most recent survey evidence from Scotland in 2008 reveals the same significant changes that had been experienced in England (Crook *et al.*, 2009). Only 14% had been inherited. Eighty percent had been purchased and of these, over three quarters had been financed with a loan, a complete reversal of the position in the previous survey in 1992/93, which showed that 76% of those that had been bought had been paid for with cash and not with a loan (Kemp & Rhodes, 1994). Notably in 2008, a very large proportion, 43%, had been acquired in the previous five years, implying that many landlords had bought at a time of rapidly rising house prices.

'New' landlords since the 1989 deregulation

Before the 1989 deregulation there had been a fairly consistent pattern of new owners entering the sector for the first time through deliberate acquisition as well as inheritance. This continued after 1989, but new landlords were mainly individuals and not companies.

In 1993 a quarter of the stock was owned by those who had first become landlords since January 1989 (Crook & Kemp, 1996a). In 1998 30% was owned by those who had become landlords since 1989 (Crook *et al.*, 2000). By 2001, 42% was owned by those who had become landlords in the previous decade (ODPM, 2003b). And by 2003 this proportion had risen to 53% of the stock, indicating how large a proportion of the stock was by then owned by those new to landlordism since deregulation (ODPM, 2006). By 2006 16% was owned by landlords who had been in the sector for two years or less, compared with only 11% in 2001, further indicating the growth in the proportion of stock owned by those very new to landlordism (CLG, 2008b). The evidence from Scotland echoes that from England and shows that far more landlords were very new to the sector twenty years after the 1989 deregulation than before. In 2008 42% of the stock had owners who had first become landlords within the previous four years (Crook *et al.*, 2009).

'New' landlords were a distinct group from 'continuing landlords'. In 1998 they were much more likely to be sideline than business or institutional landlords, to own a few properties (the median portfolio was a single property, compared with 11 for continuing landlords) and to be the landlords of addresses which had once been the landlords' own homes. Indeed 30% of addresses owned by new landlords were landlords' previous homes (Crook *et al.*, 2000).

Significantly, these new landlords were generally not companies. In 1998 only 8% of the company-owned stock belonged to new landlords, compared with 42% of the individually owned stock. Only 1 in 10 of the 1998 stock owned by those who became landlords for the first time since deregulation was owned by companies and other organisations (Crook *et al.*, 2000). By 2003 the great majority (88%) of new landlords were private individuals. Nearly three-quarters had no prior experience of property or building, nor held relevant professional or vocational qualifications. More than a third of the dwellings of new landlords had once been their own homes (ODPM, 2006). Very little, only 9%, of the stock owned by 'new' landlords in 2006 was company-owned (CLG, 2008b).

How landlords regarded their properties

As we have seen, landlords initially came into the business for many reasons but this original motivation does not necessarily explain how they later came to regard their property. In fact, since the 1989 deregulation there was a steady increase in the proportion of the sector regarded as investments, especially for capital growth but also for housing family and friends, reflections of the significant increase in house prices and of student numbers after the year 2000.

Table 4.9 shows that in 1993 nearly half of all lettings were regarded as investments. Noteworthy is the fact that 3% of all lettings (and 6% of the most recent lettings in the sample) were landlords' homes that they had been unable to sell and that 7% were properties landlords intended to live in at some time in the future. Business landlords were more likely (83%) to regard lettings as investments, institutions for housing employees (59%) and sideline landlords for other reasons including as a liability (13%). 'New' landlords were

Table 4.9 How landlords regarded dwellings

	England 1993	England 1998	England 2001	England 2003	England 2006	Scotland 1992/93	Scotland 2008
Investment: rent income	26	14	21	27	22	15	8
Investment: capital growth	22	4	8	15	25	11	23
Investment for both	na	39	40	18	23	17	41
To live in at some time	7	2	10	11	12	6	17
A home that cannot sell	3	6	2	3	2	2	2
Other non investment	23	23	9	16	12	38	4
Liability	10	7	<1	na	na	na	na
Other/don't know	10	5	10	10	4	12	4
Sample base	Dw	Dw	Dw	Dw	Dw	Dw	Dw

Dw, dwellings.
Sources: Crook & Kemp (1996a); Crook *et al.* (2000); ODPM (2003b); ODPM (2006); CLG (2008b); Kemp & Rhodes (1994); Crook *et al.* (2009).

less likely to regard addresses as investments (44%) than continuing landlords (50%). We calculated that about half the net increase in lettings between 1988 and 1993 had been as a result of the property slump, with landlords unable to sell their own homes, letting them out instead (Crook & Kemp, 1996b).

In Scotland in 1992/93, landlords' attitudes revealed a broadly similar pattern to that in England. A smaller proportion were dwellings that had been landlords' own homes that they had been unable to sell, a difference probably due to the fact that, unlike England at that time, Scotland was not then experiencing a slump in property prices and sales.

The 1998 and 2001 English surveys showed that that there had been a significant increase in the proportion of dwellings regarded as investments since deregulation, although only small proportions of dwellings had owners who relied on capital growth alone to deliver these returns. With the beginnings of the recovery in the housing market a smaller proportion in 2001 than in previous surveys were landlords' former homes that they could not sell. The proportion regarded as liabilities also fell dramatically and was confined to companies and other organisations. Indeed in 2001 properties owned by individuals were much more likely (73%) to be regarded as investments, than those owned by companies and other organisations (48%), a pattern repeated in the later surveys. The same trend was seen in Scotland where, by 2008, 72% of addresses were regarded as investments.

The later 2003 and 2006 English surveys reflect two trends. First, there was an increase in the proportion of dwellings that had recently been acquired to house friends and family members, including those of the latter going away to university. Second, is the increase in the proportion of dwellings regarded as investments for capital growth alone, particularly amongst new landlords, reflecting the growth of the buy-to-let market and the significant increases in property prices at the time. By 2006 a quarter of all dwellings were regarded as investments where the return came from capital growth alone. Scotland experienced the same phenomenon and, in 2008, amongst those who had entered the lettings business for the first time in the previous five years, much higher proportions regarded the property as an investment for capital growth alone or as a home for themselves or a family member.

Overall landlord typology

Table 4.10 shows the proportions of addresses owned by landlords classified by our adaptation of the Thomas and Snape typology. The typology confirms the findings we have discussed above.

The proportion of addresses owned by business landlords was less than a fifth and this proportion fell after the 1989 deregulation. Sideline landlords owned the majority of the sector and the proportion owned by sideline investors increased. There was a small increase in the first decade after deregulation

Table 4.10   Proportion of addresses owned by different categories of landlord

Type of landlord	England 1993	England 1998	England 2001	Scotland 2008
Business	19	22	15	7
Sideline investor	34	32	45	65
Sideline non-investor	36	27	18	26
Institution	11	19	22	<2

Sources: Crook & Kemp (1996a); Crook *et al.* (2000); ODPM (2003b); Crook *et al.* (2009).

in the overall proportion owned for business and (sideline) investment purposes: a rise from 53% to 60% between 1993 and 2001.

The questions asked in the 2003 English survey did not permit the use of
this typology, but the results found that 24% of the stock was owned by
what the survey called 'full-time landlords'. Property sector sideline landlords owned 12% and the remaining 65% was owned by what the survey
called 'part-time landlords'. The 2006 survey found very similar proportions
(CLG, 2008b). In Scotland in 2008, business and institutional landlords
owned a much smaller proportion than in England, with nearly two-thirds
owned by sideline investor landlords (Crook *et al.*, 2009).

Landlords since 1989: key conclusions

The proportion of the sector owned by sideline landlords has increased consistently since deregulation and the stock owned by business landlords has
fallen. The stock owned by individual landlords has also increased considerably, portfolio sizes have fallen, and although the proportion owned for
investment purposes has increased (especially for capital growth), a sizeable
proportion of the sector, particularly amongst new landlords, is owned for
non-investment purposes, including as homes for family members. Crucially
in relation to government policy, the proportion owned by companies has
fallen, companies own only a small proportion of new lettings, and they are
only a small proportion of the landlords entering the sector for the first time
since the 1989 deregulation.

Managing properties after 1989

We now examine how landlords managed and maintained their properties
after 1989 and whether their attitudes to letting changed. We start by looking at the extent to which they used agents and whether landlords and agents
were members of relevant trade and professional bodies.

Management and membership of professional and other organisations

While agents managed more properties after deregulation than before, many were still managed by landlords. Membership of professional bodies and trade associations was also low, even two decades after 1989, although there had, by then, been a substantial increase in the numbers of agents who had become members of trade associations.

In the mid 1990s Thomas and Snape found that landlords generally wanted to manage properties themselves. Amongst sideline landlords this was because agents' fees were high and because landlords thought they could do the job better, especially if they lived nearby. Business and organisational landlords relied on managing agents even less, considered they did a better job themselves and visited properties more regularly, thus quickly spotting problems (Thomas & Snape, 1995).

We largely confirmed this in our 1993 study (Crook & Kemp, 1996a). Landlords wholly managed almost two-thirds of lettings, although they managed fewer of the more recent lettings themselves (56%). Individuals were more likely to manage themselves than companies and other organisations. Where agents were used, they decided on the more day-to-day tasks, such as rent collection and tenant selection, but landlords tended to take investment decisions, such as major repairs spending.

After 1993 there was an increase in the proportion of lettings managed by agents. In 2001, 51% were managed by agents, especially the most recent ones (ODPM, 2003b). This may have been stimulated by conditions attached to buy-to-let mortgages. The 2003 survey showed that agents were more likely to manage the better and higher-income end of the sector and that new landlords were more likely than continuing ones to use formal letting processes. But it also confirmed that self-management by landlords was still widespread, with only 48% of dwellings let on the open market being managed by agents (ODPM, 2006).

Thomas and Snape's findings that landlords preferred to manage property themselves, especially if they lived nearby, was strongly confirmed by evidence from Scotland (Crook *et al.*, 2009). In 2008, 50% of dwellings were wholly managed by landlords, 32% wholly by agents, with the rest being a shared responsibility. There was a strong relationship between the distance landlords lived (or worked) from their portfolio and whether they managed it themselves. If they self-managed they lived on average within 2 km of their portfolio, whereas if an agent did all the tasks landlords lived nearly 6 km away. Because of landlords' preference against using agents, they managed risk by only owning properties close to their homes or workplaces, where they had a good understanding of the local property market and could keep a close personal eye on their properties.

Even though many managed their own lettings, few landlords were members of relevant professional bodies or trade associations. In 1998 in England only 38% of lettings had landlords who were members of professional or other bodies connected with letting accommodation. New landlords were much less likely to be members of these than continuing landlords. Only 12% of all lettings had landlords who were members of landlords' associations and only 29% of agent-managed lettings had agents belonging to agents' associations (Crook *et al.*, 2000). But by 2001, 55% of all agents were members of trade or professional bodies, although this was still true of only 15% of landlords (ODPM, 2003b). Even by 2006, 62% of individually owned addresses had landlords with no related experience or qualification and 83% did not belong to any relevant professional or trade association. In contrast, where agents managed property, 71% did belong to one or more of these (CLG, 2008b).

And, despite the importance attached by governments to local authority forums and accreditation schemes, by 2001 only15% of landlord managed addresses had owners involved in local authority forums, although agents were more likely to have been involved (35%). Only 9% of addresses had a landlord or agent who was a member of an accreditation scheme (ODPM, 2003b).

This lack of formal qualifications, membership of trade associations and forums and accreditation schemes, showed just how reliant the sector was on landlords and agents having access to other sources of information, especially when they faced significant problems with difficult tenants, rent arrears, regaining possession and housing benefit. Landlords generally sought advice from their solicitors, who were seen as helpful in the vast majority of cases. Landlords were less likely to seek advice for the regular day-to-day problems, including rent arrears and doing repairs, than for other less regularly occurring problems, such as seeking repossession (Crook & Kemp, 1996a).

Thomas and Snape's study confirmed that many sideline landlords were unaware of much of the legislation and that their understanding of what they did know was very patchy with a good deal of misunderstanding evident. Many tried to find out only when they needed too, but often the 'experts' consulted did not fully understand the issues. And one bad experience could result in substantial changes across a whole portfolio, even although this was sometimes the result of landlords' inexperience and naivety about their legal and other obligations (Thomas & Snape, 1995).

The potential problems that arise from this lack of knowledge were well illustrated by our 1998 survey. For example, at 86% of addresses where landlords alone took decisions on minor repairs, they had no qualification at all in building or related property matters, yet nearly half of all addresses had owners who said they experienced difficulties doing this work. And even where agents took these decisions on behalf of the owners, 49% did not have any professional qualification (Crook *et al.*, 2000).

Doing repairs and improvements

Governments hoped that deregulated rents would enable landlords to carry out repairs and make improvements as part of the normal overhead of running their businesses. This was because tenants would expect high standards and be prepared to pay for them. As a result, it would no longer be necessary to rely on local authority enforcement and grant-led action to secure improved conditions. This hope was not realised.

The evidence in Chapter 3 suggested that, although there had been an improvement in conditions, this did not principally arise from the 1989 deregulation but from the continuing transfer into the sector of properties from other tenures, consequent upon buy-to-let purchases and landlords letting out what had once been their family homes (see also Crook *et al.*, 1998a, 2000).

Evidence from the 1990s also showed that, far from market forces transforming conditions, properties that were owned for investment purposes by business and sideline investor landlords were in a worse state of repair than other properties and that their landlords spent less than did non-investor landlords who owned the better condition properties. Indeed the latter spent more than was necessary because they took a general 'stewardship' approach to property ownership and did not spend only what could be justified on investment grounds. Table 4.11 shows the median outstanding general repair costs in 1996: the worst were owned by business landlords and by sideline investor landlords and the better were owned by other sideline landlords and by institutions. The same pattern had been found in 1991 (Crook *et al.*, 1998a, 2000).

This pattern was further confirmed by examining what landlords spent on repairs and improvements between 1996 and 1998 (Crook *et al.*, 2000). Table 4.12 shows that addresses in the best physical condition in 1996 were more likely to have had major work done between 1996 and 1998 than others. Average expenditure on major work after 1996 was highest for those addresses

Table 4.11 General repair costs in 1996 prices by type of landlord as recorded in 1998

Type of landlord	Percent in each quartile range				Median costs £	% unfit	Cases
	Best	Second quartile	Third quartile	Worst			
Business	23	18	20	39	3583	23	44
Sideline: investor	19	27	27	27	2711	17	63
Sideline: other	22	34	20	24	1872	14	55
Institutions	39	26	21	13	1207	5	38
All addresses	24	27	22	26	2288	15	200

Source: Crook *et al.* (2000).

Table 4.12   The condition of addresses and the tendency to undertake major work
and expenditure between 1996 and 1998

	Economic repair costs 1996 prices: quartiles			
	Lowest 1	2	3	Highest 4
1. Proportion of dwellings where major work had been done (%)	29.0	23.7	23.7	23.7
2. Average economic repair cost in 1996 (£)	340	1400	3617	9755
3. Average expenditure on major repairs (£) since 1996	3020	2596	850	2139
4. Repairs expenditure as percentage of repair cost	888	185	24	22

Values in Row 4 are calculated as the value from Row 3 divided by the value in Row 2.
Source: Crook *et al.* (2000).

in the 'best condition' quartile in 1996. And the worse were the conditions in 1996, the lower was the subsequent expenditure relative to the assessed economic repair costs. This represented a continuation of the trend between 1991 and 1994 (Crook *et al.*, 1998a). The key determinant of the amount spent was the type of landlord. Investment-oriented landlords were less likely to undertake repairs than those who let largely for non-commercial reasons.

In the light of these findings it is important to understand the extent to which the deregulated market generated the rents and capital values to incentivise landlords. The evidence suggests that the market did so, but only in part (Crook *et al.*, 2000; Crook & Hughes, 2001).

There was no relationship in 1991 between rents and the state of repair in the deregulated market (Crook & Hughes, 2001). Since newly deregulated markets take time to mature, 1991 may have been too soon after the 1989 deregulation to expect a fully competitive market, such that market rents were systematically related to conditions. But five years later there was still no evidence of this. The 1996 evidence was broadly in line with the results from 1991. Dwelling conditions did not have any relationship with the level of rent. In other words, poor conditions commanded as much in rent as good conditions (Crook *et al.*, 2000).

Undertaking repairs did, however, lead to higher capital values. Good repair, measured in terms of outstanding repair costs, was captured by higher capital values and the results showed that in 1991 a landlord could have recovered more than three-quarters of repairs expenditure simply from the resulting increase in capital value over about two years. But because annual spending on maintenance and vacant-possession market values were highest amongst the better-condition properties, net rates of return in 1998 were, paradoxically, lowest at this top end. Hence, at the top end, rents were broadly the same as at the bottom end, but because they carried higher

Table 4.13 Rates of return in 1998 by dwelling condition

	Income (net rental) return:	
Quartiles of repairs outstanding	**Before voids and bad debts (%)**	**After voids and bad debts (%)**
Top quartile (best condition)	7.1	7.0
Second quartile	8.1	7.5
Third quartile	8.3	7.9
Bottom quartile (worst condition)	9.4	6.6

Source: Crook & Kemp, with Barnes & Ward (2002). Reproduced by permission of the British Property Federation.

annual maintenance charges and higher capital values than properties at the bottom end, net rental rates of return were actually lower – by some 2.3% (Crook *et al.*, 2000).

One explanation for the poor relationship between rents and conditions is that tenants did not place a high value on good repairs, but were concerned more about superficial aspects (Crook *et al.*, 2000; Crook & Hughes, 2001). They may have been more interested in their location, internal decorations and 'white goods' than in the state of their roofs (for later evidence of this, see Bibby *et al.*, 2007). That would not be entirely irrational for short-term tenants. Although most landlords of the worst properties still managed to find tenants for their accommodation, they had difficulty in doing so and there was also evidence of higher voids and arrears (Crook & Kemp, with Barnes & Ward, 2002). There were also capital losses amongst these very same properties (Crook *et al.*, 2000).

Because neither rents nor capital values were likely to increase commensurately with any improvement of the worst properties in these low-demand areas, it may thus not have been economically rational, even though socially desirable, for the landlords to have undertaken the work needed, unless the repair work undertaken very substantially reduced void and arrears losses. These were much higher amongst the worst properties and when these are taken into account they reduced the net income return by nearly 3% in 1998, making them equivalent to the best condition dwellings (Table 4.13). Voids were probably higher in these properties because landlords may not have been able to let them as quickly as those with better properties, where voids were much fewer and of short duration. Arrears may also have been greater because tenants kept rent back to get repairs done or because it was only low-income tenants, more prone to get into arrears than others, who would accept the conditions (Crook & Kemp, with Barnes & Ward, 2002). This suggests that landlords owning poor-condition property could get good returns from renovations because voids and arrears would fall even if rents stayed the same. But many of these properties were in low-demand areas where neighbouring properties were also in poor condition. Unless landlords were sure their neighbours would also carry out improvements, perhaps supported by council-led area improvement programmes, they could have found themselves owning the only decent home in a neighbourhood and hence still unable to attract good tenants.

Later evidence from the 2001 and 2006 surveys broadly confirmed these findings and also threw more light on the issue of conditions and landlords' strategies in low-demand areas (ODPM, 2003b; CLG, 2008b).

In 2001 just over 53% of dwellings failed to meet the new decency standard but this proportion was much higher (64%) amongst those owned by business landlords. Comprehensive repair costs for properties owned by sideline investors were much lower, suggesting that properties acquired by new buy-to-let landlords were in much better condition on acquisition than those owned by earlier generations of sideline investor landlords. In 2003, company-owned dwellings and those owned by other full-time landlords owning several properties were in a worse condition than others. Although properties owned by new landlords were in a better condition than those owned by continuing ones, they were in a worse state of repair than dwellings in the owner-occupied sector from which they had transferred.

The evidence also confirmed that landlords' decisions about repairs spending were mainly motivated by non-economic factors and that, although rents could finance minor repairs, they could not fund major repairs (ODPM, 2003b). There was a tendency for properties in low-demand areas to be in poorer condition, to take longer to let and to be owned by full-time landlords and those with larger portfolios than properties in higher-demand areas (ODPM, 2006).

We can draw two key conclusions from all this evidence. First, dwellings in the worst condition and those least likely to have been improved were more likely to be owned by landlords with investment motives. Landlords who were looking for investment returns operated within a market that did not generate the returns needed to deal with disrepair whilst those owning dwellings in the best condition pursued stewardship approaches, irrespective of investment returns. Second, the deregulated market was not producing higher rents for better properties, nor giving landlords higher net rental rates of return. This posed significant problems for policies designed to secure improved conditions within a market framework when local authority grants had been curtailed and resources for enforcement action had been reduced.

Attitudes to letting

Did deregulation in 1989 change landlords' attitudes to letting and had they become more confident? The evidence below shows that many became more positive and confident about being landlords, especially about being able to

Table 4.14 Landlords' attitudes to letting accommodation in 1982/84 and 1993 in England

Statement	Source	Agree	No view	Disagree
Law allows landlords to charge a reasonable	a	39	30	32
rent these days	b	67	19	14
Landlords are adequately protected by law	a	17	23	60
against tenants refusing to leave	b	46	33	20
Tenants generally look after accommodation	a	69	14	18
	b	58	22	21
Landlords find tenants generally good at paying	a	52	29	20
rent on time	b	70	19	11
Landlords find that wear and tear on property is	a	45	12	43
quite small	b	42	17	40
It is hard for landlords to find out how they are	a	37	27	37
affected by the law	b	33	23	44
Landlords spend a lot of time arranging new lets	a	38	20	42
because tenants move so frequently	b	33	22	45
Landlords only let if they can't sell	a	15	21	65
	b	16	17	66
Landlords find it difficult to fill their vacancies	a	9	8	84
	b	11	18	71

a, Figures from 1982/84 survey; b, figures from 1993 survey.
Sources: Todd & Foxon (1987); Crook & Kemp (1996a).

charge reasonable rents, in marked contrast to the picture before deregulation. Nonetheless two negative things stood out. Landlords still found it hard to find out about matters affecting them and many thought they were not adequately protected by the law when they sought possession.

Table 4.14 compares results from the 1982 to 1984 survey of the landlords making new lettings in England in that period with the results of the 1993 survey. In both surveys landlords were asked what it was like to let accommodation 'today' (Todd & Foxon, 1987; Crook & Kemp, 1996a). There were two areas where landlords had become more positive after the 1989 deregulation: their ability to charge reasonable rents and their protection against tenants refusing to leave, although less than half agreed about the latter. In other respects there were no significant changes. Hence landlords generally agreed that tenants still looked after accommodation and were still good at paying rent on time. They still had mixed views about the extent of wear and tear, the difficulty of finding out about the law, and the amount of time spent arranging new lettings. They still disagreed that landlords only let if they could not sell (unless they were new landlords) and that it was difficult to fill their vacancies. We can conclude that by 1993, whilst confidence in letting appeared to have improved in some important respects, in other aspects it had not done so.

Table 4.15   Landlords' attitudes to letting accommodation in 1992/93 and 2008 in Scotland

Statement	Source	Agree	Neither	Disagree
Law allows landlords to charge a reasonable rent these	a	84	5	11
days	b	74	18	8
Landlords are adequately protected by law against	a	38	17	46
tenants refusing to leave	b	19	34	47
Tenants generally look after accommodation	a	73	9	18
	b	70	8	23
Landlords find tenants generally good at paying rent on	a	78	8	14
time	b	73	9	18
Landlords find that wear and tear on property is quite	a	47	13	40
small	b	n/a	n/a	n/a
It is hard for landlords to find out how they are affected	a	28	9	63
by the law	b	33	23	43
Landlords spend a lot of time arranging new lets	a	32	10	58
because tenants move so frequently	b	n/a	n/a	n/a
Landlords only let if they can't sell	a	9	5	86
	b	n/a	n/a	n/a
Landlords find it difficult to fill their vacancies	a	7	8	85
	b	12	18	70
The law adequately balances the interests of landlords	a	n/a	n/a	n/a
and tenants today	b	43	23	35

a, Figures from 1992/93 survey; b, figures from 2008 survey; n/a, question not asked in 2008.
Sources: Kemp & Rhodes (1994); Crook *et al.* (2009).

Table 4.15 compares attitudes to letting by Scotland's landlords in 2008 with those in 1992/93 (Kemp & Rhodes, 1994; Crook, *et al.*, 2009). Most lettings had landlords who felt they could charge a reasonable rent, that tenants paid rent on time and looked after their accommodation (although that did not mean that wear and tear was small). Few lettings had landlords who found it difficult to let vacancies. On the negative side, a significant minority of landlords considered that the law did not adequately protect them against tenants refusing to leave and this proportion had increased between 1992/93 and 2008. A significant minority also felt it was hard to find out about the law. Noticeably too, many lettings were owned by landlords who were unsure about the extent to which the law protected them and considered it hard to get information about it. Finally it is important to note that in 2008 less than half lettings were owned by those who thought the law adequately balanced the interests of landlords and tenants.

These findings were problematic in terms of policy objectives since these required well-informed landlords with confidence in the liquidity of their investments. Those on whom policy was particularly targeted – companies and those with larger portfolios – generally had the most positive views, except with respect to seeking possession. But these were very much in a minority and it was individual owners, very much the majority owners of the sector, who were more likely to have negative views on repossession and finding out about the law.

Investment returns and plans

Government policy was predicated on the basis that deregulation would provide landlords with competitive returns that were sufficient to retain existing landlords in the sector, to persuade new ones to invest and for all to add to their portfolios. The evidence shows that while rents broadly covered landlords' costs after the 1989 deregulation, they were not enough to give competitive investment returns. This meant that capital growth was crucial in securing the returns landlords required.

Rates of return

It is easy to assume that landlords were well informed about their returns and had clearly defined targets, but evidence suggests otherwise. Thomas & Snape, in their qualitative work in the mid 1990s, found that not all landlords knew what their returns were and that, whilst all knew what their income was, few worked out their net income return and even fewer had a target return, although business landlords were more likely to have to be an exception (Thomas & Snape, 1995).

Our 1993 survey confirmed that few landlords expected rents to give them an investment return. Apart from rent-free lettings, landlords expected rents to cover costs, especially loans, repairs, management costs and insurances, but few expected rents to provide their investment return. Only 32% of lettings owned by business landlords and 29% of those owned by sideline investors were looking at rents to provide their returns. As Table 4.16 shows, less than half of all lettings had landlords who thought the rent sufficient to cover costs in 1993, although this rose to nearly three-quarters for the most recent lettings, many of which had been made since deregulation. But much lower proportions thought their rent sufficient to cover costs and also give returns – less than half the landlords of new lettings.

Landlords lose substantial amounts through voids and arrears. In 1993 arrears and voids constituted 2% and 6%, respectively, of the collectable rent across all lettings. On top of these, running costs were high and accounted for 26% of gross collectable rent amongst the recent lettings sample. Table 4.16 also shows the gross and net income returns based on landlords' estimates of the vacant-possession value of their addresses, their rents and costs (including voids and arrears). Returns amongst deregulated tenancies were much higher (6.5% net) than amongst those that were still regulated (3.4% net) (Crook & Kemp, 1996a).

Table 4.16   Whether rent was sufficient, rent loss, costs and rates of return[a]

	England 1993 all lettings	England 1993 new lettings	England 1998 deregulated	England 2001	Scotland 1992/93	Scotland 2008
Percentage where rent was sufficient to cover costs	49	72	70	66	44	n/a
Percentage rent lost in voids and arrears	5	9	10	n/a	n/a	n/a
Costs as a percentage of gross rent	30	26	26	40	34	n/a
Gross income return (% per annum)	6.3	8.4	10.4	8.2	6.5	4.9[b]
Net income return (% per annum)	5.5	6.8	7.3	5.5	4.6	n/a
Total net return (% per annum)	11.2	12.3	11.2	n/a	n/a	n/a
Percentage where rents from all lettings sufficient for costs and returns	39	47	n/a	n/a	n/a	68
Sample base	Dw	Dw	Dw	Dw	Dw	Dw

[a] Only calculated where addresses were not let on a rent-free basis; [b] median return.
Sources: Crook & Kemp (1996a); Crook *et al.* (2000); ODPM (2003b); Kemp & Rhodes (1994); Crook *et al.* (2009).

Even though returns were thus higher in 1993 than those obtained before the 1989 deregulation, this did not mean that they were competitive. We asked landlords what they thought a sufficient rent would be. On that basis the average sufficient gross return was 12.5% for recent lettings, with an average yield gap of 4.1%. This implied a 50% increase in rents and suggested that five years after the 1989 deregulation, rents had to rise substantially (or costs or capital values to fall) to yield sufficient returns.

Landlords also gain a total return from accruing capital gains on top of their net rental income. We calculated total returns in 1993 by computing the real capital gains, or losses, from comparing the price paid when sample addresses were acquired with the landlords' estimates of open market valuations in 1993. Median annual gains were 1.8% and 3.4% for all and for recent lettings respectively. This made the average total annual return in 1993 11.2% for all lettings and 12.3% for recent lettings.

At first sight these returns were attractive and met the benchmark of '9% gross, 6% net' set out by the British Property Federation in 1982 (House of Commons Environment Committee, 1982), a broad target confirmed by a survey of managing agents in 1993 who thought that 10% gross returns were needed (Rhodes, 1993). But, as Table 4.16 shows, fewer than 4 in 10 of all lettings in 1993 had landlords who thought the rent from all their lettings sufficient to cover costs and give a reasonable return. However, when this is broken down by landlord type, nearly 6 in 10 of lettings owned by business and sideline investor landlords had owners who thought their rent income sufficient, as did nearly 7 in 10 of lettings whose landlords sought a return in rent income rather than capital growth, of whom only 5 in 10 thought the rent reasonable (Crook & Kemp, 1996a). These findings confirmed the diversity of the sector, the very different attitudes to owning property, the different horizons over which returns were sought and, in addition, the importance of capital growth to making returns satisfactory.

The key results of our 1998 survey broadly confirmed those of 1993 (Table 4.16). Only 23% of addresses had landlords who expected rents to give returns on market value. The landlords of 79% of deregulated lettings thought rents sufficient to cover costs. Gross and net income returns had risen slightly since 1993, although total returns had fallen slightly, compared with 1993, both trends reflecting the fact that capital values were lower in 1998 than in 1993. In 1998 rents would have had to rise by about a third to ensure all landlords had sufficient rent income to cover their costs and get a sufficient return. Net income returns from deregulated lettings were 7.3%, compared with 4.8% from those that were still at that time regulated. Returns from flats (8%) were much higher than from houses (6.8%) (Crook & Kemp, with Barnes & Ward, 2002).

Later surveys confirmed the 1993 and 1998 findings. The 2001 survey showed that 66% of lettings had landlords who thought the rents sufficient to cover costs but only 40% had landlords who expected their rent to give an investment return, much lower than the 60% of lettings whose landlords said they expected an investment return from their property. This suggests that capital growth was key to getting a sufficient return (ODPM, 2003b).

In Scotland the picture was similar. Only 24% of addresses in 1992/93 had landlords who expected rents to give a return on vacant-possession value. Gross income returns of 6.5% were reported in the 1993/93 survey, comparable with returns from the 1993 survey in England. Only 56% of addresses had landlords who thought the rent sufficient. Detailed analysis of what landlords said would be sufficient suggested a need for returns to rise by four percentage points to yield gross and net sufficient income returns of 11.4 and 7.8% respectively, implying a very significant increase in rents or, instead, a need for substantial capital gains (Kemp & Rhodes, 1994). In 2008 gross income returns in Scotland were only 4.9%, a reflection of the significant increases in capital values in the preceding period (Crook *et al.*, 2009). Of those addresses where landlords were expecting rents to cover costs, only 68% had landlords who thought their rents were sufficient to cover all necessary costs and give them a reasonable return. These landlords were getting higher gross returns of 6% on average.

Evidence about returns also comes from regular rent indices. The York index of rents and yields provided a regular quarterly series from 1996 to 2001 using valuations of market values and rents as well as transactions (Rhodes & Kemp, 2002). Although rents rose from 1996 to 2001 by 20%, gross income returns fell by 6%, because capital values rose more than rents. The index had results that were broadly comparable with the survey evidence for 2001, with a net income return of 5.7% and a gross total return of 13.8% in 2000. It also confirmed that rental returns were greatest amongst smaller properties, especially one- and two-bedroom flats and that returns for these were competitive with other property and financial investments including equities and gilts (see also Coopers & Lybrand, with Kemp, Crook, & Hughes, 1995).

Scrutiny of the ARLA index (http://www.arla.co.uk/uploads/news) and the Investment Property Databank (IPD) index (http://www.ipd.com/ourproducts/indices) showed how very important capital gains were after the year 2000. For example, the ARLA index (based on evidence from small- and medium-scale buy-to-let landlords) for quarter 1 in 2009 revealed a net income return (gross rent less voids) of 4.9% but a total return of 10.2% based on average capital gains of 7.9% over the preceding five years. The index also showed the impact of leveraging to achieve higher returns on geared investments, especially when interest rates were low. In quarter 1 of 2009 an equity investment of 25% of the purchase price (borrowing the remaining 75%) gave total returns of 24.2%.

The IPD index of large residential portfolio returns enabled comparisons of returns with those from commercial property, equities and bonds. It again illustrated the significance of capital gains in the period after the year 2000. In 2000 income returns were 5.6%, but total returns were 18.5%. By 2006 income returns had fallen to 3.6% and total returns to 12.4%. By 2008 income returns were only 3.2% and total returns were negative at minus 18%. However, residential did better in 2008 than commercial property and equities, though worse than bonds. Taking a longer-term view, total returns from residential property investments outperformed commercial property, equities and bonds between the years 2000 and 2008.

Evidence can also be gleaned from a buy-to-let mortgage lenders' index of rents and values based on its loans book (http://www.paragon-mortgages.co.uk). Gross income returns fell from 8.0% to 6.4% between June 2003 and June 2008, despite a modest increase in rents, since capital values increased, on average, from £124000 to £165000. Because of this, total returns were much higher than gross income returns, for example as high as 27.4% in June 2003, but falling to 13.6% in June 2008. This data also showed significant regional variations in returns with much higher total returns being earned in the northern regions of England.

To sum up, so far, the evidence on returns shows that although a much larger proportion of addresses had rents that covered costs than before deregulation, rents were still not high enough to give all landlords an investment return as well. Competitive returns thus depended on achieving significant capital gains on top of the rents. However, the low level of net income returns did not necessarily mean they were uncompetitive since they needed to be compared with returns from alternative investments and in the light of risk and liquidity. We looked at the evidence about this in the 1990s (Crook & Kemp, with Barnes & Ward, 2002).

Table 4.17 Investment returns in deregulated sector and in alternative investments, mid-1990s

Investment	Gross income return (%)	Net income return (%)
Scotland 1992/93	7.0	5.0
England 1993/94	9.1	6.5
York Index England 1996 Q1	9.1	5.8
Commercial property	n/a	8.6
Medium-dated gilts	n/a	7.5
Equities	n/a	6.7

Source: Crook *et al.* (1998b). Based on data from Crook, Hughes, and Kemp, 1998b, *Journal of Property Research,* 15, 229–248. With permission.

Table 4.18 Investment returns in deregulated sector and in alternative investments, 1998

Investment	Net (income) return (%)	Total (nominal) return (%)
Deregulated lettings	7.3	10.6
Retail	6.5	11.6
Office	7.9	11.6
Industrial	9.2	13.2
Equities	2.8	13.7
Long-dated gilts	6.4	25.0
Treasury bills	7.9	7.9

Sources: Crook & Kemp, with Barnes & Ward (2002). Reproduced by permission of the British Property Federation.

First, we examined returns from the mid 1990s. Table 4.17 shows that net income returns earned from deregulated lettings in both Scotland and England were not competitive with those that could be obtained from commercial property, government bonds and equities, all of which were more liquid and less risky. The York index demonstrated that higher returns could be earned on one- and two-bedroom flats (7.8 and 7.2% net respectively) suggesting that careful property selection and asset management could yield higher returns than average, but these were still below or just on a par with returns from other less-risky and more-liquid investments. This further confirmed that capital gains were an important feature in helping to make residential investment competitive.

Second, we compared total returns from our lettings sample in England in 1998 with total returns from property and financial investments. In this comparison we used methods that ensured comparability with those used for analysing returns in commercial property and other investments. This involved, briefly, using nominal and not real accrued capital gains, adding 'in-year' capital expenditure and half the annual net rent to the estimated capital value. Table 4.18 shows that net rental returns from deregulated lettings performed better in 1998 than returns from retail property, but

Table 4.19 A nationally based estate management company's portfolio returns in 1999

Investment	Net (income) return (%)	Total (nominal) return (%)
Deregulated lettings	5.4	19.0
Retail	6.3	14.1
Office	7.6	14.1
Industrial	8.9	17.3
Equities	2.6	23.8
Long-dated gilts	4.9	−3.5
Treasury bills	5.5	5.5

Sources: Crook & Kemp, with Barnes & Ward (2002). Reproduced by permission of the British Property Federation.

worse than other property. It also performed better than equities and long-dated gilts, but worse than treasury bills. As far as total (nominal) returns were concerned, deregulated lettings performed worse than all other property and financial investments, with the exception of treasury bills.

We thirdly examined returns in 1999 from a nationally based managing agents' corporate clients' portfolios. Table 4.19 shows that deregulated lettings gave lower income (net rental) returns in 1999 than did other property but gave higher total returns, reflecting the high level of nominal capital growth in the residential market. Net income returns in deregulated lettings were also higher than income returns from financial investments. Total returns were also higher, apart from equities.

These findings suggest that, when compared with other investments, residential lettings' performance varied both in terms of the comparator investment and in terms of timing. In making these comparisons, three additional factors must be taken into account:

First, before deregulation, residential lettings were seen as higher risk and lower liquidity than other investments. If this was still correct after deregulation, residential lettings performed poorly, since a higher return would be required. However, reduced risk and increased liquidity since the 1989 deregulation should have reduced the premium significantly, suggesting that residential lettings have given acceptable returns, especially for flats and other small properties.

Second, most potential investors examine the manner in which assets contribute to their whole portfolio, rather than examining returns in isolation and on a year-by-year basis. In particular, residential lettings can provide additional diversification potential, since returns move in a different cycle from other property returns (Coopers & Lybrand, with Kemp, Crook, & Hughes, 1995; Crook & Kemp, 1999).

Third, timing is important, especially in relation to capital growth cycles. Hence the favourable total returns from the nationally based estate

Table 4.20 What landlords would do with vacant lettings

Intention	England 1993 (%)	England 1998 (%)	England 2001 (%)	England 2003 (%)	Scotland 1992/93 (%)	Scotland 2008 (%)
Let/improve to let	68	69	73	77	76	83
Sell/improve to sell	21	24	15		17	5
Occupy it	2	+	+	23	2	4
Other	10	7	12		5	8
Sample base	Dw	Dw	Dw	Dw	Dw	Dw

Dw, dwellings; +, data included in 'other'
Sources: Crook & Kemp (1996a); Crook *et al.* (2000); ODPM (2003b); ODPM (2006); CLG (2008b);
Kemp & Rhodes (1994); Crook *et al.* (2009).

management company's clients' portfolios in 1999 appeared much less favourable when the returns for 2000 were examined (Crook & Kemp, with Barnes & Ward, 2002). This suggests that timing of acquisitions is all-important, especially as capital gains are maximised by investing at the bottom of the house price cycle.

On this basis, returns since the 1989 deregulation could be judged competitive, but only if capital gains were taken into account, residential lettings were mixed with a wider investment portfolio, small properties were acquired and bought at the bottom of the property market cycle. It is likely that this complete prescription applied to the owners of only a handful of lettings acquired after 1989.

Future intentions

What do we know about the extent to which landlords intended to continue investing? In their qualitative study of landlords' in the early 1990s Thomas and Snape showed that, where expansion was being contemplated, it was amongst a limited number of the business landlords operating at the lower end of the market. Some were considering buying up properties at competitive prices, renovating these themselves and letting to housing benefit claimants. Landlords suggested this was then a very active market with funding coming from landlords' own resources, mortgages or commercial overdrafts. There was also the student housing market, especially where universities were prepared to underwrite against damage and rent arrears. Sideline investor landlords tended to operate at the better end of the market and here expansion was limited and constrained by the difficulties of securing funding and by the high cost of properties in this part of the market (Thomas & Snape, 1995).

Our quantitative surveys showed what landlords intended to do if their lettings became vacant 'tomorrow' and if they expected their current portfolios to grow (Table 4.20).

Table 4.21   Whether landlords expected portfolios to increase in next two (or three) years

	England 1993	England 1998	England 2001	England 2003	Scotland 1992/93	Scotland 2008
Intention	**2 years (%)**	**2 years (%)**	**2 years (%)**	**2 years (%)**	**3 years (%)**	**3 years (%)**
Increase	17	19	21	24	20	17
Stay the same	59	59	62	55	67	74
Decrease	24	22	16	20[a]	14	8
Sample base	Dw	Dw	Dw	Dw	Dw	Dw

Dw, dwellings; [a] includes 11% of dwellings whose landlords would quit the sector.
Sources: Crook & Kemp (1996a); Crook *et al.* (2000); ODPM (2003b); ODPM (2006); CLG (2008b); Kemp & Rhodes (1994); Crook *et al.* (2009).

In 1993, 68% of all lettings were to be re-let if they had become vacant, a much higher percentage than in the 1976 survey but similar to the survey of recent lettings in 1982 to 1984. Just over two in ten would be sold, with the remainder occupied by the landlord, left empty or put to some other use. Not surprisingly, addresses owned by sideline non-investors were much more likely not to be re-let and so too were addresses owned by landlords seeking their investment returns through capital gains. Landlords' main reasons for not re-letting were related far more to their personal circumstances, such as re-occupying their main home or no longer needing the accommodation for a friend or relative, than because of a poor investment return or the bother and hassle of letting. By 2001 and 2003 the evidence showed slight increases in the percentage of dwellings that would be re-let. The picture in Scotland was very similar.

These findings provided strong evidence that deregulation had changed landlords' intentions and that few had decided against continued letting because it was not worthwhile financially. The 1998 survey confirmed that many of those who become landlords for non-investment purposes were only in the market for limited periods of time (for example, whilst they had moved jobs or housed a relative for a temporary period) and were not likely to be in the letting business for lengthy periods.

Looking at whether landlords' intentions for their portfolios as a whole had changed since deregulation, Table 4.21 shows that there was a slight balance in favour of an overall decline in the portfolios of landlords in 1993, but this was in stark contrast to the results of the 1976 survey when 48% of lettings were parts of portfolios expected to decline (and only 7% to increase) (Paley, 1978). The scenario that landlords thought most likely to allow them to increase portfolios was increasing rents and stable house prices, whereas stable rents and increasing house prices would lead to contraction, a finding that reinforces the importance of rental income and not capital gains as key to sustaining investment.

The 1998 survey confirmed the broad findings of the 1993 survey and also that new landlords were not the ones most likely to expand their portfolios. By the time of the 2001 and 2003 surveys the balance had shifted towards a slight expansion of portfolios. The 2003 survey also found that 11% of addresses had landlords who expected to quit the sector completely within the following two years, including over a fifth of dwellings owned by new landlords. This confirmed the extent of 'churn' in the sector with nearly half the stock owned by landlords expecting both an increase and a decrease in their portfolios and with a very pronounced 'churn' in landlords as well as in dwellings. In so far as there was evidence of stability, it was amongst the portfolios owned by companies and property sector sideline landlords, with 43% and 39% of dwellings owned by them being, respectively, parts of portfolios expected to grow. Unfortunately dwellings owned by companies formed only a small part of the sector. Again the picture in Scotland was very similar.

Conclusions

At the beginning of this chapter we asked, first, if there had been a growth in corporate landlords, realising economies of scale, and spreading their risk, as had been hoped? The answer is 'no'. Instead there had been a significant growth in individual landlords. Portfolio sizes fell amongst both companies and individual owners. Business landlords owned only a small part of the stock and companies constituted only a small proportion of the stock owned by new landlords. Sideline landlords owned the great majority of the sector. And although a majority of dwellings were owned for investment reasons (especially since the year 2000 for capital growth), many landlords originally came into the sector for other, non-investment, reasons. Much more of the sector was funded by mortgages than in the past.

Second we asked if the changes in the legal framework and the wider environment gave landlords more confidence and if they acted in a more informed and rational way? The answer is only partly 'yes'. A large proportion of the sector was self-managed by sideline landlords in their own spare time. Membership of relevant professional and trade bodies was limited. Confidence in the legal framework had improved but there were concerns about regaining possession and a significant proportion had landlords who said it was hard to find out how the law affected them. Many properties had been brought at the height of the property boom after the year 2000, suggesting a not wholly rational approach to making property investments.

Finally we asked if landlords were getting more competitive returns and had sufficient confidence to expand their portfolios? Again the answer is only partly 'yes'. A higher proportion of the sector than before deregulation had landlords who said rents were sufficient to cover costs, but only a small proportion thought they were enough to give them an adequate return. Rental returns had risen since deregulation and were more competitive then in the past, but it appeared that many landlords looked to capital gains, and increasingly so, to provide their returns. Furthermore, deregulation had not delivered improved physical conditions of itself, as the dwellings in the worst conditions were owned by business and sideline investor landlords, for whom deregulated rents did not offer clear market signals to make repairs and improvements. Despite this, there was clear evidence that more land-lords intended to re-let properties than in the past and also expected to add to their portfolios in the future.

Deregulation had thus delivered a more confident sector getting better returns. The transformation that occurred was not the modernisation hoped for by government but the emergence of a sector increasingly dominated by small-scale part-time individual landlords, many investing for capital gains and managing in their own spare time, and not necessarily well informed about their rights and responsibilities. The sector continued to attract many new landlords, often temporarily, attracted by capital gains and perhaps often entering irrationally at the peak of the market. This is not quite the sector government had in mind when it introduced deregulation nor was it a sector that necessarily responded to market signals in the rational and well informed way on which government policy was originally predicated.

In particular, the environment since deregulation did not appear to have been conducive to the emergence of large-scale corporate landlords looking for long-term income. Instead it was conducive to the emergence of small-scale and part-time landlords seeking short-term capital gains. In the next three chapters we look in more detail at the specific attempts to create a more corporate sector and at the emergence of the buy-to-let phenomenon.

5

The Business Expansion Scheme

Introduction

As we saw in Chapter 2, the Conservative government of Mrs Thatcher was keen to achieve an expansion in the corporate ownership of the sector as well as to secure an overall revival of private renting. It hoped that the 1989 deregulation would enable landlords to earn competitive returns, not only because rents would increase but also because the greater liquidity of private renting that would arise with restricted security would reduce investment risk and hence improve landlords' confidence. Because of this, their target returns would be less than in a regulated market and with an increase in rents this should persuade existing landlords to stay in the market and new ones to enter.

But the government recognised that this would not happen overnight. By one mechanism or another, rents and security of tenure had, by 1989, been subject to controls and regulation for seven decades. It would take time for the new policies to take effect and for a mature deregulated market to emerge. Existing landlords would need time to see if rents did go up and to experience how the more limited security arrangements worked in practice before they contemplated expanding their portfolios. Any new landlords thinking of entering the sector were likely to be even more risk averse – and perhaps want more returns than existing ones – and would take even more time and need more evidence before considering an initial investment.

Hence from the perspective of policymakers in 1988, it was likely that deregulation would have not have an immediate large-scale impact, apart from perhaps persuading existing landlords not to withdraw from the market. If the desired outcome was to be achieved more quickly, some way was

Transforming Private Landlords: Housing, markets & public policy, by Tony Crook & Peter A. Kemp © 2011 Tony Crook & Peter A. Kemp

needed to speed up the impact of deregulation. The mechanism selected would need to overcome existing and potential landlords' reluctance to invest until the market matured a bit more. In effect the government needed to underwrite some of their financial risks. But it did not want to make this a permanent underwriting since the need would, in principle, only arise during the limited period before the newly emerging market fully matured.

In effect what was needed was some kind of 'demonstration project' that would provide landlords with an incentive to invest in the newly deregulated market and that would provide evidence of its profitability and the competitiveness of its returns so that by the time the demonstration had run its course the incentives would no longer be required.

To do this the government decided not to create a new way of helping private landlords, for example by creating a structure of new grants or tax breaks specifically aimed at private landlords alone, but to extend to the private rented sector, for a limited five-year period, an existing mechanism, the Business Expansion Scheme (BES), that had originally been designed to help new businesses raise investment capital. Importantly too, the BES scheme was designed to help companies, and not individuals, to raise capital. It could therefore be deployed not to incentivise investment by individual landlords, but to support the development of more corporate landlords. In this way (and in the words of the then Chancellor of the Exchequer) the government planned to 'kick start' new investment and thus encourage a revival of the sector (Lamont, 1988a). The decision to introduce these incentives had not been part of the government's original plans for deregulating private renting announced in 1987 but had been introduced as part of the 1988 Budget process and given legislative authority in the Finance Act of 1988. The Chancellor of the Exchequer spoke of the way the BES was well suited to task of speeding up the process of increasing supply because the fact that full tax relief is given immediately meant that it should bring forward new investment straight away (Lamont, 1988b).

In this chapter we review the evidence for the short- and longer-run impact of this initiative. The evidence comes mainly from our own monitoring and evaluation studies of the BES scheme, which covered its full five years (Crook et al., 1991a,b, 1995; Crook & Kemp, 1996b).[1] Related research also surveyed shareholders of these companies (Hughes & Madin, 1998; Hughes, 1999).

BES: its origins and the rules for assured tenancy companies

The Finance Act extended the provisions of the BES to companies whose main trade was letting houses on assured tenancies. Prior to this extension, rented housing was not a qualifying trade under the BES. The BES was introduced in 1983 to encourage the setting up of new businesses – and was originally called the Business Start-up Scheme. Believing that it was difficult for new and small companies to raise capital because of the risks involved, the BES gave tax incentives to those who bought shares in new small unquoted companies, the generosity of the tax relief being consistent with the high risks of making such investments. Within three years of its inception, £400 m of venture capital had been raised by companies using the BES, although mainly for larger companies with less risky ventures than had been originally intended. These had also been marketed as tax shelters rather than as long-term investments (Peat Marwick, 1985; Mason *et al.*, 1988).

Companies that raised funds through the BES were not originally meant to be asset-backed, such as property companies, but instead to be trading companies operating in new high-risk areas, as well as in general commercial and industrial businesses, including transport, where, if successful, the rewards could be commensurate with the high risks taken by investors.

The Finance Act of 1988 amended the BES in two important ways. First, for a five-year period, up to the end of 1993, the scheme was extended to companies letting housing on assured tenancies, but not assured shortholds on the implicit basis that the government did not think the underwriting of investment in the provision of more short-term rental housing was justified. Second, the upper limit on what a company could raise in any one tax year was limited to £500 000 except for those in the new qualifying trade of assured tenancies and those in shipping, where the limit for both was set at £5 m in any one tax year. At the same time a limit was placed on the maximum purchase price of property acquired by BES assured-tenancy companies (including all costs, fees and spending on capital improvements): £125 000 in London and £85 000 elsewhere (in 1989, average prices of newly built dwellings in London and Britain were £85 000 and £76 000, respectively). Properties could not be let at the time they were acquired, had to meet the, then, fitness standard, and must not have previously benefited from capital allowances under the 1980 assured tenancy scheme. In addition 80% of a company's business had to be in the qualifying trade to qualify for BES status.

The scheme was designed to incentivise the retail investment of share purchases by individuals, and not wholesale investment by financial institutions. The incentives were twofold. First, individual investors got income tax relief on investments of up to £40 000 each tax year in BES firms provided they owned the shares for at least five years. Shareholders were exempt from capital gains tax on any gains realised from selling their shares after five years. Until October 1989 investors could get additional tax relief on loans taken out to fund shares (this tax concession was stopped in April 1989 for share purchase in close companies – those controlled by a limited number of people). The 1994 Budget enabled those holding shares in a company that was taken over by or merged with another one at the end of its qualifying period to roll over their capital gains relief, provided the shares were exchanged on a one-for-one basis. The highest rate of income tax in 1987/88 was 60% (the standard rate was 27%), falling to 40% (25%) a year later.

Because the original conception of BES was to raise funds for start-up companies they were inevitably small in scale and new. Nor were they to be listed companies -whose shares would trade on a stock exchange. Hence those devising new companies needed to address liquidity issues if they were to attract investors, who would be concerned to get their capital back at some stage. Clearly too, the BES assured tenancy scheme could not be used to attract new capital into existing residential property companies, although these could sponsor new assured tenancy companies. The BES was thus well suited to the government's objective of creating more companies in the sector and of providing investors with the chance to invest without individually owning the properties themselves. However they would be investing in companies that were initially, and inevitably, going to be small in scale and would offer a relatively illiquid investment, unless the companies found ways of enabling shareholders to exit at the end of the five qualifying years.

For investors, income tax relief on the purchase of shares was equivalent to a nominal gain of around 10% a year over the five-year BES period. Those setting up the companies offered the prospects of additional and tax-free gains by establishing companies that would benefit from expected house price inflation through skilful property buying and management or by setting up other companies where there would be guaranteed uplifts on legally enforceable buy-back deals.

Launching the companies

Given the size of the incentives it is not surprising that the BES scheme had a significant impact, albeit, as we shall later see, a short-run one. Large sums were raised – £3.4 bn over five years – and many new companies, 903 in all, were formed. However, this success was short-lived and, as we shall see, many companies were dissolved shortly after the initial five years, enabling their shareholders to exit with tax-free capital gains. During the five-year life of the scheme it was transformed from an initiative to raise funds for lettings in the newly deregulated sector to one that was used for two other purposes. First, at a time of high interest rates, it enabled universities, colleges and housing associations to raise cheap finance through sale-and-leaseback schemes for new (but also existing) housing. Second it enabled mortgage lenders to remove repossessed properties from their balance sheets by selling them to BES companies, sometimes with provisions to buy them back after five years. This was a time of a pronounced property slump in Britain. Mortgage interest rates were high (the Bank of England base rate was 14% in 1989), house prices fell in many areas of Britain (the price of newly built homes fell from £97 000 in 1989 in south-east England to £88 000 in 1993) and repossessions by mortgage lenders grew (over 532 000 court orders were issued over the period 1989 to 1993).

The process of setting up the companies and of raising the capital involved one of four possible routes. The first three involved the issue of a public prospectus or memorandum. Using the first route, a prospective company published a prospectus inviting investors to buy shares in it. In the second route, a fund published a memorandum inviting the public to buy shares in the fund, which subsequently invested in BES rental housing companies selected by the fund managers. The third route involved inviting the public to invest in a 'scheme' involving a preselected range of companies. The money raised under the BES assured tenancy initiative was very largely through these three types of public issues and half were launched through schemes. The fourth route involved money being raised by private placings, including groups of individuals who set up and invested in their own companies. Since private placings were not allowed to advertise for subscribers, nor to produce a prospectus, it was virtually impossible for anyone to gather any systematic information about them. They were therefore largely excluded from our analysis, although we were able to use the Inland Revenue aggregate data of the time to make estimates of the total funds raised by all private placings. However, we had no information about the individual companies themselves.

Companies that issued prospectuses often enlisted the help of sponsors to prepare the prospectuses and market the issues. Many sponsors were instrumental in setting up the companies in the first place. The incentives for sponsors to get involved in BES issues were the fees that they earned and their constant need to provide their high net-wealth clients with new investment opportunities. Many had been involved in earlier BES issues before the introduction of assured tenancies to the BES. We found that almost nine out of ten companies raising funds by prospectus issues used sponsors and that these sponsors were very largely (80%) in the financial services business. Although they had no prior experience of residential letting they gave the BES companies they were sponsoring access to their financial acumen, reputation and, crucially, their client base. Sponsors were keen to protect their share of the BES market in general and thought these companies would offer a very attractive tax-efficient and low-risk investment to their existing clients. Once they had got involved in sponsoring these companies they helped develop their property investment strategies and as the market evolved and more and more companies were launched, they worked hard to develop new ideas and products to continue to attract investment.

Most of them sponsored only five companies or less, but three sponsored more than ten each. Hence, while most companies (57%) were sponsored by firms for whom it was not a core business, just over a third (37%) were sponsored by a few major BES sponsors. The latter were particularly active in the formation of contracted exit companies (see below) and sometimes issued single prospectuses for schemes of up to 15 companies. Companies with sponsors were more likely to achieve their minimum subscription than others and to have raised, on average, more than others (£3.4 m compared with £2.6 m for companies without sponsors). In return for their efforts, sponsors were rewarded with fees that on average were 4.4% of the funds subscribed. Some had additional bonuses that were related to share options at discounted prices and which were based upon share performance of the companies once launched. An additional role of the sponsors was to monitor the companies of behalf of shareholders to make sure they operated within the BES regulations, although there was very little evidence that they had done much due diligence on the demand for private lettings for their sponsored companies nor that they got involved in the running of the companies once successfully launched. Many were in fact concerned about the limit of £500 000 placed on what other types of BES companies could raise.

BES funds involved investors subscribing a minimum of £2000 in a fund that then invested in a minimum of four rental housing companies on behalf of the funds' shareholders. The investments were made at the discretion of the fund manager and during the first five years the funds' shareholders had no effective control over their investments. In contrast, schemes involved the offer of shares in a specified set of companies, within one issue document, gave investors the choice of where their money should go. In effect, schemes were a series of individual discretionary investment portfolio management agreements. Funds and schemes were set up by a variety of mainly financial institutions, including mortgage lenders, life assurance companies and corporate finance companies.

Unlike the sponsors of prospectus issues, those running funds and schemes had property as well as finance experience and were more involved in the running of the companies into which funds were invested, including in property-acquisition, asset-management and tenant-selection policies. They were also concerned to create viable companies that could operate in the long run and were critical of the short-term nature of most companies launched in other ways (see below).

Most companies had a promoting director with previous property experience. For those with previous property connections, including the few that were private landlords already, the availability of capital via the BES scheme was a good alternative to borrowing, especially at a time of (then) high interest rates and more cautious lenders. The BES also offered them the chance to expand their core property business, whether it was estate agency or property development. In addition, the BES scheme offered them the possibility of establishing a 'family' of companies (including via funds and schemes), all with the same shareholding ownership and management and with the intention of a merger and the possibility of a stock market flotation at the end of the five qualifying years for BES status. But these promoting directors with property experience were in a minority and our research showed that, looking at all the BES companies formed in the first two years, directors with property experience were far out numbered by those from financial services backgrounds. Directors either received salaries or a fee payment was made to directors' employers for their services. Many directors had invested in their companies (and in those cases a fee for their services was paid to their company in order to protect their tax relief). Many also had targets which, if achieved, were rewarded with share options.

In summary, those setting up these 903 companies had a mixture of motives. For many it was simply part of their core business as financial services firms enabling their clients to invest in as tax-efficient a way as possible and protecting their share of the BES market. For some others, who had property backgrounds, it provided a chance to access additional equity and add to their existing businesses. But for all of them the tax incentive was crucial. Without it, none of them would have set up a new company and the BES scheme was much more important as a factor in the setting up of new companies than deregulation itself. The latter was a necessary, but not a sufficient condition.

Numbers and types of companies formed

Most companies had set minimum subscriptions (£700 000 on average) and a quarter had their minimum subscriptions underwritten (three in ten of these drew on the underwriting).[2] Overall, a fifth of companies and a tenth of the funds failed to attract the minimum they required. But overall the scheme was a success and between the 1988/89 tax year and the end of the 1993 calendar year 903 companies were set up, almost a third of them in the final nine months of that period.

The nature of the tax incentives on offer, combined with the wider property and finance market context of this five-year period, fostered a short- rather than a long-term approach to the use of the BES scheme for assured tenancies. Although the scheme got underway at a time when house prices had been rising, it was developed during a period of a significant property slump.

There was much emphasis in prospectuses and other issue documents on the way investors could realise tax-free capital gains at the end of the qualifying five-year period over which they had to hold onto their shares before they could benefit from this tax break. Prospectuses spoke of the expectation

of significant capital gains that might be expected from a five-year investment. All companies offered this prospect, but they were of two types:
'entrepreneurial' and 'contracted exit'.

First, were those we called 'entrepreneurial' companies. These offered the
prospect of returns from both rental income and from capital growth in
the value of companies' properties. They were characteristic of many of the
companies launched in the early part of the BES assured tenancy scheme.
They relied on the skills of the directors and managers to increase share
values by astute use of the funds they raised, both in property acquisition
and in efficient management of the subsequent lettings. The companies set
up in 1988 and 1989 were based on the expectation that property prices
would continue on an upward curve and, although shareholders ran the risk
that these gains would not occur, the companies adopted a number of strategies to generate capital gains on properties. These included both care in
selecting the regions and the types of property where they most expected
gains to occur and care in tenant selection, management and rents policies
to get vacant possession at the end of the qualifying five-year period. Many
companies were explicit about raising rents at the end of the five years. This
was necessary because, to enable their shareholders to qualify for the tax
incentives, they were required to let on assured and not assured shorthold
tenancies; it was anticipated that the threat of a rent hike would persuade
tenants to move on.

Through all this careful planning, companies expected to be able to
increase share values significantly by greatly increasing the underlying net
asset value of the companies' properties. This would provide three potential
exists for the founding shareholders: as the properties became vacant at the
end of the five years they could be sold, the company liquidated and the assets
distributed to all shareholders (after the company paid tax on these gains), or
the company might be sufficiently profitable for its shares to trade at a value
that gave shareholders an opportunity to realise gains through selling shares,
or, instead, selling the company as a going concern to another residential
property company.

Initially, 150 of these companies were formed in the tax year 1988/89 but
this fell to 65 in the following year. Entrepreneurial companies continued to
be formed between 1990 and 1993, but because the housing market had
moved into a slump by then these later entrepreneurial companies adopted
new approaches to property acquisition to try to capture capital growth for
shareholders. These included redevelopment, bulk buying with significant
discounts, exploiting local knowledge and predatory purchasing from repossessions auctions and from distressed housebuilders. They also offered a
higher risk–reward profile than the later contracted exit companies and enabled those investing in several BES companies an opportunity to acquire a
portfolio of BES assured tenancy company shares, spread between the two

types. The later entrepreneurial companies also benefited from the subsequent recovery of the residential property market and the collapse of the commercial property market, offering both good prospects for capital growth and a safer haven than commercial property.

But the property slump also produced a radically different approach by most sponsors and promoters, one which was designed to attract investing shareholders with a promise of capital gains, whatever happened to house prices. They devised contracted exits, whereby third parties guaranteed to buy the shares or property of the newly formed companies at a pre-arranged uplift in share face values at the end of five years. Three types of organisations were generally involved in these arrangements: housing associations, universities, and mortgage lenders. They entered into mutually beneficial arrangements with BES companies and their shareholders. From the shareholders' perspective, the guaranteed exit offered a lower but safer risk–reward ratio and for the institutions involved in buying back after five years it offered access to cheap capital at a discount to normal rates because of the investors' tax relief. The latter meant that institutions could offer to buy back the properties at a price that meant that their effective borrowing of the capital sum when they first sold the properties was less than if they had borrowed the funds at normal commercial rates, whilst still leaving the shareholders with decent gains.

Universities were faced with a significant expansion in student numbers but without the funds to construct new student housing. Housing associations were likewise experiencing increased demands but faced shortages of grant funding from the government. Not only did the BES companies provide universities and housing associations with much-needed accommodation, but also by judicious arrangements the latter agreed to sell land and property to the companies with agreements that they would buy it back at pre-arranged prices from the companies after five years. Often these contracted exit buyback arrangements were underwritten by banks or other guarantors. Although the institutions themselves got involved in setting up the companies, the initiative largely came from sponsors who were keen to tap the strong demand for these share issues to maximise their fee income. Companies linked to universities and housing associations began to appear from the third year of the BES initiative onwards, although the majority were formed in the last two years.

Mortgage lenders also benefited from the BES initiative since it allowed them to dispose of repossession stock and enter into arrangements to either buy these properties back in five years time or to buy the BES companies' shares, in the meantime benefiting from the disposal of the stock and the capital raised from the sale. Once again, sponsors tended to take the lead in setting up these companies and it took mortgage lenders some time to satisfy themselves about the potential impact on their reputations of getting involved and also that they could satisfy the Building Societies Commission that such arrangements for disposing of repossessed stock would protect the interests of dispossessed mortgagors. This took time and it was not until the last two years of the BES initiative that these types of contracted exit companies were launched.

In the case of contracted exits, the average guaranteed uplift was high. For example, for those set up in 1990 the average uplift on share value was 40% with an exit in 1995. This equated to an annual nominal capital gain of 17.5%, of which about 7% derived from contracted uplift and about 10% from the tax relief on the share purchase.

Overall, 52% of BES companies offered contracted exits and these dominated the market after 1990, representing 68% of the new companies formed and taking 72% of subscriptions. They helped renew investors' confidence once the property slump had set in but they also reinforced the short-term nature of the initiative. The BES rules themselves encouraged investor withdrawal after five years but since most contracted exit companies relied on voluntary liquidation of the company after selling the properties this did not nurture anything other than a short-term boost to private renting. A longer-term boost to private renting by the BES relied very heavily on the entrepreneurial companies becoming profitable and creating a liquid market in their shares at the end of the five years.

Funds raised

Over £3.4 bn was subscribed over the six tax years when BES assured tenancy companies were able to raise funds. As Table 5.1 shows, most was raised by public issues but 13% (£440 m) was raised through private placings. The cost of raising the funds came to £185 m, or 5% of what was raised, covering sponsors fees, marketing, legal and other costs. Companies raised very little additional funding through borrowing (only £48 m in all) so that BES companies were significantly under-geared. Taking account of this limited borrowing meant that a total of £3278 m was available to spend on property acquisitions.

As Table 5.2 shows, entrepreneurial companies dominated fundraising in the first two years and were still raising significant sums in the last two years as well, despite the competition from contracted exit companies. They raised just over a third of the funds raised by all BES assured tenancy companies. It also shows that the guaranteed exit companies raised most of their funds in the last three years of the scheme, reflecting the property price climate at the time. Indeed just under two thirds (65%) of all BES funds were raised in the last two years, a reflection of how attractive these guaranteed exits were to investors at the time. Those linked with mortgage lenders

Table 5.1 BES funds raised by public issues and private placings

Tax year	Public issues (£m)	Private placings (£m)	Total subscriptions (£m)	Issue costs (£m)	Available for investing inc. borrowing (£m)
1988/89	361	90	451	22	458
1989/90	101	80	181	9	180
1990/91	208	100	308	18	295
1991/92	376	70	446	24	422
1992/93	976	50	1026	59	970
1993/94	953	50	1003	53	954
Total (£)	2975	440	3415	185	3278

Source: Crook *et al.* (1995). Reproduced by permission of the Joseph Rowntree Foundation.

Table 5.2 BES funds raised publicly by type of BES company

Tax year	Entrepreneurial companies (%)	Guaranteed exit: university (%)	Guaranteed exit: housing association (%)	Guaranteed exit: mortgage lender (%)	All companies (%)
1988/89	34	—	—	—	12
1989/90	8	1	—	—	3
1990/91	7	9	18	—	7
1991/92	12	20	24	—	13
1992/93	24	13	35	67	33
1993/94	15	57	23	33	32
Total (£)	1059	819	1351	747	2975
Total (%)	35	28	12	25	100

Source: Crook *et al.* (1995). Reproduced by permission of the Joseph Rowntree Foundation.

raised all their capital in the last two years. It will be noted from Tables 5.1 and 5.2 that funds raised were substantial in 1988/89 but fell in the following year. This was partly because of changes in the tax rules but also because 1989 saw the start of the housing slump, which reduced the confidence of investors in entrepreneurial companies about their ability to exit at the end of the five years because the net asset value of companies would have fallen. As we have already seen this led sponsors to create the innovation of contracted exit companies to address potential investors' twin concerns about the high risk and low liquidity of entrepreneurial companies. As a result, company formations expanded rapidly in the last three tax years.

Although the grand total of £3.4 bn funds raised was substantial, the amounts raised by each company were inevitably small because of the cap placed on the maximum that could be raised in any single tax year. Although companies could raise additional funds in the year following their initial call for funding, this created complications in arranging the exit for share-holders, especially for guaranteed exit companies. Nonetheless 22% of the companies established in the first two tax years had second share issues. Even so, most companies were small in terms of capital raised, none raising the maximum permitted in any one year. Entrepreneurial companies raised an average of only £2.13 m in the first two tax years, with an increase to £3.6 m each over the following years. University companies raised £3.05 m, housing association companies £4.36 m and mortgage lenders £4.61 m. As we shall see, the limits imposed by the BES rules meant that each company could acquire quite limited numbers of properties and was in principle unable to achieve economies of scale, unless of course it was part of a scheme or was linked through shared directorships and sponsors to a number of other companies with which it could share fund and asset management services. The BES rules were thus too restrictive for the scheme itself to enable the development of the large companies envisaged at the time of deregulation.

Property acquisition and management

As Table 5.3 reveals, just under two thirds (£2.2 bn) of the funds raised was to be invested in London, the south-east and east of England. In the first two years, much more (40%) was targeted at other regions and nations than in the later years, especially in the northern regions of England, where property prices were low and income returns high, and in Scotland, where economic recovery and economic activity generated by North Seal oil had increased the demand to rent privately.

The subsequent property slump and wider economic recession heralded a different approach. More investment was targeted at southern England, especially the south-east region. BES companies thought that the economic recovery would begin here and that increased house prices would follow. It was also an area where rental demand was strong and rents high. This was important to entrepreneurial companies since they needed to assure potential investors, in the light of the uncertainty, that capital gains would be enough to enable shareholder exits to be achieved. Our detailed analysis of specific locations of intended investments showed that BES companies were targeting locations that were not typical of the private rented sector as a whole but were distinctly more upmarket.

BES companies bought over 80000 flats and houses. As Table 5.4 shows, a quarter were repossessed stock acquired from mortgage lenders. Almost 40% were dwellings belonging to or intended for housing associations and nearly 10% were student and other housing for universities. Only about a quarter were dwellings acquired by entrepreneurial companies. Most of the dwellings were acquired in southern England: 51900 being in London and the south-east.

Table 5.3 BES property investment 1988/89 to 1993/94 by nation and region

Nation/region	Total invested £m[a]	Percentage
England		
Greater London	1195	35
South-east and east	1005	29
South-west	140	4
East Midland	207	6
West Midlands	32	1
North-west	186	5
Yorks and Humber	168	5
North	54	2
Scotland	241	7
Wales	131	4
Northern Ireland	56	2
Total	3415	100

[a] Taken from information in prospectus issues; issue fees not deducted.
Source: Crook *et al.* (1995). Reproduced by permission of the Joseph Rowntree Foundation.

Table 5.4 Numbers of dwellings acquired 1988/89 to 1993/94 by type of BES company

Tax year	Entrepreneurial companies	Guaranteed exit: university	Guaranteed exit: housing association	Guaranteed exit: mortgage lender	All companies
1988/89	7508	—	—	—	7508
1989/90	2574	442	—	—	3019
1990/91	1717	2987	2000	—	6614
1991/92	2770	5168	1935	—	9873
1992/93	4439	3755	2308	14183	24685
1993/94	2893	19028	1458	6069	29448
Total	21902	31290	7701	20252	81145

Source: Crook *et al.* (1995). Reproduced by permission of the Joseph Rowntree Foundation.

In 1993/94 BES companies paid an average of £40000 for each dwelling acquired but there was a considerable range both in terms of location and of acquiring company. Dwellings in London cost £56000 compared to £24300 in the north-west (where older terraced properties were favoured by some companies). University companies paid only £24300, reflecting the small size of the typical student flat. Entrepreneurial companies paid the most at £60500 and those connected to mortgage lenders paid only £40700, a sum reflecting the downmarket locations and poor repair state of much repossessed property. Companies appear to have paid prices that were well within the capital value limits allowed, although this meant that acquisitions had to be flats rather than houses in London and other parts of southern England.

The total acquired was only a small part of the private rented stock. However, it was nonetheless a not insignificant part of the gross inflow of new dwellings into the sector over the period 1988/93. We calculated that in England it constituted about 70000 of the total gross inflow of 450000 dwellings, or about 16%. Put another way about 1 in 6 of the additional dwellings coming into the sector after deregulation in 1989 were owned by a BES company (Crook & Kemp, 1996b). Whether these constituted long-term additions to the stock is a matter we consider below.

As far as the management of the stock was concerned, the university and housing association contracted exit companies had management agreements with the relevant institution or association. Nine in ten of those connected to mortgage lenders used managing agents, who were often linked to the companies' sponsors. Entrepreneurial companies also used external agents, with only 10% having in-house management. In the first two years, a third of the entrepreneurial companies had changed their agents, not because their fees were too high (the average was 11% of the rent collected) but because of concerns about the quality of their service (an issue we will return to in the next chapter).

Companies were keen to take on tenants who would not stay too long since, for most, their strategy was to empty their properties after five years and sell them. However, rapid tenant turnover was also to be avoided because this built up a heavy cost in lengthy voids periods. Thirty-nine percent of BES companies intended to house students (and not only those linked to universities). Students are, of course, a traditional part of the demand for private tenancies, but the expansion of higher education occurring during this period was also a factor that BES companies took into account when devising their tenant-selection policies. Nurses and armed forces personnel were attractive, especially to the early companies, of whom 15% targeted these groups. Professionals were the other group most often mentioned in prospectuses. Most companies reported strong demand for their accommodation but increasing competition, especially in London where the property slump appeared to have increased letting by homeowners unable to sell their property but who had meanwhile relocated elsewhere. As a result of this competition, many BES companies had to adjust their tenant-selection policies, with more being willing to let to unemployed people. This appeared to have worked well, with the exception of delays to their cash flow caused by problems in processing housing benefit claims. In general, despite letting on assured tenancies, companies welcomed tenant turnover (provided this did not give rise to high rent losses through long void periods) as they depended on this to generate vacant-possession sales at the end of the five-year qualifying period. As a result of competition, companies' reported rents were flat in the latter part of the five years, although those in London and the south-east were still able to command rents that were 20% higher than elsewhere.

Our survey of BES tenants undertaken in 1990 revealed very high levels of satisfaction and this contrasted markedly and positively with the previous experience of those who had been private tenants at their last address. The tenants were similar in demographic and socio-economic make up to those in the rest of the deregulated sector at that time, although the spread of incomes was greater and suggested that BES companies had attracted more upper-income groups. This was particularly the case in southern England and in Scotland.

Returns

We were able to calculate the portfolio returns of BES companies by using information in their published annual accounts when these had been filed at Companies House. We used their income as a measure of rents and examined all their operating costs in their income and expenditure accounts. We used the valuation of their properties as the basis for calculating returns. Accounting and reporting requirements meant that they had to make an estimate using RICS valuation rules. The results are shown in Table 5.5.

Not unexpectedly, the gross returns rose over the years. This is because companies were initially focused on acquiring properties, with rental income being derived later. Once properties had been let the results of our analysis suggest gross returns were good, much higher than those being earned in the rest of the sector (see Chapter 4). Gross returns were higher in the south-east. Since property prices were higher here than in most other regions, this must have been the result of higher rents. The rise in returns over the years reflected not just the build up of lettings, and hence rental income, but also the decline in valuations of their properties as a result of the property slump.

Table 5.5 Average income returns from BES companies

Year	Gross income return (%)	Net income return (%)	Number of companies
1988/89	2	–7	11
1989/90	4	–4	110
1990/91	9	–2	155
1991/92	13	2	155
1992/93	15	3	127
1993/94	15	1	22

Source: Crook *et al.* (1995). Reproduced by permission of the Joseph Rowntree Foundation.

Larger companies did not achieve higher gross returns from their ability to buy at lower prices by bulk acquisitions from housebuilders or at auctions of repossessed property, although they did achieve higher net returns. The overall average portfolio returns were only 3% net in 1993, well below that earned by all landlords in 1993 (see Chapter 4). This is partly because companies' costs were much higher than those for individuals. Costs for entrepreneurial companies came to £2779 per dwelling, compared with the £1005 for all dwellings in England (see Chapter 4). BES company costs included property management and maintenance, professional fees, including audit, directors' remuneration, office costs and fixtures and fittings. Many of these costs are not borne by the typical individual landlord, including the audit costs of a company's accounts and the money costs of an individual landlord's time. In many cases, some of the costs of repair and maintenance are borne by individual landlords who may do the work on a DIY basis, not charging for their time. BES companies were trying to keep costs down, especially directors' fees (which cost them about £600 per dwelling) with a number taking steps to reduce the number of directors.

The largest companies had net returns of 5% to 6% compared with the 1% to 2% achieved by smaller companies, the former being approximately comparable with those earned by all private landlords at that time (see Chapter 4). This appears to demonstrate that economies of scale are possible in the sector, although the ability of BES companies to demonstrate this was limited by their maximum capitalisation of £5 m. As we have seen, the average funds raised by each entrepreneurial company were only £3.6 m, enabling them to purchase 59 dwellings at the average price they paid. This is not the basis for achieving economies of scale unless they were part of a group of companies launched as part of a scheme, which together might have had a much larger portfolio. Even so, the larger companies did get better net returns.

Evaluation

The main objective of the initiative was to deliver a kick-start to private renting's revival and to help generate more corporate landlords. How far was this aim achieved, how much of the investment and the stock was additional – and at what cost to the taxpayer?

Most of the directors of the BES companies were clear that the scale of funds invested could not have been raised without the initiative. They thought it most unlikely that they would have set up these companies and that the shareholders would have put money into them without the tax incentives.

However, only a few BES properties were genuine additions to the housing stock. Repossessed dwellings accounted for 20000 of the total, existing dwellings that were temporarily recycled into private renting. It is difficult to know exactly how many of the remaining 60000 were newly built and not transfers from other tenures but our estimate, based on company prospectuses, was that only 20% of the total were newly constructed, which means that the BES financed only 12000 new units. The other 69000 were simply transferred into private renting from other tenures (or from another segment of the sector in the case of existing university accommodation that was recycled into the ownership of BES companies under the guaranteed exit arrangements).

But even this boost to private renting was only temporary. We estimated at the time we did the research that most repossessed stock would revert to owner occupation once the companies had been wound up and the stock sold, the pace and timing of this change depending on the state of the housing market. All the housing association and university accommodation would revert to those institutions at the end of the qualifying period (and did). This leaves the 22000 dwellings owned by the entrepreneurial companies. We estimated on the basis of interviews with directors and from information in company prospectuses that up to 50% might be sold and only 50% retained, with the companies consolidating through mergers and perhaps also achieving stock exchange flotations (which some did – see below).

Hence we calculated that, of the 81000 dwellings acquired by BES companies, only 11000 or so would remain as private rented dwellings by the year 2000, that is the end of the qualifying period by which all companies would have facilitated exits by their founding shareholders. Thus, although the share capital subscribed to these companies was probably wholly additional investment in private renting, not all the dwellings that were acquired were additional and even fewer would be in the long term.

Whatever the short- and long-run impact of the BES initiative, it was expensive in terms of tax expenditure, by which we mean the tax income that the government would otherwise have collected had it not set up this initiative. Table 5.6 shows that we estimated the total cost in tax expenditure was £1.7bn at 1994 prices.[3] This equates to £20874 per dwelling acquired at 1994 prices. This figure fell consistently over the period because property prices were falling and because of the increased prominence of contracted exit companies, where purchase costs were lower on average. This tax cost to the government represents the subsidy tied up in the scheme and constituted 44% of the average cost of each dwelling. For entrepreneurial companies the tax cost was £28800 per dwelling, or 48% of the acquisition cost. One of the ironies of the tax arrangements is that the tax expenditure was higher if the companies continued trading than if they liquidated, since in the former case the government receives the corporation tax paid on the capital gains before these are distributed to shareholders.

Table 5.6   The tax costs of BES at current and 1994 prices

Tax	1988/89	1989/90	1990/91	1991/92	1992/93	1993/94	Total
Tax relief on share issues: current	237m	70m	118m	168m	384m	375m	1352m
Corporation tax paid by companies: current	(0.3m)	(0.3m)	(0.3m)	(0.3m)	(0.3m)	(0.3m)	(1.8m)
Tax income foregone: current	26m	10m	17m	21m	38m	25m	137m
Tax cost: current	263m	79m	135m	189m	422m	399m	1487m
Tax cost at Nov. 1994 prices	355m	101m	160m	209m	450m	419m	1694m
Tax cost/dwelling at current prices (£)	35052	26256	20358	19145	17088	13565	18239
Tax cost/dwelling at Nov 1994 prices (£)	47285	33345	24206	21192	18233	14221	20874
Tax cost/dwelling at real net present value (£)	63366	42557	29423	24534	21102	14932	24362

Source: Crook *et al.* (1995). Reproduced by permission of the Joseph Rowntree Foundation.

We calculated that had the government used the tax expenditure to provide grants to registered housing associations under the capital subsidy system under which they operated at that time, it would have provided approximately 60% to 80% of the dwellings that had been provided under the BES (the range reflects assumptions about the location and procurement mix of the alternative investments). Although fewer than the numbers of BES dwellings, they would have been permanent additions to the social rented stock, whereas the BES dwellings were largely only a temporary addition to the private rented stock. This suggests that not only were the BES dwellings not additional to the private rented sector in the long run, but that the tax expenditure involved represented a significant opportunity cost for the government. This ignores, however, the possible (and potentially important) side effects of the scheme, including the way the institutions and individuals involved in the finance industry (including financial advisers) as well as the individual shareholders came to learn a lot more about the private rented sector as a result of the BES than they would have done through deregulation on its own.

The longer term

At the time we undertook the surveys, most company directors were sceptical about the ability of their companies to survive beyond the initial five years and to make a permanent contribution to the market rented sector. Most were convinced that their shareholders would want to exit from the companies and the sector as soon as possible without losing their tax breaks, a view that was subsequently confirmed by a later study of BES shareholders, which also showed that, whilst BES shareholders were interested in investing in private renting, they would rather own property themselves than hold shares in a residential property company (Hughes & Madin, 1998). Apart from the fact that the 39 000 dwellings belonging to university and housing association-linked companies were to return to these institutions and hence would be outside the market rented sector (although statistically the university owned ones would be part of the private rented sector), the directors of these and the companies linked to mortgage lenders did not think it was possible to make private renting viable without incentives, even though they foresaw a growth in demand.

The views of the entrepreneurial company directors were equally pessimistic. The directors of the companies formed in the first two years thought demand for private renting had picked up and, although they saw the market maturing, they thought there was some way to go before the future was assured. Directors of companies formed in later years also had mixed views. Some stressed the need for more government action, others for stability in the legal framework (which did of course subsequently happen) and some talked of the need to get the major financial institutions involved. Only 3 of the 40 we interviewed were unambiguously enthusiastic about the future of their own company.

Many spoke of the need for government assistance. They tended to favour tax incentives over grants and spoke of the need to structure the assistance to favour longer-term horizons for investors, for example tax relief on dividend payments and not on capital gains. Several were in favour of capital allowances. In addition, many were in favour of some system of approving or accrediting landlords in order to get rid of the bad landlords so that their own reputations would not be tarred by the behaviour of the few.

After we conducted the research it was evident, mainly from reports and commentaries in the professional property press, that the great majority of BES companies had been dissolved and their properties sold off, often at auctions (for example see Collett & Theakston, 1996). But some companies survived and grew. Some merged with others (often these were families of companies originally part of schemes) and some of these got listings on the stock exchange, for example Artesian Estates and City North, which floated in 1998 (*Estates Gazette*, 1998a). The former also acquired portfolios of BES company properties to add to its own (*Estates Gazette*, 1996a), but has since disposed of them having been taken over by another company which concentrated on commercial property. One financial services firm, the Capital Ventures group, which had serviced 167 BES assured tenancy companies, acquired four of them and floated on the Stock Exchange as Pemberstone, adding additional BES portfolios later (*Estates Gazette*, 1995a; 1996b; 1997). However, this was not solely with the purpose of continued letting as it intended to sell stock when vacant possession was secured (*Estates Gazette*, 1998c).

Many companies sold off their holdings at auction shortly after the five-year qualifying period expired and once market conditions provided acceptable prices (and if they did not, after long negotiations with any insurers who had underwritten the gains expected at launch). The professional press carried regular reports of these sales over the period 1995 to 2000, with reports of BES being a huge source of auction lots (*Estates Gazette*, 1995b). Reports also suggested that many of the disposals represented capital losses for shareholders but that the tax relief on their share purchases offset these. They also suggested that, whilst many properties were being disposed of piecemeal, some were being sold as as going concern portfolios to private landlords (*Estates Gazette*, 1995c). For example the Bradford Property Trust acquired 470 dwellings that had originally been part of the Link Assured Group of BES companies at a price of £21 m in 1995 (*Estates Gazette*, 1995d). The Pears Group was similarly involved in acquiring BES portfolios with the apparent intention of breaking them up and selling them onto owner-occupiers once vacant, an ironic echo of the way blocks of flats were broken up for sale in the 1970s and 1980s (Catalano, 1999). Other BES stocks were acquired by individual, unincorporated landlords whilst at least one new property investment company, Fairbridge Estates, was formed with equity from private investors and loans from the Nationwide Building Society, in order to acquire maturing BES companies' portfolios but with plans to sell some of the properties off once vacant possession had been obtained (*Estates Gazette*, 1998b).

UK companies were not the only ones involved. A USA investor, Amresco, purchased 900 BES properties in 1998 (Rose, 1998), the Dutch-based property investment company IBUS bought 243 properties from a BES company in 1998 (*Estates Gazette*, 1998d) and ING, the Dutch insurer, was reported to have bought a large portfolio including BES stock (*Estates Gazette*, 2001). Auction reports also suggest that some of the properties were acquired by newly formed buy-to-let landlords (see Chapter 7), thus moving out of corporate and into individual ownership (*Estates Gazette*, 1998e).

It is impossible to trace what happened to all the properties within the entrepreneurial group in any systematic way, but the press reports suggest that our initial estimate that only half the dwellings owned by these companies would remain in the sector is not far off the mark on the basis that about half the reports talk about piecemeal auctions and that other half about acquisitions by property companies (some previous BES companies themselves). For example, auction reports in 1998 suggested that only 50% of the stock sold was tenanted (*Estates Gazette*, 1998e). What the reports also suggest is that BES companies were acquired by other BES companies or taken over by vehicles specifically set up to acquire BES stock, either at auction or by taking over the companies. Some of these were listed but many were private trusts and some were offshore for tax purposes. A few hoped to be able to sell off the stock they had acquired into the proposed Housing Investment Trusts (Rose, 1999) (see Chapter 6).

We have attempted to track what happened to the 40 companies that we studied in detail as part of this research (the ones involved in case study interviews). These covered the full range of BES companies and included contracted exit as well as entrepreneurial ones. We undertook searches on the Companies House website, searched through reports in *Estates Gazette*, the weekly journal of the property world, and searched the web using Google. We could find no information on five of the companies. Twenty-two had been dissolved (including all the contracted exit companies). Four had been acquired by other (non-BES) companies, two after they had themselves floated (one on the Stock Exchange and one on the Alternative Investment Market). Of these one is now part of a wholly commercial property company, two are now part of companies with mixed commercial and residential port-folios, and the fourth is part of one of the largest and longest-established quoted residential property companies. Only nine of the original BES assured tenancy companies appear to have survived in their own right, but not all are in residential investment and five are listed as dormant or exempt from making annual returns on the Companies House register. One of the four other companies that are still active pooled its family of BES companies and floated on the stock exchange, acquired a portfolio of other BES companies, but has now disposed of all its residential portfolios and is wholly focused on commercial property. Hence out of these 40 com-panies only three are still active in their own name as residential property companies, one is part of a large quoted residential property company (that existed long before the BES scheme), and two are part of other companies with mixed commercial and residential holdings. At the most, then, only six of the original BES companies we studied in detail survived until 2010 when they were still making residential lettings, albeit three operating now as part of other companies.

Conclusions

On almost all criteria to assess a policy initiative, the BES must be regarded as mainly a failure. Although it delivered the hoped for kick-start and a lot of companies were set up and much capital raised, this success was short-lived and was at considerable cost to taxpayers. None of the companies achieved competitive returns and thus the initiative did not deliver one of its key objectives – to provide a demonstration effect of the renewed profit-ability of the sector. Part of the reasons for this failure are that the tax incentives within the BES encouraged, if not guaranteed, a short-term approach to the investment, targeted at achieving capital gains in the short run and not good income returns in the longer run.

Most of the companies and much of the stock has since disappeared from the sector. Most companies went into liquidation but some companies have survived. A handful are listed on the stock exchange. Some of those that have been liquidated had their stock acquired by existing listed and unlisted residential property companies or by unauthorised property unit trusts. One outcome has been the development of a small number of additional residential property companies that might not have come into existence but for the BES, but this number is much smaller than had been hoped for when the BES initiative was launched in 1988.

Despite this, the initiative had four important results. First, it reintroduced the financial services industry to private renting and improved their knowledge and understanding of it. This was an important development and ensured that when Housing Investment Trusts were introduced more of the industry knew about the sector than would otherwise have been the case. Second, it demonstrated a strong demand for good-quality rented housing by professional groups willing to pay high rents for it. Third, it showed how very difficult it was to create a viable corporate sector without longer-run financial support, whether in the forms of tax incentives or grants, with the former much preferred by directors of the BES companies. Fourth, it demonstrated that the problems of adapting support structures developed outside the sector for private renting. It meant that the rules did not provide the necessary degree and type of support. The BES, designed as it was to get initial venture capital into new high-risk companies, was ill-suited to the longer-term task of fostering a fragile corporate private rented sector. When it was adapted to enable universities and housing associations to use guaranteed buyback schemes to access cheap funds for their own housing purposes, the scheme ran the risk of being abused. That and the fact that the development of the BES scheme for assured tenancies led to a severe decline in funding for other trades targeted by the scheme led to its abolition in 1993 and its replacement by the Enterprise Investment Scheme (HM Treasury, 2009a).

We return to these issues in our last chapter but first we must examine, in Chapters 6 and 7, two other key initiatives to create more modern landlords: one by government and the other by the private sector.

Notes

1. In this study we collected information on every company formed, including the capital they raised and how this was spent, based on their prospectuses and questionnaires we sent to all of them. We examined their annual reports and audited accounts lodged at Companies House. We interviewed the directors of a sample of 40 BES companies

and of their funds and sponsors, and conducted interviews with a sample of tenants living in BES assured tenancy companies' lettings.

2. Underwriting involved guarantees by third parties, usually financial institutions, to take up any of the unsold share issue.

3. To make this calculation, we assumed that 82% of BES investors were top-rate taxpayers (and 100% of all who were involved in private placings) (60% tax rate in 1987/88 and 40% thereafter) and that all were able to carry back some tax liabilities to 1987/88. We assumed that all shareholders would have otherwise invested in equities and paid income and capital gains tax on their dividends and gains, respectively. Because of the latter assumption we have not therefore included the loss of capital gains tax on the sale of the BES shares. Had all investors otherwise invested in other types of BES companies the tax expenditure would have been zero but the evidence of the scale of the funds raised and the investment behaviour of BES shareholders (on the latter, see Hughes & Madin, 1998) suggests that this is not a tenable assumption. Most of those who invested would not have invested in other BES companies had the assured tenancy initiative not have been taken.

6

Financial Institutions and Rented Housing

Introduction

As we saw in Chapter 2, the Thatcher government was keen not only to create new company landlords but also to attract institutional investment into the newly deregulated sector. The last chapter showed how its attempt to create new company landlords through the BES scheme did not have the desired long-lasting impact. The BES scheme was designed to attract retail investment into the sector through share purchase by individuals. Financial institutions such as building societies, pension funds or insurance companies were involved only if they lent funds to enable assured tenancy companies to gear up the investments made by individual shareholders or if, as mortgage lenders, they set them up in order to sell off their repossessed property. They did not make equity investments.

The introduction of Housing Investment Trusts (HITs) in 1996 can be seen in retrospect as the second stage in the government's drive to get new capital into the deregulated sector and to create more corporate ownership. If the BES scheme was about retail investment, the HITs scheme was aimed at getting wholesale, or institutional, funding into the sector, both in terms of equity (buying shares, etc.) and in terms of debt (making loans). To do this the government announced in 1995 that it would enable the creation of HITs to provide a vehicle for financial institutions to invest in private renting (DoE, 1995). These 'would provide the opportunity for institutions to invest ... (and) it will be for the market to judge whether the opportunity is right and if the return from renting as compared with alternative investments, is attractive' (DoE, 1995, p. 22).

Transforming Private Landlords: Housing, markets & public policy, by Tony Crook & Peter A. Kemp © 2011 Tony Crook & Peter A. Kemp

As we shall see, no HIT was formed and a second attempt, building on some of the lessons of HITs and, even more, on experience overseas, was later made to attract institutional investment by enabling the formation of Real Estate Investment Trusts (REITS) (Barker, 2003; HM Treasury, 2004, 2005). Legislation was enacted in 2006 but, at the time of writing no residential REIT had been established. However attempts were still being made to revive the initiative and to explore other ways of securing institutional funding.

In Chapter 2 we identified the arguments for creating more corporate landlords. The creation of larger organisations with shareholding ownership would, it was hoped, enable individuals and institutions to invest indirectly in residential property companies, instead of having to own it themselves. These would be run with professional management, achieve efficiencies through economies of scale (including through the ownership of large-scale developments on single sites as well as on portfolios spread geographically), cope with market risk through diversified holdings and take a long-term view in seeking income returns based on rental growth and rely less on capital gains for their investment returns, hence fostering stability in the market. Crucially, the setting up of such companies would improve the reputation of private renting because blue-chip organisations would invest who would jealously guard their reputations by ensuring that good housing management practices were adopted. They would also enable the large-scale investment that was seen by some commentators to be vital to the creation of a modern private rented sector. Only institutional ownership would create the scale of investment required (Best *et al.*, 1992; Coopers & Lybrand, 1993b, 1996). To illustrate this, a calculation we did in 1998 suggested that if the sector's share of all housing were to rise by 1% from the then current level of 11% of the housing stock, it would need £11.3bn of funding, over three times as much as had been raised by the BES scheme over five years (Crook *et al.*, 1998b).

The aim of this chapter is to examine the barriers to institutional investment in Britain, to describe the HIT and REIT initiatives, and to examine the reasons why the HIT and (so far) REIT initiatives have failed to overcome these barriers. We draw on the research we did in studying a panel of financial institutions' involvement in the equity and debt funding of the private rented sector and their specific involvement in particular initiatives, including HITs and later REITs (Crook *et al.*, 1995, 1998b; Crook & Kemp, 1999, 2002).

Barriers to institutional investment in residential lettings

Britain, as we have shown in Chapter 4, is still characterised by small-scale and mainly part-time individual landlords, many seeking their investment returns from capital growth rather than long-term income growth. Far from there having been an increase in property company ownership since deregulation, these companies now own a smaller share of the market than ever before and the attempts to use the BES framework to stimulate the formation of more companies did not succeed in the long run.

Although this pattern of ownership also characterises many other advanced economies, including in the rest of Europe and in North America, some institutional investment is not uncommon in them, including Canada, Finland, The Netherlands, Sweden, Switzerland and the USA (Priemus & Maclennan, 1998). Nor, as we saw in Chapter 1, has institutional ownership being wholly absent in Britain. Historically, financial institutions were important investors and owners in the nineteenth century and, to some extent, also in the interwar years of the last century, their activities including the creation of blocks of flats in London and the main provincial cities in the 1930s (Kemp, 1984). However, in the 1960s and 1970s they disposed of these portfolios almost in their entirety, often selling them off to companies that specialised in the subsequent break-up of the flats through leasehold sales to sitting tenants or to owner-occupiers (Hamnett & Randolph, 1988). At the same time, taxation changes in 1965, which introduced tax on shareholders' dividends (previously all the tax was paid by companies), reduced the returns institutions obtained from owning shares in property companies of any kind (Whitehead *et al.*, 1995). Hence institutions very substantially reduced both their direct and indirect ownership of residential lettings.

At the same time as they were disposing of their residential portfolios, institutions were also building up significant direct ownership of commercial property portfolios (Ball *et al.*, 1998; Scott, 1996). Commercial property is now a key asset class for institutions, alongside investments in equities (shares) and bonds (commercial as well as government bonds, or gilts as the latter are also known). Investing in property became important to institutions from the 1960s and 1970s onwards, although more recently exposure to commercial property assets has been on the decline.

These investment opportunities presented themselves because the boom in service employment and retail spending was underpinned by large-scale office and shop developments in city centres, often as part of the comprehensive redevelopment of Victorian city centres (Marriott, 1967). Unlike manufacturing industry, where factories and related floorspace tend to be owned by the companies themselves, most shops and offices do not own the floorspace they occupy. There are of course exceptions (for example, the major food retailers and DIY stores generally own their superstores), but much retail and office space is owned by property companies and financial institutions, who lease out the space for varying lengths of time but on arrangements whereby the occupiers bear the full insuring and repairing costs of occupation and have also historically faced 'upwards-only' rent reviews.

Property companies and financial institutions play separate roles in pro-viding this space. The former use their accumulated skills to assemble sites, negotiate planning consents, hire architects to design the proposed build-ings, and tender and then project manage their construction. These compa-nies have typically funded these projects with a combination of their own equity and development finance provided by bank loans. Once constructed, the completed projects are sometimes retained by the property companies, who replace the loan finance with longer-term equity funding from institu-tions. Alternatively, completed developments are sold on to financial insti-tutions, which become the owners and managers of the properties.

These property investments became important assets to financial institu-tions because they were good investments at a time when inflation was becoming a key feature of the economy. It was expected that office and shop rents would rise in line with inflation (unlike controlled and registered resi-dential rents), as measured by wages as well as by retail prices, and hence rise in accordance with the institutions' liabilities to their pension and life assurance policyholders. Property has the added attraction that returns move in different cycles from returns from equities or bonds, and this diver-sification of income streams was important in ensuring a steady income stream from all assets in relation to liabilities. Investments in residential lettings have the characteristics of both bonds and equities. In the case of the former the investor is buying primarily for income. In the case of the latter capital appreciation is also important. Residential lettings offer both – an income from rents and the possibility of long-run real capital growth with the two often moving in different cycles (Coopers & Lybrand, with Kemp, Crook, & Hughes, 1995).

Given the attractiveness of commercial property as an asset class, what is it that has prevented institutions from investing in residential lettings? After all, as an investment class it has many of the same attributes as com-mercial property, especially given the evidence that rents from residential lettings tend to rise in line with earnings (as Chapter 3 has shown) and thus in line with institutions' needs to honour liabilities such as pensions that are formulaically related to pensioners' final or career-average salaries. There are strong *prima facie* arguments for this being much more than the very small amount (£22 bn) currently held by property companies and funds. UK institutions' exposure to residential assets is only 1% of their total property exposure, compared with, for example, 43% in The Netherlands (PIA, 2008).

There are, however, a number of barriers, some of which are directly related to residential lettings as an asset class and some of which are related to ways of structuring indirect investments in assets like property, including in par-ticular the taxation consequences. Many of these were identified in a quali-tative study of a panel of financial institutions that we undertook in the years just before and soon after the introduction of the HIT legislation – the years were 1994 and 1998.[1] The study assessed their appetite for making investments in this sector – and later their experience of the HIT initiative (Crook *et al.*, 1995, 1998b; Crook & Kemp, 1999, 2002).

Most of these financial institutions had substantial sums in commercial property. It was particularly important to pension and life insurance companies, who had to allocate assets between bonds, equities, and property in order to ensure that total returns matched their liabilities. Typically they invested in commercial property through direct ownership. They generally let their properties to tenants on full repairing and insuring leases often with upwards-only rent reviews and no break clauses. These lease structures minimised the management cost and hassle of direct property ownership. Commercial property not only gave them stable and predictable returns from rental income but also the prospect of capital growth in the value of their property portfolio. They believed that the income and capital growth cycles of commercial property did not synchronise with those for equities and bonds and this additional diversification in their assets helped to spread risk and smooth out fluctuations in their income. Because they owned the properties, the income flowed to them directly and was taxed in accordance with their own tax liability. This meant that 'gross funds', such as pension funds, paid no tax on the income they received from their property portfolios.

Lending on commercial property was a significant part of retail and investment banks' loans books. The cost of debt to borrowers, typically property companies, depended on the track record of the borrower, on the nature of the project and the likely resilience of rental streams, with funds for the construction of developments intended for blue-chip tenants in prime locations attracting the cheapest terms. Lenders also expected borrowers to have sufficient asset cover to provide security in the event of defaults. By 1998 some of these banks also had significant exposure to the loans they had made to housing association and to private landlords.

Residential mortgage lenders (and these included those who later demutualised as well as those who continued as building societies) had significant experience of lending, including to private landlords, although capital adequacy rules meant that that they had to charge higher interest rates in 1994 than on their loans to housing associations, usually requiring landlords to have a 30–50% equity stake and setting rates than were 2.5–3% higher than the London Interbank Offer Rate (see Chapter 7 for later developments that reduced the cost of buy-to-let mortgages). As we saw in Chapter 5 they had also had the experience of using the BES scheme to offload repossessed properties from their balance sheets. In 1994 some were actively considering whether to set up subsidiaries to own and manage private rented dwellings and saw this as a logical extension of their core business.[2] However, this exploration was mainly within niche markets, such as student and nurses' homes, as most felt that returns from mainstream market tenancies were inadequate to provide equity returns or to cover debt charges.

These institutions were keen to compare the performance of their property assets against industry-wide benchmarks. The ready availability of consistent market information about the returns being earned on commercial property throughout the UK was crucial to them for seeing how well their assets were performing against other property investments and also against returns from bonds and equities. Property needed to deliver equity-type returns over the long run. At the time of the research in mid-1994 they sought running returns of between 8% and 10% on commercial property assets, compared with the 5.6% then being earned on gilts. In 1998 institutions were in general looking for total returns (rental income plus capital growth) of 3–4% above gilts to allow for the additional risk that property investment involved compared with risk-free government bonds – much the same uplift as in 1994.

If property in general was underperforming in relation to these benchmarks or a particular property itself was underperforming, institutions would reduce exposure by cutting new investments and by selling poorly performing properties. The ability to sell properties was important to maintaining the liquidity of investments. The general strength of commercial property has meant that occupied property tends to command a higher price than empty property (in contrast to residential lettings). Having a property fully occupied by tenants with a good covenant enabled institutions to readily trade in property, disposing of what were seen as poorly performing assets whose performance could not be enhanced and acquiring other ones that appeared to be underperforming but whose performance could be enhanced, for example through additional investment. Investments tended to be substantial: typically the minimum lot sizes of individual property acquisitions were in tens of millions of pounds.

Despite the notional attractiveness of residential lettings, given their inflation-proofed earnings and additional diversification potential, it was a far from attractive asset class to financial institutions in so far as equity investment was concerned. The barriers were fivefold.

First, institutions considered that the earnings potential of residential lettings depended very much on the market segment. These were thought to be almost non-existent at the bottom end of the market but more likely to be present at the middle and top end where both rental income and capital growth was thought likely to be more secure. In addition there was some interest at the time in exploring niche markets such as student accommodation where some underwriting by universities (such as taking subleases or guaranteeing occupation rates) provided attractive covenants. It was therefore vital to explore the potential of residential investments very carefully indeed and the lack of reliable benchmarking at that time was a problem when undertaking due diligence.

Second was the issue of political and reputation risk, although by 1998 the former was considerably less of a deterrent than it had been in our initial 1994 study. In 1994 our panel referred to the risk of rent controls being re-introduced and of further cutbacks to housing benefit support for tenants, the latter in the light of the cuts to benefits that had then recently occurred. These were mentioned far less often in 1998. This was because the new Labour government had made it clear that it was in favour of responsible private landlords and had repeatedly reassured landlords that it would not re-introduce rent controls. Reputation risk was also important in 1994 and by 1988 potential investors were much more concerned about this than about political risk and were concerned that their own reputations might be tarnished if the market perceived them to be investing in a less than wholly reputable sector. They were therefore keen to see minimum standards and some form of regulation (preferably voluntary) to ensure that bad landlords were eliminated. They were also less than keen in 1994 to have their names on rent books if tenants in arrears had to be evicted.

Third, were the problems associated with acquiring the asset class itself. Investors were used to acquiring high-quality commercial property in prime locations with each acquisition running often into tens of millions of pounds. They perceived (quite rightly) that it was impossible to find the equivalent large lot size in residential property. There was no bespoke production line of newly built property in locations with a vibrant rented market and of the type where income returns met benchmarks. Investors did not want to spend their money on 'penny packet' purchases: it was simply not an efficient way of investing. The ideal purchase was to spend, say £50m, in the purchase of a job lot of, say, one- to two-bedroom flats in central locations, with good public transport links and spreading the purchases across one or two regions so as to have a differentiated portfolio to help spread market risk and to limit their exposure to the vagaries of market demand in one location. Instead, at that time, newly built properties tended to be in suburban areas, available in smallish lot sizes and of the wrong type.[3] The alternative to buying newly built property was to acquire (or invest into) an existing portfolio, but this was equally problematic because few existed. This obstacle was the consequence of the dominant structure of rental housing provision, which, as we have seen in Chapter 4, consisted of very small-scale portfolios owned by amateur landlords with the few larger-size portfolios tending to consist of older properties less suitable to the target markets for potential investors and often with long-term sitting tenants and which were generally geographically scattered rather than concentrated in one or two prime locations. Hence the available product simply did not match investors' requirements.

Fourth, were the problems of managing these assets. Here the proposition was totally different from commercial property. In the latter the tenants undertook most of the management functions (doing repairs, paying for insurance) and accepted long leases. In residential lettings the landlord does all this, and more, and tenant turnover is high. As we have seen in Chapter 4, the costs of management and maintenance, including voids and arrears, constitute between a quarter and a third of gross rents. To make the proposition work, investors needed to secure high-quality management and also to keep costs down if the gross income returns obtainable were to provide competitive net returns. Potential investors thought that the scale of portfolios that might yield management efficiencies simply did not exist and that the quality of services they needed could not be obtained from the existing structure of small-scale and locally based residential managing agents. The latter presented only high costs and poor-quality services. Getting high-quality management was crucial, given their need to protect their reputations. Thus the kinds of portfolios, with large-scale and geographically diverse holdings, and the management services to support economies of scale and to manage market and reputational risk simply did not exist.

Fifth, and most significantly (and partly as a direct consequence of their concerns about management risks for their reputations and the costs of mitigating these), most institutions did not want to own residential assets themselves. Instead they would want to invest indirectly by acquiring shares in residential property companies. There were some limited exceptions amongst the few who had already invested or who were, at the time of the research in 1998, on the verge of doing so. They had opted for direct ownership because it was tax-efficient (see below), gave them greater control over the asset, and provided them with more predictable and transparent income returns than the alternative of holding shares in a listed property company. In particular these institutions argued that such shares tended to reflect the wider performance of the equities market and not the fundamentals of residential property and that also they would be exposed to the tendency of shares in property companies to trade at a discount to the net asset value of the properties owned by the companies. These institutions had invested, or were intending to invest, in niche markets and their number included overseas institutions that had experience of direct ownership of residential investments in their own countries.

However, the majority of institutions would, if investing, opt for indirect ownership. This had the advantage of liquidity (shares being easier to sell than property) and avoided them being involved in managing property and having their names on rent books. They were willing to explore avenues other than listed property companies, including authorised property unit trusts and limited partnerships, despite the latter's lack of liquidity. If they were to get involved in buying shares in residential property companies they required them to have four key characteristics: liquidity, large portfolios, good-quality housing management, and tax transparency. Many thought that private renting was too illiquid and even though this could be overcome through indirect ownership they thought that the lack of an active market in tenanted property would in practice restrict the liquidity of even an indirect investment vehicle.

In fact the lack of tax transparency was a major barrier to institutional investment at the time, given the majority preference for indirect ownership. This is a key issue for those institutions, like pension funds, who are not liable for tax on the profits on investments that they directly own, including property, although they are liable for tax on transactions including stamp duty. They do, however, suffer a tax liability when they invest indirectly in property by purchasing shares. This is because property companies are liable for corporation tax on their profits and hence pay dividends net of tax to their shareholders. Although they were able, at that time, to claim back some of this corporation tax through the tax credit system (see below) they were still at a tax disadvantage compared with direct property ownership.

If these barriers were to be avoided through indirect investment in the shares of a residential property company, such companies were very thin on the ground and in any case pension and other gross funds suffered tax leakage. Indeed, because of these problems, property companies reported considerable difficulties raising equity finance compared with loan finance. This lack of equity funding prohibited growth, as companies needed a larger equity base on which to gear up with borrowing. They also pointed out that small property companies had particular problems raising equity through share issues because share-price movements could be sparked off by only a few shareholders selling and this made large investors cautious about buying shares in them.

Taking all these five barriers together made investing in residential lettings an unattractive proposition, despite its appeal in principle. The right type of property in a large-enough portfolio was nearly impossible to find, management costs were high, propositions were difficult to benchmark, and it was crucial to find the right market segments to get the necessary income returns and to ensure reputations were secure. All of this uncertainty made residential lettings a novelty investment that required a high risk premium and a high hurdle rate of return above that acceptable for commercial property investments. Although in 1994 the institutions found it hard to identify the returns they would need, the hurdles they stated ranged from 10% to 13.5% net income returns (most at the bottom end of this range) with, at that time, little expectation of significant capital gains.

In general all those interviewed in 1994 and 1998 took the view that these required yields were in fact unlikely to be generated by the deregulated market except in some niche markets (as we have seen in Chapter 4) and were unlikely to fall until institutions had considerable and positive experience of the asset. Moreover, even if subsidies were introduced in the forms of tax incentives or grants to make returns more attractive, the respondents in our panel in 1994 said that they were still unlikely to invest as they regarded returns underpinned by subsidies as too fragile a basis for a long-term investment. If at all, they preferred to see an investment underpinned by an upfront grant rather than an ongoing tax abatement.

This did not mean that pension and life funds in 1994 would not invest in any circumstances. A number thought the market needed to mature a lot more and to demonstrate competitive returns before a proper judgement could be made. A number speculated that if tax distortions in the housing market generally diminished and demand for renting rose, returns might rise. If that happened profitable residential property companies would emerge and financial institutions might then take equity stakes in them – but not before.

Housing Investment Trusts: initial proposals and legislation

Given all the barriers that had been identified, the prospects for securing the billions of equity that could potentially transform the sector looked poor and because of this a number of commentators put forward proposals in the mid-1990s to create a new kind of investment trust that would own and manage private rented dwellings and that would also foster indirect investment, but without the tax leakage described above.

Those putting forward these proposals based many of their arguments on the tax disadvantages suffered by private renting. Coopers and Lybrand, the management services consultancy (now Price Waterhouse Coopers), in particular argued that in many other countries landlords received more favourable treatment, especially in the form of depreciation allowances and the ability to offset losses on rental property against taxable income from other sources (so called 'negative gearing'). In some countries both of these tax treatments were available. In the UK neither was. In almost all other countries chargeable capital gains could be deferred (by roll-over relief) if gains were applied to new acquisitions. From their own modelling, Coopers and Lybrand argued that rental housing was capable of producing total returns of 6% in real terms but that this was below the 6–9% the institutions wanted, being comparable to nominal returns of 10–13% (and also comparable with the evidence from our work). They argued that some way needed to be found of enhancing the achievable rates by about 2% and their preferred approach was to introduce initial capital allowances of 40% of the cost of dwellings, with the balance allowable against tax at 4% for 15 years (something familiar to the UK tax authorities and thus not a novel way of dealing with companies' taxes). They also proposed placing the tax treatment of rental income on a trading basis, giving landlords greater flexibility for relief on losses and exempting landlords from capital gains tax provided property was held for at least ten years. Their proposals would have cost the Exchequer the equivalent of 10% of the initial capital costs of dwellings (the latter then £50 000, excluding land costs, on average). It was their expectation that institutions would not initially want to invest themselves but that they would so do via residential property companies, provided these demonstrated the returns required. In the longer run a new residential investment trust would be needed to provide tax transparency for those not paying tax. (Coopers & Lybrand, 1993a; see also Coopers & Lybrand with Kemp, Crook, & Hughes, 1995).

These proposals were not dissimilar to many put forward by other commentators (Crook & Kemp, 1991; Crook, 1992b; Barnes, 1993; Kleinman *et al.*, 1996; Whitehead, 1994; Whitehead *et al.*, 1995). Many proposals had the not unimportant disadvantage of requiring the government to introduce subsidies in the form of explicit tax breaks for private landlords, something that would not necessarily command support, not the least in the light of the cost of the BES scheme and because of the difficulty of adequately targeting subsidies to avoid 'deadweight loss'. Nor would they impact directly on non-taxpaying investors if these invested directly, although they would in principle improve the post-tax returns of any residential property companies in which such gross funds held shares. More likely to command support and also to directly address the needs of gross funds were measures to introduce some form of tax transparency. What was needed was a new kind of vehicle to provide passive, indirect and liquid investment to non-taxpaying investors. The tax regime would be 'as transparent as possible but based on established principles' and would not involve any 'positive' tax breaks (Robertson & Rowe, 1993).

Tax transparency occurs when the tax liability of a company is not assessed in accordance with its income and expenditure account. Instead, all profits pass straight through the company directly to its shareholders, who are then taxed fully in accordance with their own individual or corporate tax liabilities. This avoids the double-taxation problem of indirect property investment.

Although indirect investment through unauthorised unit trusts or limited partnerships achieves the objectives of passivity and tax transparency, these vehicles are not very liquid. A proposal was thus developed for a new type of investment trust to be known as Authorised Housing Investment Trusts, although it was thought that without some kind of incentive investment would not occur, even if these new vehicles came into existence, because of investors' uncertainty about the asset. Recognising that explicit tax breaks were not likely to be acceptable it, was proposed that grants of up to 20% of the cost of dwellings should be provided and could be allocated in a competitive manner (Robertson & Rowe, 1993; see also Mew, 1994).

Following these and other reports, the property industry lobbied for the introduction of 'approved investment trusts' the aim of which was to provide an indirect investment vehicle with the full tax transparency that comes with direct ownership.

Legislation to introduce HITs was enacted in the Finance Act of 1996. When introduced, they were not fully tax-transparent but they were liable to pay only the small companies' rate of corporation tax, which in 1996 was 24% compared with the standard rate of 33%, and they were exempt from paying tax on capital gains. Post-tax profits were then to be distributed as dividend payments to shareholders. Shareholders were to pay tax on the dividends they received from an HIT but were also able, under the tax rules in place in 1996, to receive tax credits on the advance corporation tax paid by the company prior to paying out their dividends, which they could then use to offset their own tax liabilities. Gross funds would not have paid tax on any HIT dividends they received and would have been able to reclaim the tax credit.

Tax credits reflected the fact that companies had already paid tax on the dividend income they distributed to shareholders by virtue of the corporation tax paid on their taxable profits. The system was designed to prevent an element of double taxation on these profits whereby they were taxed first because the company paid corporation tax and second because shareholders paid tax on any dividends received. Up to 1997, pension funds, like all shareholders, were able to reclaim the tax credits on their income from share ownership. This offset some of their tax liabilities.

To qualify for the special tax arrangements, HITs had to meet three sets of criteria. First, they had to meet the normal criteria for all investment trusts. Investment trusts are companies that perform the tasks of fund management on behalf of their shareholders. Their shares tend to trade at a discount on the underlying value of investment trusts assets (Piesse *et al.*, 1995; Ball *et al.*, 1998). HITs were required to invest only in eligible residential property and not in other types of property or in shares or securities. They also had to conform to all the legislation governing investment trusts in general: to be based in the UK, to have their shares listed on the London Stock Exchange, to distribute 85% of their income to shareholders, but not to distribute capital surpluses.

Second, the Finance Act of 1996, which enacted the HIT legislation, defined 'eligible residential property' as dwellings acquired by a company after 1 April 1996. Dwellings had to be vacant when acquired or let on assured shorthold tenancies (short assured in Scotland), to have a value of no more than £125 000 in Greater London or £85 000 elsewhere (including acquisition costs and any renovation costs). These cost limits were the same ones that had been prescribed for BES-assured tenancy companies.

Third, because of the listing requirement, HITs also had to meet the London Stock Exchange's rules. These rules were drawn up independently and after the HITs legislation was enacted. The Stock Exchange waived its normal requirement that those seeking a listing had to have been trading for at least three years before listing, but instead required that the directors and managers demonstrated a track record of at least three years' experience in the management of a similar size and type of portfolio as that envisaged for a listed HIT. It stipulated that HIT directors had to be independent of their property advisers and managers. Any newly listed HITs also had to have net assets of at least £30m, including any funds raised at the time of the listing. Gearing (or borrowing) was limited to a maximum of 50% of a HIT's gross assets. At least 75% of the value of the gross assets of a HIT had to be invested in physical property assets within two years of a listing and the proportion of a HIT's portfolio that was not earning income from lettings was limited to 25% of the company's value.

Housing Investment Trusts: the experience

Despite some initial commentary suggesting that HITs would succeed, albeit with a slow start, raising £1bn for 20000 homes in the first three years (Robertson & Rowe, 1996), most early commentators disagreed and suggested that few, if any HITs were likely to be formed (for example, see Barnes, 1996; Crook *et al.*, 1997). In the end, none were formed,[4] which suggests that the HIT initiative failed to overcome the barriers to institutional investment. Our research confirmed this and identified a wide range of reasons.

The failure of HITs could not be attributed to ignorance of the initiative, as all of the financial institutions in our survey panel were aware of its existence, many had active involvement with residential lettings and kept up to date with government policy, and all but one had given HITs a lot of consideration, including doing due diligence on the limited number of putative HITs that were being explored by fund and property managers (Crook & Kemp, 1999, 2002).

The three mortgage lenders (including former building societies) considered HITs from two angles. First as an avenue for equity investment in residential lettings and second as a way of disposing of the stock of repossessed dwellings that had accumulated on their balance sheets. They had all been involved in BES schemes and some of the BES companies they had launched had been bought back by them. Both of these avenues were explored, but proved unattractive. In the latter case the stock was so badly repaired that the investment needed to make it attractive enough for letting would have resulted in poor income returns. In the former case it was concluded that becoming landlords was not part of their core business. They were experts in debt funding, including to private landlords, but did not wish to diversify into ownership. One had looked at providing debt funding to a proposed HIT but this did not proceed. Another was, at that time, selling off all its BES companies as portfolios. In addition, in all cases where detailed propositions had been explored, the returns were not attractive enough and were well below what they were earning across their businesses as a whole. These views were in marked contrast to those expressed at the earlier stage of the work before the HIT initiative had been launched (see above). All had plans to expand their lending to private landlords, including through the buy-to-let scheme for small landlords (see Chapter 7) and through commercial mortgages to larger landlords.

All but one of the six clearing and investment banks in our survey panel had been involved in HITs, either in discussions about placing equity in some of the well publicised HIT proposals or in providing loans. All the clearing banks had lent to housing associations and, with one exception, also lent to private landlords, especially focusing on longer-term lending to the more professional landlords. The investment banks were less involved in lending to private landlords, although they were involved in raising funds for housing associations. One had bought a private rented portfolio and another had considered underwriting a HIT proposal that intended to purchase a large portfolio of BES schemes, but this did not proceed.

The experience of the six life assurance and insurance companies and four pension funds (who together managed funds worth over £500 bn) varied, but only a few had not actively considered getting involved. This was in complete contrast to their views in 1994 when they were especially negative in their opinions about investment in the sector. Although none of the four pension funds had made investments in residential lettings, two were actively considering propositions.

By 1998 only two insurance and assurance companies had deliberately decided not to invest in residential lettings. These two did not think residential lettings a suitable asset. Many of the others spoke of having gone through a transformation in their attitudes to residential property. In all other cases, however, the exploration of specific proposals had shown that returns from HITs were simply not sufficient to justify an equity investment. This did not mean that they were uninterested in making investments. Two insurance companies (including one overseas insurer) had already invested (approximately £20 m each) and had acquired lettings themselves rather than acquiring shares in a listed residential property company. Another was actively considering a proposition. The other was on the brink of putting clients' funds into rented property. In both these latter cases indirect vehicles and not direct ownership was being considered. In all these four cases, although they considered that HITs had failed, this had not deterred them from making investments via these other routes. Nonetheless, despite this interest, only relatively small sums were being talked about at that time.

All of the property fund managers in our panel, who were amongst the largest in the UK, had looked very closely at HITs. Two had concluded they were not viable but one had worked hard to get a proposal off the ground. This firm had a great deal of experience in residential lettings, having got BES companies launched, managing portfolios for private clients, acting as fund managers for them as well as for pension funds, and managing £3.5bn of property funds in total. The other two had limited experience of residential assets in the UK and their main expertise was in commercial property, although one had an overseas partner that was one of the largest owners and managers of private rented housing in the USA. This suggests that prior knowledge of running portfolios may be crucial to getting investment projects to work, by giving other funders some confidence in the asset itself as well as in the fund management aspects of such proposals.

The five property companies had varying backgrounds. Two were listed, having been set up in the interwar period, one had reverted from a listed to a private company, one concentrated on providing management for others and two were BES companies, one of which was listed. All had investigated HITs very closely, including trying to persuade financial institutions to help them set up HITs, but had concluded that these would have provided too much competition for their companies. To avoid this, two had considered converting into a HIT but had been prevented from doing so since this was outside the rules.

It cannot be said therefore that HITs failed to get off the ground because of any lack of knowledge or due consideration. What barriers had come to light as a result of all the due diligence?

First, all our panel thought HITs did not fully address the tax problem. They did have to pay some tax and so were not fully tax-transparent and hence they were less attractive to gross funds than direct ownership. Our own modelling in 1996 confirmed this and showed that although gross funds would have received better post-tax returns from a HIT than from buying shares in a normal residential property company, they would still be below those obtainable had the lettings been directly owned. At that time corporation tax rates were 33%, with 24% being charged for small companies (the rate HITs would have paid) and the tax credit arrangements were in place.

As Table 6.1 shows, an ungeared 11-year investment made wholly in a portfolio of flats gave an aftertax total net return (allowing for tax credits) from direct ownership of 8.4%, from a dividend payment from a residential property company of 6.8% and from returns from an HIT investment of 7.5%. If the investment had a gearing of 40% debt funding, returns would have been 10.3% (direct ownership), 8.5% (dividend from property company) and 9.3% (from a HIT). This showed that, whilst a HIT investment gave a

Table 6.1   Average annual net returns on open-market vacant-possession value on an 11-year investment by gross fund in 1996

Type of dwelling	Direct ownership (%)			Invest in residential property company (%)			Invest in HIT (%)		
	a	b	c	a	b	c	a	b	c
Flat after tax: with tax credits	8.4	10.3	10.2	6.8	8.5	8.2	7.5	9.3	9.0
Flat after tax: no tax credits	8.4	10.3	10.2	6.6	8.3	7.9	7.4	9.2	8.9
House after tax: with tax credits	7.8	9.3	9.5	6.4	7.7	7.7	7.1	8.5	8.4
House after tax: no tax credits	7.8	9.3	9.5	6.2	7.5	7.4	7.0	8.4	8.3

a, ungeared; b, 40% debt funding; c, 50% efficiencies in running costs.
Source: Crook *et al.* (1998b). With permission from Journal of Property Research, Taylor and Francis.

better return than from shares in a property company, it was still significantly less than from direct ownership. The calculations also showed the positive impact of potential economies of scale in management and maintenance, which it was assumed a HIT with a minimum capitalisation of £30 m could achieve. If a 50% efficiency could be obtained the returns from an ungeared HIT investing in flats could be increased from 7.5% to 9% net. Intriguingly, this would have raised HIT returns close to the bottom end of the target range of returns respondents spoke of. Our modelling thus showed that getting efficiencies out of management and maintenance costs had as much of an impact on returns as the partial tax transparency built into the HIT arrangements.[5]

This modest improvement in indirect investment was, however, set back when, as part of a wider review of corporation tax unrelated to the HITs initiative, the government changed the arrangements whereby pension funds could reclaim tax credits on share dividends. At first, tax credits for gross funds on advanced corporation tax were abolished and then the latter was abolished altogether. This came into effect in 1997 and increased the tax leakage of any investment in HITs, making them even less tax-transparent and even less attractive than direct investment, although the rate of corporation tax was reduced to 21% for small companies (i.e. the rate HITs were to pay) and 31% for others. But poor returns were not the only barrier.

Second, the maximum cap placed on the value of property acquired by HITs was regarded as too low, making it difficult to find suitable property, especially in London and the south-east, and to put together a portfolio that would generate competitive returns. In particular, our panel believed a mixed portfolio of both high- and lower-value property was essential to generating long-term returns as this enabled HITs to operate across several market segments.

Third, the restriction on 'trading', that is the active disposal of poorly performing dwellings and the acquisition of new ones, made it difficult to get competitive returns across the whole of a portfolio. Trading is a normal activity in a property company. It does not signal the short-term investment horizons that characterise some individual landlords (see Chapters 4 and 7) but is good portfolio management, selling poorly performing properties and replacing them with ones expected to do better. In the view of our panel, these restrictions made it very difficult to operate a property investment and management business and to generate the returns that funds needed, especially as they were driven by the imperative of at least matching industry-wide benchmarks.

Fourth, financial institutions felt hamstrung by the rules imposed by the Stock Exchange. They considered it almost impossible to raise the required minimum funds of £30m and then spend all this prudently to acquire a good, performing portfolio within two years. The small scale and fragmented nature of residential lettings meant that there were hardly any existing portfolios of suitable size for acquisition. This was made even more difficult by the need to acquire properties either on a vacant-possession basis or an assured shorthold sitting-tenant basis because most large portfolios that then existed were dominated by regulated tenancies with sitting tenants. The alternative of putting together a portfolio of newly built property of the right size and location and within the value limits and all within two years was equally problematic. The fact was that the large-scale residential property companies that some had anticipated might emerge when we interviewed them in 1994 had simply not come to fruition. And no one seemed prepared to take the risk of developing an embryonic HIT by building up a portfolio and then listing it as a HIT when it had reached the right size, in the meantime attracting the necessary launch funding on the basis of prospective HIT status.

A fifth concern was the perceived probability that the founding shareholders of a HIT would suffer from the way investment trust and property company shares tended to trade at a discount on the value of their underlying net assets. This probability was further compounded by the way residential property values tend to trade at a discount of perhaps 10–20% on their vacant-possession value once let (unlike commercial property where the opposite can apply). Hence founding investors would suffer a double discount if the HIT was to invest in vacant property and the potential returns that could be earned were not thought sufficient to compensate for this.

A sixth difficulty was with liquidity. In theory, stock exchange listings should overcome this by turning physical assets into tradable financial assets but the respondents in our panel were not convinced. This was because they thought few HITs would be set up and thus the market in shares would be fairly limited.

To sum up, it was felt that the structure for HITs was too complex and restrictive. The rules would make HITs difficult to set up and would prevent them being run as a normal property business, thus preventing them from managing their assets to produce competitive returns for shareholders. All the due diligence showed that returns were not only below those obtainable on direct ownership (which itself was unattractive to most) but they were simply uncompetitive, given the risk, liquidity and novelty of the asset, compared with continuing to invest in commercial property, equities and bonds. Just as in 1994, institutions found it difficult in 1998 to specify the hurdle rate that would persuade them to invest and tended to discuss what they required in terms of an uplift on the returns they were then getting from commercial property. Potential equity investors found it more difficult than lenders because they had so little experience of the sector, but the uplift above commercial they thought was required varied from 2% to 5%. Insofar as they had some idea of net income returns required, they specified returns of between 7% and 10%, provided these were in low-risk markets and provided also that there was sufficient capital growth to generate total returns of 18–20%. Those that had made direct investments were getting acceptable returns of 6–9% net income (and 10–14% total returns) but this seemed to be the result of careful market selection and tough cost control. Lenders on the other hand, because of their experience, felt that competitive equity returns could not be earned, which is why they had, in the end, settled for being lenders and not owners. One lender that had made an initial investment said that it was then getting 6% net return but that this did not justify the investment.

The general view of those who had investigated HITs was that the desired returns were not obtainable except in low-risk and niche markets and that a significant yield gap existed because of high running costs, high management fees involved in administering indirect vehicles, the way the underlying assets were priced by the owner-occupied market, and the novelty and risk premiums investors required. The latter seemed a crucial barrier, with some who had invested in other ways being resigned to finding it difficult to attract institutional partners until they had demonstrated their returns over a longer period and had built up more substantial portfolios.

Real Estate Investment Trusts: the background and rules

Despite the difficulties the HITs initiative revealed about attracting major City funding into the sector and of creating a new corporate form of private rented ownership, the New Labour government was as committed to this as was the previous Conservative government. Indeed, as we have seen in Chapter 2, very early in the new administration it made it clear that it would not re-introduce rent controls. It announced very clearly that it intended to make no changes to legislation for the deregulated sector or to the general policy objectives about the sector. The first Minister of Housing in the New Labour government also said, in a speech to a conference of private-sector managing agents, that 'real prospects for significant long-term growth depend on attracting the institutions back into the residential lettings market' (Armstrong, 1997). It later stressed its commitment to expanding the corporate sector and to fostering increased investment by major financial institutions, since without them a step-change in the size of the sector was unlikely and they would also bring 'economies of scale, efficiency and quality' (DETR, 2000a, p. 47). Whilst it said that it was willing to consider whether tax measures could help, it also stressed that it did not want to introduce artificial tax breaks that would distort investment choices and that did not tackle the sector's problems. In the meantime its stated intentions (see Chapter 2) to deal with irresponsible landlords would enhance the sector's reputation and hence improve the climate for institutional investment.

Instead of tax breaks,[6] the government adopted the tax transparency route noted in the Barker Report on Housing Supply (Barker, 2003, 2004). This report was commissioned by the government in the context of a growing overall shortage of housing, especially of affordable housing. It suggested that the government should examine the merits of establishing bespoke tax transparent investment vehicles like US Real Estate Investment Trusts (REITs). The attraction is that the REITs themselves pay no tax on their profits. Instead these are distributed to shareholders, who then pay tax accordingly to their own marginal tax liability. Hence a pension fund would pay none, putting tax liabilities for this indirect holding on the same basis as its direct property assets. Likewise, individuals preferring to hold property indirectly through shares and not through direct ownership would pay tax according to their income tax liabilities.

Although the majority of the US residential lettings are owned by individuals and there is comparatively little direct ownership by pension and life funds, residential REITs have been successful residential property companies in the USA. Following a set of tax reforms in 1986 they grew significantly, with investments from both individuals and funds, although more from insurance than pension funds, which tend to favour direct investment. Commentaries suggest that the competitive returns of REITs in the USA derive from their large scale and efficient management. They still account for only a small proportion of residential lettings (1% in the USA), but evidence shows that they are particularly viable on large-scale development sites in growing cities. As well as in the USA, they have also been successful in a number of other countries, for example Australia (see Crook,

2000; Ball, 2004; Ball & Glascock, 2005; Jones, 2007, for reviews). Barker hoped that, if introduced in the UK, they would help expand supply by commissioning new build, and that their long-term investment horizons would ensure they maintained properties and managed them professionally. She also hoped that their long-term investment horizon would promote stability in the housing market because such investors rely less on debt funding than individual landlords and are less exposed to changes in borrowing rates (Barker, 2003).

Although such arguments were not new and had indeed been urged on the government by a number of commissions and lobbyists (see, for example, Urban Task Force, 1999; Shelter, 2002) the status of the Barker report gave added weight to the case. Indeed, the government accepted her recommendation before it came to its conclusions on the rest of the Barker report. In its consultation on what were initially called Property Investment Funds (PIFs), it stated its belief that there was great potential to increase institutional investment through PIFs, to promote better standards, to provide an alternative to the highly geared buy-to-let market and to improve the liquidity of supply, which would help with increasing labour mobility, especially for key workers in areas where house prices were high (HM Treasury, 2004).

Although the initiative originated from a housing review, the property industry then lobbied for it not to be restricted to residential investment but to cover investment for any type of rental income, including commercial property. It had long argued for tax transparency to be applied to all property assets in order to improve liquidity. Double taxation had undermined investment in all forms of property, with many property companies delisting and going private, where they could achieve higher returns through borrowing, whilst many property funds were being held offshore. The government agreed, and in its initial reactions to the Barker interim review it accepted that REITs would improve efficiency and liquidity, thereby lowering the cost of capital for property and generally bring more flexibility to the whole property investment market, whilst also increasing scrutiny, and hence benefits to the UK economy (HM Treasury, 2003). It therefore consulted on the scope for a wider reform of the tax treatment of all property investment and not residential lettings alone (HM Treasury, 2004).

As a review by a House of Lords Committee pointed out, the tax and legal framework for property meant that there was little scope for small investors to buy shares, liquidity was poor, the use of commercial property was inefficient, there were variable standards of provision in the private rented sector, which relied heavily of debt financing and not equity investment, whilst there were also considerable tax distortions in the housing market. It noted that the government believed that the introduction of REITs would address all of these points, but was committed to ensuring that any reform was introduced at no cost to the Exchequer (House of Lords Economic Affairs

Committee, 2009). In general, the view was taken that REITs would benefit the UK economy, making it more competitive and attracting equity investment from overseas, given that many other developed economies already had REIT structures. So what was initially recommended as an initiative to address the needs of private rented housing became a wider reform to improve efficiency and liquidity in the property market generally.

As a previous Conservative minister of housing, referring to tax transparency, said during the second reading debates on the legislation in the House of Commons:

> ... the clauses contain the necessary changes to introduce that measure and I welcome that – it avoids double taxation. However, something has happened in the intervening period that I find very worrying. Instead of housing investment trusts, they are now real estate investment trusts. As I will show in a moment, the emphasis is very much on commercial property and the original idea, if not abandoned, is certainly no longer centre stage. There was never an equivalent argument for REITs for commercial property, compared with residential property. If one wants to invest in commercial property, there are listed property companies and one can do that with great ease. There is no shortage of institutional capital to invest in shops and offices, whereas in many parts of the country, as I said, we need more good quality new accommodation for rent ... The argument that I was developing was that what had been perceived initially as a vehicle for investment in residential property has now become a vehicle for investment in commercial property, where the underpinning argument of the need to increase supply is not so strong ... (Young, 2006).

Following its 2004 consultation on PIFs, the government then sought more specific views on the establishment of REITs, the industry-favoured term for the vehicle (HM Treasury, 2005). Subsequently the Finance Act of 2006 enabled REITs to be formed from January 2007 onwards. The intention was to enable them to closely mirror the nature of direct property investment vehicles with rules on listing, conversion, gearing and profit distribution. REITs must be listed on a recognised stock exchange and they enable full tax transparency, provided at least 90% of rental profits and capital gains are distributed to shareholders within 12 months of the accounting period. The latter are then taxed on this as property income and not as dividends (KPMG, 2007). At least 75% of the profits must be derived from property rental and at least 75% of assets must be in the tax-exempt part of the company (see also HMRC, 2009). The requirement to distribute such a high share of profits was designed to distinguish REITs, as vehicles that delivered returns from managing property, from trading companies that need to re-invest significant proportions of profits in further property development. Thus REITs might not suit companies developing property, although they would provide a vehicle to buy these properties. There are restrictions on borrowing to ensure that interest payments do not reduce profits distributed to shareholders and hence make a tax loss for the government. Unlike HITs (and the BES), there is no maximum limit placed on the type or value of property in which REITs may invest.

During the preliminary consideration of REITs there was a debate about the extent to which their introduction would constitute a loss of taxes without any compensating benefits to the UK economy as a whole. Clearly this would arise if existing (essentially) commercial property companies were able to covert themselves into REITs (they were) and hence the final legislation required them to pay a charge of 2% on the fair market value of their gross assets on conversion as compensation. This charge provided good value to property companies that had built up significant liabilities for tax on capital gains.

Real Estate Investment Trusts: the experience

Since January 2007, many large listed commercial property companies have converted to REITs. On launch, these REITs had £33bn worth of assets and accounted for 73% of the assets of listed property companies (*Estates Gazette*, 2007a). There was initially some limited indication of interest in residential REITs. For example, Invista (owned by the bank HBOS) originally stated an intention to convert to a REIT with £500m of existing assets. Twenty not-for-profit housing associations, including Affinity, Genesis and Sovereign, were also putting together a REIT with £250m from existing unencumbered assets (i.e. those dwellings that had not been funded through government grants) (Jolliffe, 2006).

But the general expectation at the time of writing (early 2010) is that few, if any, new residential REITs will now be launched, with commentators pointing out that net returns are inadequate and that adequately sized portfolios are difficult to source (which, as we have seen, was one of the stumbling blocks in the way of setting up HITs). And, unlike the conversion of existing commercial property companies who have mainly converted to REITs, the few existing residential property companies have not done so because their business models, which depend on significant trading, do not fit the requirements for REITs (Grainger Trust, 2004). Only two of the UK REITs that had been set up by early 2010 had a small element of residential properties within their largely commercial portfolios and no wholly residential REIT had been formed (HM Treasury, 2010).

Indeed announcements in the property press strongly suggested that the fate of residential REITs will be no different from that of HITs. Both the Invista and joint housing association proposals were shelved (*Estates*

Gazette, 2007b). That part of the Invista portfolio of 1518 dwellings, worth £325 m, which had originally been built up from acquisitions from British Land was sold to a large charity, the Wellcome Trust, as part of Wellcome's direct property holdings. Nor was the remaining part of Invista's portfolio, acquired from the Ministry of Defence, to be used to construct a REIT (*Estates Gazette*, 2007c). The principal barriers to residential REITs have been identified as the costs of converting existing companies to a REIT structure, the low gearing that is possible, the high overhead (management and maintenance) costs of running residential portfolios, and the problems of recovering VAT (Owen, 2007). The quality of housing management (but not the costs of it) now seems to be less of a barrier than it was at the time HITs were under discussion, given the development of a number of residential fund managers looking after private funds (BPF, 2003).

In addition, a further disincentive is stamp duty land tax thresholds. Stamp duty is not charged as a constant percentage of transaction prices. Instead there are a series of tiered rates depending on the price. At the time of writing these rates were zero for those under £125 000, 1% for those between £125 000 and £250 000, 3% for those between £250 000 and £500 000 and 4% for those over £500 000. If REITs were to efficiently acquire a portfolio of, say, 100 properties, each worth the average dwelling price in Britain of £237 000 (in quarter 3 of 2009), the value of the total transaction would require stamp duty to be paid at the highest rate of 4% of the transaction price of £2.37 m, i.e. £948 000. If instead, a REIT acquired each of the properties on an individual basis it would only pay a lower rate of 1% on the basis of the value each individual transaction, a total of £237 000 in total for all 100 transactions (but incur the added transactions costs of doing so).

All these difficulties meant that the returns from residential portfolios were simply insufficiently attractive to those seeking income returns, rather than total returns. Investors continued to indicate that they were looking for net income returns of between 6% and 7%, a level of return in excess of the 3–4% that the market had been consistently generating in previous years (HM Treasury, 2010).

Real Estate Investment Trusts: lobbying for reforms

Despite this lack of progress, the government announced a year after REITs were launched that, whilst it was keeping the viability of residential REITs and their listing requirements under review, it did not feel there was a compelling case for change (HM Treasury, 2007). There have been minor changes in the REITs rules in general (for example, mitigating the current gearing restriction on the interest cover ratio, which restricts profits to a ratio of

125% of loan charges and which, if breached, would have led to REITs paying corporation tax on excess financing charges). But there was no change to the fundamental restrictions that lobbyists claim have prevented a residential REIT being launched, including the need to allow income from property sales to be included in the interest cover test, which made it harder for residential REITs to cover interest without sales income than commercial REITs.

In its review of REITs a year after they were launched, the Property Industry Alliance argued that the REIT rules worked well for existing listed property companies who wanted to convert to a REIT by paying the 2% charge on gross assets to do so, but did not work well for the establishment of new residential REITs. It argued for an alignment of the REIT legislation more closely with residential business models to allow some trading to take place, and for amendments to rules on VAT, stamp duty and the limits on borrowing (PIA, 2008). Implicit was the argument that, having agreed with Barker that a REIT structure was needed to foster institutional investment in residential property, the government had responded to the wider commercial property lobby and created a REIT structure that met the needs of that wider lobby rather than those of the residential sector.

Similar but additional arguments came in a Centre for Cities and Smith Institute report, where several of the authors argued that the following changes were needed to enable institutional investment to take place. These included the following: S106 agreements attached to planning consents should oblige developers to provide dwellings for market rental for a period of 15–20 years,[7] allied to a separate-use classes order for private rented dwellings, tax arrangements should be amended to level the playing field between individual and corporate landlords by enabling corporate owners to reclaim VAT payments on management expenses and to be exempted from stamp duty, and residential REITs should be allowed to be established without a stock exchange listing (Bill *et al.*, 2008).

These proposals were very similar to those put forward by the British Property Federation, who at the same time also argued for listing on the Alternative Investment Market, for capital gains rollover relief for those who sold property to a REIT, a reduction from 90% to 80% on the requirement for the proportion of profits that must be distributed and for changing the threshold of properties sold before a business's income would be classed as trading. It also argued that concessions like these should only be granted to landlords who were accredited (BPF, 2008). These proposals were also an echo of some of those made by the All-party Parliamentary Urban Development Group, which was explicitly concerned that an apparent government policy void on these issues made it appear that 'policy across government often supports individual rather than institutional investment', whereas what was required was the long-term commitment that institutional investors would make to the wider management of local communities, essential to safeguarding their investments as well as to the communities themselves (APUDG, 2009, p. 21). A report for the Mayor of London also argued that a modification of the planning consent regime to define a specific use class for private rented housing would reduce land values and improve returns (GLA Economics, 2008). A report from the leading quoted residential company urged that any tax incentives should be tied to registration and membership of industry trade bodies (Grainger Trust, 2008).

The government did not act on these proposals and its decision not to do so has caused much disappointment within the property industry and amongst other lobby groups. In the government's own 2008 review of how far it had got in meeting the targets it had set out in a 2007 Green Paper on housing need and sustainable communities, it reinforced its view that:

> Success in designing a financial model that supports new build designed for a broader private rented market would be an attractive product in the housing market. Such investment models could support more professional approaches to being a landlord and help improve the overall quality of the sector.

It had set up a review of the sector (the Rugg review – see Chapter 8) and would give further consideration to this issue when it had considered any recommendations (CLG, 2008c). But in its later response to the commons select committee's report on the supply of rented housing it appeared to have closed the door to any amendment to the tax regime. The committee had urged investigating the tax reforms necessary to 'promote greater institutional investment in the private rented sector' and to enable the 'greatest possible amount of money to be available for improvement of the supply of rented housing' (House of Commons Committee on Communities and Local Government, 2008, Vol I, p. 113). In its response the government argued that it kept the REIT regime under review but that it was 'not currently clear that changes to the REITs regime would have the desired effect and offer value for money to the taxpayer' (CLG, 2008c, p. 40).

The Rugg review, whilst somewhat skeptical of the arguments for getting more institutional investment to improve management of the sector, nonetheless accepted the arguments of the lobbyists about the changes that would secure more funds and recommended that liability for stamp duty should be disaggregated into liability for the value of individual properties within any bulk transaction and that there should be rollover relief for taxation of capital gains (Rugg & Rhodes, 2008). In its response the government indicated it would await the lessons emerging from the Homes and Communities Agency initiative (see below) before taking any further action and would consider what further support was needed, which would be subject to value-for-money and state aid considerations (CLG, 2009b). However, it decided to consult further on the barriers to investment in the sector as a whole

(HM Treasury, 2010) and indicated that it wanted to create a virtuous circle where a high-quality sector attracts investment that further improves the sector and so attracts further investment (CLG, 2010b).

Meanwhile, there was continued exploration by the industry of other ways of attracting City funding. For example, it was reported that house-builders were exploring joint ventures with their banks, whereby the latter accept dwellings at cost and place them in a joint ventures, with the builders and the banks being joint owners and managers of the rental business (*Estates Gazette*, 2008a). There were also reports that some consideration was being given to setting up REITs to buy 'distressed portfolios', which banks had taken onto their balance sheets during the 2008/09 credit crunch, an echo of the similar use of the BES initiative during the property slump of the early 1990s (*Estates Gazette*, 2009a). There were also reports that some commercial property companies were considering investing in residential portfolios, for example British Land was reported to be contemplating acquiring a small stake in, as well as managing, a proposed £300 m fund to be launched to buy 500 prime London properties with funding from high net wealth individuals (*Financial Times*, 2010). Nonetheless the history of these initiatives is not encouraging and in the past many such proposals have not emerged with funding in place and no development has been undertaken. This suggests that many, if not all, such proposals are still very fragile.

The next step: pump-priming institutional investment

These and similar initiatives reflected the way the industry was seeking other ways of establishing residential funds, but they also reflected the property-market climate. The credit crunch of 2008/09 led to much reduced sales by private housebuilding firms and they and their banks were keen to find ways of keeping their businesses going. At the same time the credit crunch created a larger demand for private lettings, with many first-time buyers having to defer purchase because mortgage lenders were requiring much higher deposits than their current savings can provide, notwithstanding the fall in prices and interest rates. The depressed property market, allied to a higher demand for renting along with stalled private-sector development sites provided a major opportunity for a new government agency operating in England to seek ways of attracting institutional funds into the private rented sector.

In 2008 the Homes and Communities Agency was set up as a merger of the Housing Corporation (which funded housing associations) and English Partnerships (a property-based regeneration agency). The overall state of the property market impacted on the ability of the new agency (HCA hereinafter) to use its funds to support the development of new affordable homes.

For many years most new affordable homes had been built on private-sector sites, with developers being obliged through planning agreements to contribute both land and some funding to their construction. In this way developers met agreed targets that a proportion of what they build had to be for affordable housing. This was usually then acquired by housing associations with the help of private funding but also with grants from the HCA. The credit crunch meant that as private development slowed down so too did the production of the associated affordable homes.

The HCA thus sought new ways of ensuring that developers continued to build out their sites so that they could also continue the construction of the affordable element of the sites. It launched its Private Rental Sector Initiative in 2009 (a so-called 'build-to-let' initiative) whereby it offered to institutions the prospects of access to well-located sites, a pipeline of dwellings, and the possibility of some short-term (five-year) occupancy guarantees (HCA, 2009). It asked for bids, each with minimum funding of £50m, to participate in this initiative, which it had designed to help foster, but not subsidise, the return of institutional investors to the rental market at a time when depressed prices and access to sites and properties potentially offered attractive yields.

If this scale of operation delivers significant operational efficiencies then (just as our earlier analysis of HITs returns had suggested) this should hold the promise of competitive income returns being delivered from high-quality and professionally managed dwellings. Reports in the professional press indicated that the HCA had received 64 expressions of interest, including from overseas funds (*Estates Gazette*, 2009b). It is perhaps not surprising that these major City institutions are considering investing in residential assets at this time. Apart from the attractions of buying at the bottom of a cycle, the credit crunch has also reduced their returns from other assets, including commercial property and equities. Investing in residential assets made good sense for them if they could buy at the bottom of the market and anticipate a long-term earnings-related rise in rental income.

There were thus early signs of a positive outcome. A major insurance company, Aviva (previously Norwich Union), which is the largest insurance group in the UK, announced in the summer of 2009 that it had submitted a bid to take part in the HCA initiative. It planned to set up a fund of £1bn, funded by a 50:50 mixture of equity and debt, to buy newly built and mass-produced properties in south-east England. These were designed to its own brief and were situated on sites near public-transport hubs and on stalled regeneration sites. They would then rent them out, with the management being done by Pinnacle, a well-regarded and large management company from the USA (*Financial Times*, 2009). This business model is not unlike that used by those in the specialist student accommodation market, such as Unite and Opal, who have provided mass-produced apartments with occupation levels underwritten by local universities (see below). Another declared bidder was Legal and General, who indicated that it hoped to be able to build 12 000 dwellings for rent for letting to key workers (*Sunday Times*, 2009).[8]

Potentially this breaks some, although not all, of the barriers we have identified in this chapter, but if it does succeed it will have done so under special circumstances: countercyclical investment at the bottom of the market, allied to support, although not subsidies, from a government agency, and at a time when alternative assets, including commercial property and equities, were earning less than in the past. While these specific circumstances are unlikely to endure (specifically, the HCA support for more than its initial commitment to getting the market going), if this programme takes off, it will have broken another key barrier because City funding of the sector will no longer be seen as quite the novelty it was during earlier efforts, a feature that has bedevilled attempts to secure funding up until now. The so-called 'herd behaviour' of the financial institutions, driven by benchmarking information to allocate their assets, should then tempt more investors into the sector. It is just possible, therefore, that new economic circumstances may succeed in getting institutional funds into the sector, despite the failure of the REITs structure to provide the appropriate investment vehicles. Some sceptics are, however, doubtful that income returns alone will provide an adequate incentive and believe that success will ultimately depend on total returns and hence capital growth returning to the market. However, if good income returns are achieved, long-term investors will be more willing to grant longer-term assured tenancies than small-scale individual investors, who use assured shortholds to safeguard their ability to achieve the required capital gains. This will significantly add to the range of contracts available in the sector and should increase the demand for dwellings owned by institutional investors.

But not all obstacles have been removed. Some feel that the government's decision not to remove the high stamp duty payments on portfolio transactions was a missed opportunity to enable the HCA initiative to get off the ground. So too was its refusal to allow REITs to distribute their profits in equity to shareholders rather than in dividends, a step that would have enabled them to boost liquidity (*Estates Gazette*, 2009c).

In other words the structural problems within the REITs system may ultimately prove a fundamental barrier that specific market circumstances and government agency support will not be able to overcome. A report from the House of Lords Economic Affairs Committee reinforces this view and quotes its witnesses, who argued that the government needed to make the changes needed, such as stamp duty and gearing restrictions, if advantage was to be taken of the opportunities available in 2009 to acquire property (House of Lords Economic Affairs Committee, 2009).

If this proves to be the case, the initial optimism about residential REITs may, just like that which followed the warm welcome. to HITs, prove to be short-lived, notwithstanding the parallel HCA initiative. The government, having said, as part of its response to the Rugg review, that it will await the impact of the HCA initiative before contemplating further action on changes to REITs, may yet need to consider further intervention if the HCA initiative does not fulfil its early promise.

Niche market players

In contrast to the difficulties of establishing funds for the residential lettings market as a whole was the success of two companies in successfully establishing a presence in the student housing market.

Apart from university-owned halls of residence and other university-owned properties, university students have traditionally occupied shared houses owned by individual landlords, one of the subsectors where competitive returns were possible prior to regulation (see Chapter 2). The significant expansion of student numbers in Britain, growing 27% to 2.4 m in the 10 years to 2009, provided both a challenge to universities and an opportunity for investors. The expansion was a challenge for universities, who did not have adequate loan finance to expand their own student housing but who needed to compete with their peers to attract students, with the residences offer being a key factor. It was an opportunity to potential investors if they could enter into agreements with these universities to acquire land to build flats for these students, allied to some form of arrangement whereby universities would steer their students to this new form of accommodation, perhaps involving rental or occupancy guarantees or leasing the properties (both kinds of deals structured to ensured they were off universities' balance sheets).

The Unite Group is the UK's leading developer and manager of student accommodation (http://www.unite-group.co.uk). It started up in Bristol in 1991 and now provides accommodation to 38 500 students throughout Britain. Initially focusing on converting old office block for student flats, its properties are now purpose-built and it manages all its accommodations itself. The accommodation is in ensuite rooms and includes broadband, communal kitchens and shared gyms. It uses modular construction to keep costs down and has initiated its projects through careful involvement with universities and local communities, and through playing an active part in urban regeneration, particularly in the case of universities with urban campuses. It has had a stock exchange listing since 2000 and had a market capitalisation of £149 m in December 2009. It consistently outperformed returns in the IPD pooled funds for all property and in June 2009 was earning a 6.8% net initial yield. An important part of its strategy is the Unite Student Accommodation Fund in which other investors can co-invest and into which Unite Group sells its properties, enabling it to access additional capital for further development. The fund had total assets of £2.5 bn in December 2009.

The Opal Group is another example of the student niche market. Established in 1982, it is a private company with 17 000 bed spaces in its lettings, mainly for students but also for professional and executives in some 'high end' developments (http://www.opalgroup.com). Like Unite it manages its own lettings in-house and its accommodation is self-contained with communal facilities, including gyms and swimming pools. Its portfolio was valued at £1 bn in 2009 and it has debt funding from many of the major UK banks. It has developed close relationships with many universities and has formal partnerships with some of them.

Conclusions

We have seen how two significant initiatives to attract City funding, HITs and REITs, have foundered despite the fact that there was much background work on the concepts and the details from independent commentators and industry lobbyists. Only in limited niche markets were the barriers overcome. Why was this? In Chapter 8, where we set out our conclusions, we offer two main explanations: that the politics of private renting made if difficult for the governments of the day to legislate for structures that fully met the needs of the City and the industry, and that the dominant structure of a cottage industry made it extremely difficult to graft on a new institutional structure. Before we examine these arguments in more detail we first need to examine, in the next chapter, the buy-to-let' initiative, a measure whose success is in stark contrast to the failures of the HIT and REIT initiatives.

Notes

1. We studied 17 of these institutions in 1994, revisiting them in 1998 (and adding an additional 10 institutions to our original panel). They covered the full range of institutions: clearing and investment banks, mortgage lenders, including building societies, life insurance companies, pension funds and fund managers. Some of these were overseas institutions. We also included property consultants (some of whom were also fund managers) and property companies. We interviewed senior staff with the responsibility for investment decisions.
2. Two did set up subsidiaries: Quality Street, funded by Nationwide, and Woolwich Assured Tenancies, funded by the then Woolwich Building Society.
3. Subsequently, a large number of high-rise apartments have been built in such locations, with many of these presold to the buy-to-let market and not to institutional investors (see Chapter 7).
4. A potential fund was launched in November 1997 – the Savills Residential Property Trust – sponsored by Dresdner Kleinwort Benson and intended to raise £80 m from

institutions and borrow an additional £100m in order to create a portfolio of 3300 properties within two years. The fund did not succeed in raising the money it needed and did not proceed.

5. Although the existence of scale economies and benefits of risk diversification have been put in doubt on an a priori basis by some commentators (see, for example, Ball, 2004).

6. Apart from those primarily focused on regeneration, including 100% capital allowances for creating flats over shops and a change to VAT to enable additional conversions of buildings for use as dwellings (see Crook & Hughes, 2003).

7. When developers are seeking planning permission, s106 of the Town & Country Planning Act, 1990 allows local planning authorities to negotiate agreements with developers to oblige them to contribute to the costs of the infrastructure needed to support the development and to make contributions towards new affordable housing needs.

8. Press reports suggested that a handful of major institutions, such as Aviva and Legal & General, were in four front-running consortia being considered by the HCA for participation in this initiative, which may overcome many of the barriers to their investment we also discussed in Chapter 6. To help succour the initiative the HCA was considering ways of linking the initiative with some of its other funding mechanisms, putting in land on an equity basis and keeping open the option of rental guarantees, albeit needing to avoid breaching state aids rules in doing so (Roxburgh, 2009; Lee & Meyler, 2009).

7

The Buy-to-let Boom

We saw in Chapters 5 and 6 that recent Conservative and Labour governments have sought to promote investment in the private rented sector by property companies and financial institutions. While the Business Expansion Scheme did attract a substantial amount of new investment into new property companies, its impact was relatively short-lived. Meanwhile, despite the introduction of new investment vehicles aimed at enticing financial institutions into private residential lettings, no Housing Investment Trusts or (to date) residential Real Estate Investment Trusts have been set up. There has been some investment in the sector by financial institutions such as ING and Aviva (formerly Norwich Union), but this accounts for a very small share of the overall market. Indeed, as we saw in Chapter 4, the proportion of private lettings owned by property companies and other organisations has fallen while the share owned by private individuals has increased.

The growth of the privately rented sector over the past two decades has in fact been driven mainly by individuals and couples operating on a small-scale – 'mom-and-pop' landlords as they are sometimes referred to in the USA. Much of this growth has been fuelled by mortgaged acquisition of properties. This phenomenon has widely been referred to as 'buy-to-let' (BTL) and is the subject of this chapter. It begins by charting the growth of BTL lending by banks, building societies and other mortgage lenders. The second section then examines the main reasons for the unexpected growth in BTL investment by private landlords. The third section considers the nature of BTL landlords, assesses whether the new generation of BTL landlords are any different from their predecessors and addresses several widely expressed concerns about BTL landlords. The final section examines the impact of the global financial crisis on BTL.

Transforming Private Landlords: Housing, markets & public policy, by Tony Crook & Peter A. Kemp © 2011 Tony Crook & Peter A. Kemp

The buy-to-let mortgage market

If the financial institutions were proving highly circumspect about investing in housing to let, that was not true about private individuals. Perhaps the most striking development on the supply side of the privately rented sector at the turn of the century was the re-emergence of leveraged investment in the privately rented sector – often referred to as 'buy-to-let' – by private individuals (Kemp, 2009). In contrast to the top-down government initiatives such as the BES, HITs and REITs, BTL was an industry initiative rather than one promoted by government (Kemp, 2004; Gibb & Nygaard, 2005).

BTL was originally introduced by the Association of Residential Letting Agents (ARLA) and a panel of mortgage lenders in September 1996. It involved the provision of loan finance to moderate and high net-worth individuals wishing to invest in housing to let. Previously, the mortgage lending criteria and products available to landlords were 'strictly limited, relatively expensive and quite inflexible' (Heron & Stevens, 1999, p. 30). Private landlords typically had to pay a premium of around 2% over the mortgage rates charged to owner-occupiers (Kemp, 2004). Under the BTL scheme, however, landlords were charged mortgage rates that were closer to those paid by owner-occupiers. One condition of the scheme was that the borrower had to agree to the property being managed by a member of ARLA, thereby providing the lender with the comfort that the security for the loan was being professionally managed. The advantage for ARLA was that its members would gain extra business, which was particularly important at that time because house prices were beginning to recover and 'property slump landlords' (who entered the sector in the early 1990s housing slump) were at last able to sell their unwanted properties (Kemp, 2004).

In due course, other mortgage lenders that were not part of the official BTL panel of lenders began marketing loans under a 'buy-to-let' label. If these other mortgage lenders also required borrowers to use a managing agent, it was not a condition that was enforced in practice, since some of these BTL landlords did without them. As BLT gained in popularity, it soon came to refer to mortgaged investment in private rental housing (Kemp, 2004). However, in everyday discourse the term 'BTL landlord' is often used more generally to refer to individuals who are private landlords.

BTL has proved to be highly successful business for mortgage lenders. As Table 7.1 shows, there has been a very marked expansion in BTL lending. The number of BTL mortgage loans outstanding increased from only 28 700 in 1998 to 1 156 000 in 2008, an increase of over a million in just 10 years. According to the Council of Mortgage Lenders (CML) many BTL borrowers were private individuals investing in private rental housing for the first time

Table 7.1   Buy-to-let mortgages outstanding at end of period

Year	Number	Value £bn	Percentage of all mortgages by value
1998	28700	2	<1
1999	73200	5	1
2000	120300	9	2
2001	185000	15	2
2002	275000	24	3
2003	417500	39	5
2004	576700	57	6
2005	699400	73	7
2006	835900	93	9
2007	1025700	121	10
2008	1156000	138	10

Source: Council of Mortgage Lenders.

(Pannell & Heron, 2001). The total amount of BTL loans outstanding increased from £2 billion in 1998 to £138 billion in 2008. They accounted for fewer than 1% of all residential mortgage loans outstanding in 1998, but for as much as 10% by 2007.

Hence, after the turn of the century, lending to private landlords had switched from being a very small part of the market to being a substantial outlet for mortgage funds. Indeed, BTL became a separate subsector of mortgage lending, one that involved former building societies such as Bradford and Bingley, Cheltenham and Gloucester, and Northern Rock, major high street banks, including Barclays, Bank of Scotland and NatWest, and new, specialist BTL lenders such as Paragon Group. New mortgage products aimed at BTL investors developed to cater for this growing market. Indeed, by the summer of 2007, several thousand BTL mortgage products were available to investors, from a wide range of lenders.

Not all of the BTL loans in Table 7.1 were for house purchase; many of them involved remortgaging of existing properties. Indeed, between 2002 (when separate data for house purchase loans and remortgaging became available) and 2008, the proportion of new BTL loans that involved remortgaging increased from a third to about a half of the total. However, some of the remortgaging was undertaken to enable landlords to acquire new properties on the back of the rising value of their existing portfolio.

A postal survey of BTL borrowers from 12 lenders active in the BTL market in 2004 found that the most common type of product was interest-only loans. Landlords with more than 20 properties were especially likely to have interest-only loans. As we saw in Chapter 1, this was also true of the mortgages taken out by private landlords prior to the First World War. An important advantage of interest-only loans is that landlords can deduct mortgage interest from their taxable income, which thereby lowers the net cost relative to repayment mortgages. But, of course, interest-only loans by definition do not involve the repayment of principal and hence the full amount of the principal has to be paid when the mortgage comes to an end. As with the homeowner mortgage market, BTL landlords also made use of short-term fixed-rate, short-term discounted-rate and tracker loans (Scanlon & Whitehead, 2005).

The growth of buy-to-let

Why did BTL develop into such a significant market? We examined the demand-side reasons for the growth of private renting in Chapter 3. Here, we focus on the supply-side, drawing heavily on Kemp (2004, 2009). The legislation introduced by the Thatcher government in 1988 (and amended in 1996) was undoubtedly an important factor, for it significantly improved the terms on which private landlords could let their accommodation. As explained in Chapter 2, the 1988 Housing Act had deregulated rents, thereby allowing landlords to charge market rents on new lettings. That legislation also modified the assured and shorthold tenancy arrangements and made it easier for landlords to obtain vacant possession. The latter was important, not just for landlords, but also for lenders because it meant they could get rid of the tenant relatively easily in the event of the landlord defaulting on the mortgage (Rhodes & Bevan, 2003) and sell the property on the open market.

The election of the self-styled 'New' Labour government in 1997 was also important. In particular, it kept its promise to leave the letting framework introduced by the Conservatives in place, thereby minimising the political risk for landlords investing in the rental market. Both the Conservatives and Labour emphasised the importance of private renting and, indeed, a political consensus emerged about the role that private renting could and should play in the modern housing market (Best *et al.*, 1992).

While the 1988 legislation and the political consensus over private renting were important, they were arguably necessary rather than sufficient factors behind the BTL boom. Indeed, these housing policy developments occurred in the 1980s and early 1990s, whereas BTL really took off from the late 1990s and accelerated after the turn of the century. The BTL boom was in fact part of the wider credit and property bubbles that developed in this period in Britain and globally (Kemp, 2009). Here, we focus on those features that were specific to the rental property market.

First, from the mid-1990s, interest rates fell to historically low levels, making it financially viable to borrow money to invest in rental housing for the first time in decades. The reduction in the interest premium for lending to landlords compared with owner-occupiers further reduced the rate at which they could borrow money. As noted in Chapter 1, borrowing money to buy rental property enables landlords to gear up their investments and thereby achieve a higher rate of return (Kemp, 1982). It also enables them to purchase more properties than would otherwise have been possible (Rhodes & Bevan, 2003). Typically, the properties purchased were new or modern flats and to a lesser extent houses, which were seen as having low maintenance costs and the maximum potential for sale (if necessary) to the owner-occupied market. However, some full-time or 'business' landlords invested in older property in need of refurbishment (Rhodes & Bevan, 2003), thereby doubling up as developers in order to maximise the opportunity for capital gain.

Second, the banks began to see the attractions of lending to private landlords when previously they had been relatively circumspect about it and largely focused on lending to owner-occupiers. During the housing market slump of the early 1990s, lenders gained experience of the landlord market. This occurred both when some of their borrowers let their home when they could not sell it, and when lenders took possession of properties of borrowers in arrears and let them for the duration (Crook & Kemp, 1996b). This revealed that mortgage arrears and possessions were often lower than on owner-occupied property and, therefore, that lending to landlords was not as risky as had previously been thought (Kemp, 2004). Meanwhile, the decline in first-time buyers meant that lenders had to find new outlets for their loans. One result of these developments was the emergence of a wider range of mortgage products, including many geared specifically at the needs of private landlords (Rhodes & Bevan, 2003).

Third, financial market deregulation, the relaxation of capital-adequacy requirements by the regulatory authorities and the emergence of new sources of funding on the international capital market meant that mortgage lenders had plenty of money to lend from the late 1990s. These developments also enabled specialists BTL lenders such as Paragon to emerge. Competition among lenders encouraged them to provide new products in order to attract borrowers, including landlords. Mortgage lenders gradually relaxed their BTL lending criteria, requiring lower deposits and reducing the minimum rental cover (the amount by which the anticipated rental income had to exceed the mortgage payments).

As Table 7.2 shows, the average maximum loan-to-value (LTV) ratio offered by CML lenders on BTL mortgages gradually increased from 76% in 1998 to 85% by 2005. Meanwhile, the average minimum amount by which lenders required the rental income to exceed the repayments on BTL loans fell from 30% in 1998 to only 20% by 2007. This relaxation of lending requirements meant that landlords could purchase rental properties with proportionately lower equity stakes. However, higher LTV ratios made them more vulnerable to the risk of future falls in house prices, and reduced rental cover ratios meant that BTL landlords had a smaller cushion of protection against subsequent rises in interest rates or increases in voids.

Table 7.2   Maximum loan-to-value ratio and minimum rental cover on buy-to-let loans

	Maximum LTV (%)	Minimum rental cover (%)
1998	75	130
1999	75	130
2000	78	130
2001	80	130
2002	80	130
2003	80	130
2004	80	130
2005	85	125
2006	85	125
2007	85	120
2008	80	120

Source: Council of Mortgage Lenders.

However, it is important to note that the figures in Table 7.2 are maxima (LTV ratio) and minima (rental cover). In practice, BTL landlords as a whole exhibited a wide range of LTV ratios on their rental portfolios. The 2004 CML survey, for instance, found that two-fifths of BTL borrowers had overall LTV ratios of 50% or less across their portfolio as a whole. Only about a fifth had LTV ratios in excess of 75% (Scanlon & Whitehead, 2005).

Fourth, low interest rates also meant that the returns available on building society and bank deposit accounts were low, thereby increasing the relative attractiveness of property as an investment. Low interest rates also reduced the return on annuities that people are required to purchase when their personal private pension scheme matures, which helped to increase the attractions of rental property as a source of income in retirement.

Fifth, at the turn of the century, the stock market fell for three years in a row, reducing the attractiveness of investment in shares. This highlighted the volatility of the stock market, but also meant that the performance of pension funds deteriorated over this period. Meanwhile, many companies were beginning to switch from final-salary pension schemes into defined-contribution schemes, which carried much more risk for their employees. These developments further increased the attractions of rental property as a way of saving for retirement (Kemp, 2004). Certainly, research has found that some BTL landlords view their property as their pension (Rhodes & Bevan, 2003; Scanlon & Whitehead, 2005).

Sixth, the rapid increase in house prices from 1997 also encouraged many new investors to enter the BTL market. For instance, a survey of BTL landlords in 2004 found that about a quarter of those who had invested in rental property in the previous three years had done so mainly in order to benefit from capital growth (Scanlon & Whitehead, 2005). Rising house prices allegedly resulted in the emergence of so-called 'buy-to-leave' owners buying new flats and keeping them empty in order to re-sell at a higher price (Cobbold, 2007). The fact that they had not been lived in meant that they traded at a premium over new flats that had been occupied. In reality, these investors were not landlords but property speculators (see Kemp, 2004).

While the prospect of capital gains is widely seen as one of the main drivers of BTL investment, some commentators have argued that investment by BTL landlords was pushing up house prices and thereby making it more difficult for potential first-time buyers to become owner-occupiers. In other words, critics have claimed that BTL was, in effect, crowding first-time buyers out of the ownership market, forcing them to rent instead (Sprigings, 2008). Gibb and Nygaard (2005) concluded from their analysis of the Glasgow market that the claim that BTL was crowding out first time buyers was not proven. Meanwhile a study conducted for the Government's National Housing and Planning Advice Unit found that BTL had affected house price inflation, but not by much (7% at most), with factors such as rising incomes, low interest rates, household growth and limited supply being much more important (Taylor, 2008). Thus, at the margin, BTL investors' search for capital gains was to a small degree self-fulfilling in the property bubble up to 2007. However, since rents are more 'sticky' than house prices, the increase in house prices meant that these prospective capital gains were partially offset by declining rental yields (Kemp, 2009).

Are buy-to-let landlords different?

The BTL boom involved a substantial surge of investment in private rental housing in Britain and brought many new landlords into the sector. The large-scale postal survey of BTL landlords sponsored by the Council of Mortgage Lenders in 2004 (Scanlon & Whitehead, 2005) has provided much quantitative information about those landlords who have taken out loans to purchase or refinance their residential property portfolios. Meanwhile, an in-depth, qualitative study provided insights into the thinking of BTL landlords and the strategies that they employ (Rhodes & Bevan, 2003; Rhodes, 2007).

Some press commentators suggested that many BTL landlords are amateur or naïve operators, ill-informed about the lettings market and with only a short-term investment horizon. These assertions implicitly assume that pre-BTL landlords as a whole were more professional and had a longer-term investment outlook and hence were different from those that got involved in the BTL boom. In fact, it has been shown that, even before BTL emerged, private landlords were not necessarily the well-informed, economically rational investors that housing policy and orthodox microeconomic models often assume (Kemp & Rhodes, 1997).

However, the criticisms of BTL landlords do raise the question of whether they are qualitatively different from landlords who entered the market before the BTL boom. We have already shown in Chapter 4 that there were, in some respects, shifts in the *stock* of private landlords in both England and Scotland after the turn of the century when compared with the 1990s. For example, the proportion of properties owned by private individuals had increased and the share owned by property companies and other organisational landlords had declined. Largely as a result of that change in ownership, the average size of landlord portfolios decreased. In addition, by the mid-2000s, private landlords as a whole were more inclined to be investment-orientated and less likely to let their property for non-commercial reasons.

In this section, we explore this issue in more detail, drawing on data from a large-scale representative survey of private landlords in Scotland that we conducted in 2008 (see Crook *et al.*, 2009). For this purpose, BTL landlords are defined as those that first began letting residential property in 2000 or later. We compare key characteristics and attitudes to letting of landlords who first began letting property before deregulation in 1989 with those of landlords who entered the market in the period from 1990 to 1999 and those who became landlords from 2000, when the BTL boom took off in Scotland. Of course, the characteristics of these three groups are likely to differ somewhat because those who continue letting for many years are likely to differ in some respects from more short-term landlords. Thus, by 2008, pre-1989 entrants were by definition long-term landlords. Hence, even if there were no differences between these three landlord cohorts when they entered the market, we could expect to see differences between them by 2008. However, as noted above and in Chapter 4, the stock of landlords did change, so not all of the differences between the three cohorts can be attributed to landlord attrition over time.

One striking characteristic of Scottish landlords in 2008 is that the majority of them were new entrants to the letting business. Indeed, three out of five privately rented addresses in Scotland had landlords who first began letting accommodation after the turn of the century (Table 7.3). In other words, in 2008 the majority of Scottish private tenants were renting their home from landlords whose experience of letting property was relatively brief. Hence, BTL has not only brought many new landlords into the private rental market, but in Scotland at least they also outnumber more longstanding landlords, especially those extant from the regulated era. By comparison, the 1992/93 survey of private landlords in Scotland found that three-quarters of private tenants were renting from a landlord who had not acquired any properties in the previous four years, i.e. since January 1989 (Kemp & Rhodes, 1994).

Table 7.4 shows key characteristics for the three landlord cohorts. It confirms the shift toward private individuals and couples and away from other types of landlord such as property companies. Nine out of ten addresses let by

Table 7.3 Date landlords in Scotland first started letting

Date	%[a]
Before 1989	14
1989 to 1999	23
2000 or later	62
Total	100

[a] The percentages refer to addresses.
Source: 2008 survey of landlords in Scotland.

Table 7.4 Characteristics of landlords in Scotland in 2008[a]

Date landlord first started letting	Pre-1989	1990–99	2000+
*Type of landlord**			
Individual or couple	66	85	92
Other	34	15	8
*How address was acquired**			
Cash or equity	16	26	17
Mortgage or loan	25	59	74
Inherited	33	9	6
Other	26	6	4
*No. of dwellings in portfolio**			
1	13	28	51
2–4	25	37	35
5–19	49	27	11
20 or more	14	8	3
*Business model**			
Full-time landlord	14	10	4
Part-time landlord	86	90	96
*How managed**			
Solely landlord managed	60	55	46
Agent does some tasks	21	19	17
Agent does all tasks	18	26	37
*How landlord regards address today**			
Investment for rental income	15	9	5
Investment for capital growth	10	14	30
Both rental income and capital growth	41	52	38
Future home for self or family	5	13	13
Other	29	12	15

[a] The percentages refer to addresses. Significance: *$p < 0.001$.
Source: 2008 survey of landlords in Scotland.

landlords who first entered the market after the turn of the century were owned by private individuals and couples It is also noteworthy that there has been a feminisation of landlordism in Scotland. In 1992/93, the great majority of private landlords were male: among addresses let by individuals, 81% were owned by men and only 19% by women (Kemp & Rhodes, 1994). But by 2008, the gender profile of private landlords was more equal. Among addresses let by individuals in 2008, 49% were owned by women and 51% by men. This shift, of course, reflects wider changes in gender relations over this period.

One consequence of the BTL boom is that, compared with the 1990s, many more landlords have geared up their investment by purchasing their properties with a mortgage. As Ball (2006b) has pointed out, prior to BTL, private landlords as a whole were substantially under-geared (see Chapter 4 above). In 2008, among addresses let by landlords who first entered the sector after the turn of the century, three-quarters had been purchased with a mortgage or other type of loan. This compared with only a quarter of addresses owned by landlords who first let accommodation before 1989 and who were still doing so in 2008 (Table 7.4).

The downward shift in portfolio size under the BTL boom is also highlighted in Table 7.4. Among addresses let by landlords who entered the market after the turn of the century, half were the sole rental property owned in Scotland by the landlord. In total, six out of seven privately rented addresses were owned by landlords whose total rented portfolio in Scotland was less than five properties. Not surprisingly, there were very few full-time landlords among this group. However, just over half of addresses owned by BTL landlords were managed either wholly or in part by agents. The shift towards investment motives is also confirmed by Table 7.4. It additionally highlights the greater emphasis placed by BTL landlords on capital growth as the primary way in which they expect to get a return on their investment. Capital growth was the main orientation for the owners of about twice as many private rental properties owned by BTL landlords compared with those owned by landlords who first entered the market before 2000.

Even when other landlord characteristics are controlled for, landlords who first entered the market after the turn of the century were significantly different from those who became landlords in the 1990s (Table 7.5). They were

Table 7.5   Logistic regression estimates of the odds of being a post-1999 landlord

	Odds ratios
Bought property with mortgage or loan	1.72
Agent does some/all management tasks	1.41
Property regarded as investment for capital growth	1.84
Portfolio size (comparator = 1 property)	
2–4 properties	0.60
5+ properties	0.20
Base	1063

Significance: $*p = 0.05$, $**p < 0.01$, $***p < 0.001$. Base: respondents who first began letting in 1989 or later.
Source: 2008 survey of landlords in Scotland.

more likely to have bought the property with a mortgage, more likely to regard the property as a source of capital gain, more likely to use an agent to manage the property and less likely to have more than one property in their portfolio.

Finally, BTL landlords appear to be less knowledgeable about the business of letting property than those who became landlords before 1999. When asked whether they agreed or disagreed with ten statements about what it is like to let property nowadays, there were significant differences between the three landlord cohorts in relation to five of them. Table 7.6 shows that, for most of those five statements, higher proportions of BTL landlords neither agreed nor disagreed but instead said they were 'Not sure'. This indicates that a sizable minority of privately rented addresses are owned by BTL landlords who lack knowledge about important aspects of the business in which they have invested money. In that respect, therefore, there is some truth in the claim that many BTL landlords are not well-informed about the lettings market (Crook & Kemp, 1996a; Kemp & Rhodes, 1997).

In summary, this Scottish evidence suggests that landlords who entered the residential lettings market after the turn of the century were different in important respects from those landlords extant from the pre-BTL era. However, this contrast applies to landlords as a whole rather than one between landlords who invested in property with a loan and those who invested without one. A more narrow definition of BTL landlords is 'individuals who first began letting after the turn of the century *and* purchased their properties with a mortgage'. Three-quarters of post-1999 private individual landlords in Scotland bought the sampled address with a mortgage and thus fitted this description. They accounted for two out of five privately rented addresses in 2008.

This raises the question of what distinguishes BTL landlords on this definition with other post-1999 private landlords who did not make use of a

Table 7.6 Landlords who are not sure about selected aspects of letting

	Pre-1989 (%)[a]	1990–99 (%)	2000+ (%)
The law adequately balances the interests of landlords and tenants today	13	12	27
The law allows landlords to charge a reasonable rent these days	13	10	17
Landlords are adequately protected by the law against tenants refusing to leave	18	26	40
Landlords have a lot of disputes with tenants over the return of deposits	20	21	37
Many tenants behave in an anti-social way to other tenants or neighbours	20	13	22

[a] The percentages refer to addresses. Percentages of landlords who agree or disagree with these statements are not shown.
Source: 2008 survey of landlords in Scotland.

Table 7.7   Logistic regression estimates of the odds of having bought the address with a mortgage

	Odds ratios
Female*	0.64
Aged under 45 years***	4.49
Agent does some/all management tasks	1.29
Only one rented property in Scotland*	0.59
Property regarded as investment for capital growth***	4.60
Sideline investor landlord***	0.34
Base	784

Significance: $*p = 0.05$, $**p < 0.01$, $***p < 0.001$. Base: respondents who first began letting in 2000 or later.
Source: 2008 survey of landlords in Scotland.

mortgage to purchase the sampled address. Table 7.7 presents the results of a logistic regression that aims to shed light on this issue. It shows that BTL landlords who geared up their investment with a mortgage were significantly different in several respects from those landlords who did not make use of gearing. Other things being equal, they were less likely to be female, more likely to be under 45 years of age and less likely to have only one rental property in Scotland. They were no more likely to use an agent, but much more likely to regard the property mainly as a source of capital gain.

Buy-to-let and the credit crunch

As with owner-occupied housing, the private rental market was significantly affected by the global financial crisis. The BTL mortgage-lending boom, and the house-price bubble, both came to an abrupt end during 2007 with the onset of the credit crunch and the subsequent economic recession in Britain and overseas. The gross number of BTL mortgage advances reached 176 500 in the second half of 2007 and then slumped to only 44 000 by the second half of 2009 (Figure 7.1). House prices rose continuously from the mid-1990s until 2007, increasing in nominal terms from a trough of £61 643 in the fourth quarter of 1992 to a peak of £199 766 in the third quarter of 2007. Thereafter, the average UK house price fell until the second quarter of 2009, at which point it was £156 930, a decline of 21% in just under two years (Figure 7.1).

The decline in house prices exposed the risky nature of the mortgage lending that took place in the final years of the property bubble. Moreover, in retrospect it is evident that the BTL boom was fuelled by highly leveraged lending by banks and other mortgage lenders, much of it backed by bundles of securitised sub-prime mortgage debt. What is perhaps surprising is that,

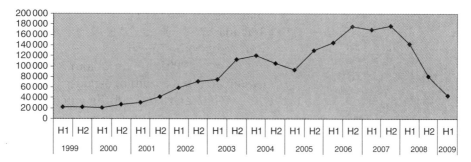

Figure 7.1 Gross number of buy-to-let mortgage advances. Note: H1 is first half of year; H2 is the second half.
Source: Council of Mortgage Lenders.

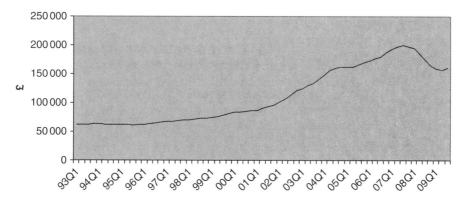

Figure 7.2 Average quarterly UK house price (seasonally adjusted).
Source: Halifax House Price Index.

in the second half of 2005, banks increased maximum LTV ratios and reduced the required minimum rental cover, possibly in response to the decline in BTL lending over the previous year (see Table 7.2). Yet, in the same year, both the OECD and IMF (among others) had warned that house prices in Britain were seriously overvalued. Thus, it was not just borrowers but also lenders that were suffering from 'irrational exuberance' (Shiller, 2008) in the latter part of the house price bubble.

The decline in house prices highlighted the myopic outlook of some highly leveraged BTL landlords and speculators who bought rental properties in the expectation of making short-term capital gains during what turned out to be the latter stages of the house price bubble. In some respects, this behaviour mirrors the sales pitch in many of the early BES rental housing company prospectuses, which emphasised the opportunity for investors to make capital gains, just at the point at which the late 1980s house price boom was turning into a bust. By 2009, significant numbers of BTL

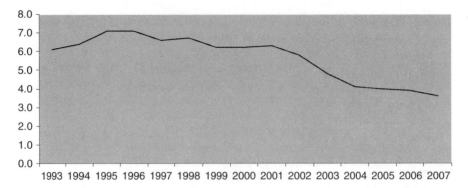

Figure 7.3   Estimated average gross rental yields.
Sources: Survey of English Housing (mean rents for assured and assured shorthold tenancies); Halifax House Price Index.

landlords who invested in rental properties at the average maximum LTV ratio (85%) in the final two years of the house price bubble would have been in negative equity as a result of the 21% decline in average house prices from the third-quarter peak of 2007.

Moreover, the highly leveraged borrowing by a minority of BTL landlords was not confined to only the mortgage advance. The evidence suggests that a significant minority of landlords borrowed money in order to finance their deposit as well. For instance, the 2004 CML survey of landlords who had taken out BTL mortgages with 12 major lenders (Scanlon & Whitehead, 2005) found a variety of sources for the deposit, some of which were not equity. Examples of the latter include bank loans (14% of landlords), remortgaging within the BTL portfolio (43% of landlords) and remortgaging their own home (33% of landlords). While only a very small proportion of these landlords had LTV ratios of 81% or more, some were making highly risky investments that were based on the speculation of continued high levels of house-price inflation.

It seems unlikely that these property speculators (see Kemp, 2004) were investing for long-term rental income. As we saw in Chapter 3, the inflation in house prices in the 2000s greatly outweighed the increase in private rents on assured and assured shorthold tenancies. The result is that average rental yields fell during the house price bubble after the turn of the century (Figure 7.3). By the time house prices peaked in 2007, average rental yields were relatively uncompetitive at around 4%.

Focus groups that we conducted in Scotland with private landlords at the more professional end of the spectrum found that many felt house prices had become too high and thereby eroded rental yields to uncompetitive levels. Hence, they felt that investment in additional properties did not stack up financially. They were somewhat dismissive of what they referred to as

Table 7.8 Buy-to-let mortgages three or more months in arrears

Year	No.	Percentage of BTL mortgages	BTL as percentage of all arrears
1998	200	0.70	0.1
1999	400	0.50	0.2
2000	600	0.47	0.4
2001	1 000	0.55	0.7
2002	1 100	0.40	0.9
2003	1 400	0.33	1.4
2004	2 800	0.54	2.8
2005	4 600	0.65	3.7
2006	4 900	0.58	4.2
2007	7 500	0.73	5.9
2008	26 700	2.31	12.2

Source: Council of Mortgage Lenders.

'buy-to-let landlords', who were buying at such high prices (Crook *et al.*, 2009). Meanwhile, a Shelter survey of 440 members of the National Landlords Association (NLA) found that just over half had expanded their portfolio between 2005 and 2007, about a quarter of whom (12% of all respondents) had expanded rapidly. Landlords who described themselves as 'struggling' financially in the recession were slightly more likely to have expanded during the period from 2005 to 2007 than were landlords as a whole (Reynolds & Smith, 2009).

Scanlon and Whitehead (2005) estimated that about 5% of their BTL sample of borrowers was vulnerable to future interest rate rises owing to high LTV ratios and a high proportion of their debt being at variable interest rates or on short-term discounts or fixes. But interest-rate risk is only part of the story; highly leveraged landlords with high LTV ratios and whose deposit is based on borrowed funds or remortgaging their own home are particularly vulnerable to falling house prices. It is perhaps not surprising, therefore, that when boom turned to bust, and the credit crunch turned into a global recession, that some BTL landlords came unstuck. The fallout in the BTL market included higher levels of rent arrears among tenants as well as increased mortgage arrears and repossessions among landlords. A minority of landlords initially experienced higher voids and rent reductions in some localised areas of oversupply.

BTL mortgage arrears rose to higher levels than among borrowers in the owner-occupier sector, whereas previously it had been the other way around. The number of BTL mortgages more than three months in arrears increased from only 200 in 1998 to 26 700 in 2008 (Table 7.8). Most of this increase took place in the final two years of this period and especially in the second half of 2008. These figures exclude cases where a 'receiver of rent' was acting on the landlord's behalf, which rose sharply from only 500 at the end of

2007 to 7900 a year later. Meanwhile, the number of BTL mortgages taken into possession by lenders trebled, rising from 1100 in 2006 to 3400 in 2008. By the end of 2008, lenders had 2300 BTL-mortgaged properties on their books (CML, 2009a, accompanying data).

An online panel survey of 500 private landlords by BDRC has provided some important insights into their experience of letting property in the 2008/9 recession. In the first quarter of 2009, three out of ten landlords had experienced rent arrears in the previous 12 months. About half were affected by voids, with average void periods being 19 days. Landlords were funding rent lost due to voids from a variety of sources, principally savings (49%), rental income from other properties (36%) and other sources of regular income (25%). However, a minority of landlords were using a credit card or other sources of credit (9%) to cover the shortfall, while others were missing the mortgage payment either with (4%) or without (4%) lender approval. About one in five landlords admitted that they were facing repossession (BDRC, 2009).

Possession action on rental properties had consequences, not only for the landlords and the banks that had lent them money, but also for their sitting tenants. Tenants that had a tenancy agreement were protected in law and could remain in the property for the duration of the lease provided they fulfilled its terms and conditions. But tenants that did not have a tenancy agreement could be evicted by the lender once they had taken possession of the property. The latter was particularly a problem for so-called 'unauthorised tenants', that is, people who were renting from a landlord who was letting the property without the lender's permission, often having originally taken out the loan as an owner-occupier of the property. Even if they had signed a written tenancy agreement, unauthorised tenants could be evicted from their home by the lender in possession (CML, 2009b).

After the crash

The credit crunch severely restricted the availability of mortgage finance in both the owner-occupied and the BTL market. Indeed, the BTL mortgage market more or less collapsed in September 2008, with a very sharp drop in the availability of such products for landlords. Paragon, one of the most prominent specialist BTL lenders, was forced by the lack of wholesale funding to withdraw from the market for the time being. By May 2009, the number of BTL mortgage products was reported to be only 213, compared with 4384 in 2007. Meanwhile, lenders still in the BTL market reduced LTV ratios (and hence required larger deposits) and increased the minimum amount by which rent was required to exceed the mortgage payment. In addition, the spread between mortgage interest rates on owner-occupier and BTL loans increased, as banks now viewed lending to landlords as riskier.

However, by the end of 2009 evidence from a variety of sources suggests that investor confidence was returning to the BTL landlord market. Thus, the 2009 Shelter/NLA survey found that about half of all landlords agreed that the recession was a good time to expand their portfolios and this was especially true of those letting in the housing benefit (local housing allowance) market. Indeed, three out of ten NLA landlords responding to the survey reported that they planned to expand their portfolio in the next 12 months (Reynolds & Smith, 2009). Meanwhile, in the third quarter of 2009 BDRC's panel survey found that landlords as a whole were increasingly optimistic. As with the Shelter/NLA survey, a larger proportion of landlords in BDRC's survey expected to buy than expected to sell properties (in the next three months). The BDRC panel also found that landlords were also increasingly confident about meeting their borrowing commitments. In both the Shelter/NLA and the BRDC surveys, landlords were reported as having benefited from the unusually low level of mortgage interest rates. The overall impression from the BDRC survey was that landlords felt that the worst was over for the private rental market (BDRC, 2009).

CML data on BTL mortgages also started to improve for the first time in two years during the third quarter of 2009. The value of BTL lending and the number of loans both increased by 10% compared with the previous three months. Meanwhile, although BTL-mortgaged properties taken into possession were still rising, the number more than three months in arrears fell by 10% in the third quarter of 2009 (CML, 2009a). At the same time, the BTL mortgage specialist Paragon reported that there had been significant improvement in the wholesale funding market on which they relied to fund their mortgage lending business. As a result, it was expected to resume lending for the first time since its withdrawal from the market in 2007 (Kavanagh, 2009). However, in the immediate future a substantial resurgence of mortgage lending is dependent on recovery in the wholesale funding market.

Conclusion

The emergence and growth of BTL involved a very substantial, but largely unanticipated, resurgence of investment in the privately rented housing sector, which turned into a boom after the turn of the century (Kemp, 2009). This development was facilitated by the changes in the letting framework discussed in Chapter 2 in 1989 and the fine-tuning in 1996. However, the main driver on the supply side was not innovations in landlord–tenant law, but what was happening in the economy and especially the financial markets. The BTL boom was part of, and made possible by, the credit and housing market bubbles that occurred in Britain in the decade up to 2007. These bubbles in Britain and other advanced economies were in turn fuelled by the growth of securitised debt finance and the prevalence of low interest rates over that period. Ultimately, the credit and property market bubbles were related to the global imbalances between creditor and debtor nations (Schwartz, 2009).

While the BTL boom reflected these wider economic developments, it seems likely that the impact of the latter related more to the scale and extent of the boom than the fact that there was a return to mortgaged investment in the private rental market. It might well have happened anyway, but probably on a much smaller scale. However, the evidence presented in this chapter suggests that during the property bubble in the early years of this century, a small minority of what might be described as 'marginal BTL landlords', as well as some speculators, entered the rental market. The marginal landlords were highly vulnerable to investment risk in the privately rented sector and some of them came to grief when the boom turned to bust during the global financial crisis and subsequent recession. Nevertheless, as we discuss in the final chapter, taken as a whole, the new class of BTL landlords is unlikely to disappear anytime soon.

8

Conclusions

In our final chapter we summarise the evidence for the way the cottage-industry nature of landlordism has been reinforced since deregulation, offer explanations for why this happened, consider whether a broader consensus on policy emerged and finally examine whether this new consensus is likely to help overcome the barriers to creating a more modern form of landlordism.

The transformation of private landlords

Since the 1980s governments have sought to create a more market-oriented sector to meet the needs of newly formed and mobile households whilst also creating a more modern landlordism. They hoped that a market-based sector would offer better returns and attract more 'modern' landlords, be better informed about markets (as well as their responsibilities as landlords) and thus be better able than existing landlords to respond to the deregulation opportunities. The growth of corporate landlords funded by City institutions was also desired to bring in the substantial additional investment needed, and to create more stability because they would seek income returns over the long term and provide good-quality and well-managed accommodation. Better management was especially important to New Labour which, as well as continuing the Conservative governments' commitment to a market-based sector, wanted to eradicate substandard accommodation and irresponsible landlords, especially in the light of the continuing way the sector housed some poor and vulnerable households. Although New Labour did not change the legal framework for tenancies

Transforming Private Landlords: Housing, markets & public policy, by Tony Crook & Peter A. Kemp © 2011 Tony Crook & Peter A. Kemp

and rents, it extended and modified the framework for physical and management standards and their enforcement.

Since deregulation in 1989, the sector has grown considerably. It grew steadily from 1989 to 1996 following the effects of deregulation, the property bust of the early 1990s and the temporary stimulation of the BES initiative. It then stabilised in size until the turn of the century, after which it grew significantly, not the least because buy-to-let investors responded to the opportunities afforded by the growth in house prices in the early years of this century. In England the sector's share of total households rose from 9% to 14% between 1988 and 2008, an increase from 1.7m to 3m households. There were some variations between the nations of Britain (for example, growth in Scotland came largely in this century) but the statistics for England illustrate the key point about the sector's substantial growth.

Whilst the aims of creating a more market-based and larger sector were therefore substantially achieved, many of the objectives about transforming the nature of landlordism were not. There was, in particular, a significant growth in ownership by individual landlords, while average portfolio sizes fell. Although a large majority of landlords were new to the market, very few were companies. Many new landlords were not well informed about their rights and obligations. Landlords were getting good total returns because capital gains had been attractive over the period in general, but income returns were generally less competitive. The average standard of accommodation got better due to the injection of existing good stock from other sectors plus, for the first time in many decades, some newly built stock, particularly high-density developments in city centre locations fostered by planning policy and acquired by buy-to-let landlords. Latterly, the sector appeared to have become an important driver of new build homes. While, at the top end, the market worked well and standards improved, in contrast poor quality stock at the bottom end of the market did not.

The sector also failed to attract City funding except at the margin and for niche markets, such as student housing. The specific initiatives to create more corporate landlords did not work as intended. Taking each initiative in turn, the BES attracted significant retail investment in large numbers of small new companies and led to a short-run increase in supply, but there was little long-run net addition in either stock or companies and it came at a high cost in tax expenditure with much tax efficient recycling of existing stock by universities, registered social landlords and of repossessed stock by mortgage lenders, but with little new building for rent. Few of the companies that were then formed have survived. HITs did not attract wholesale investment by pension and other funds into the sector, despite the political risk of making such investments having declined considerably since deregulation. The failure to launch any HITs was partly because full tax transparency for 'gross funds' was not achieved and partly because there were few opportunities to acquire the size of portfolios needed, to ensure they were well managed and to give the income returns required. Despite the greater familiarity of the City with private renting, the new REIT structure has not yet led to any residential investment via these vehicles. Whilst REITs offer full tax transparency there still remain many other barriers.

Whilst some new property companies have been formed and the City has invested in them, they have been small in scale, focused on niche markets and use existing structures that provide less liquidity for investors than the HITs and REITs structures. By contrast, debt funding has, at least until the 2007/08 credit crunch, become more readily available on very attractive terms for small-scale individual buy-to-let landlords, particularly in comparison with the period before deregulation.

Thus, the intended transformation into a more modern form of landlordism did not occur. Rather the opposite happened. This was not necessarily because government policy failed and that deregulation was not a success. It was because deregulation of itself was only a necessary condition for success, not a sufficient one. Many other factors were important and some worked against the modernisation, not the least the way the housing and capital markets evolved following the deregulation of financial markets.

Lessons

Whilst much government policy has therefore succeeded (for example, the overall expansion and the entry of new landlords through buy-to-let which, although not government-sponsored, was nurtured through the wider financial deregulation of the times), the specific initiative to transform ownership and create more large-scale corporate landlords has not so far succeeded. What might therefore explain this apparent failure to modernise the structure of private landlordism in Britain? We offer four lessons, all of which need to be taken into account in any attempts to transform the ownership of the sector: the politics of private renting, the problems of grafting a new ownership structure onto the sector, the wider market context of the attempted transformation and the reliance on the market to address a wide range of policy challenges.

First, the politics of the private rented sector. Despite the growing acceptance of the legitimacy of landlords as part of the supply of housing in Britain and a much more bipartisan approach to the politics of the sector, past debates have continued to haunt policy making. In particular, this appears to make it difficult to develop explicit policies to support private landlords, whether it be through subsidies, grants or the use of tax-transparent vehicles. Unlike other parts of Europe where such support is commonplace, British governments have been wary of introducing legislation newly designed to support landlords. Instead, they have made available, with modifications, measures originally designed for other sectors, like the BES and investment trusts. Whilst these avoided creating custom-built measures, they did not wholly address the sector's needs and had unintended consequences that militated against the desired outcomes.

The BES tax structure was originally designed to incentivise investment in new businesses by substantially rewarding short-term investment (where there was a high risk of failure and a complete loss of investment) and was inappropriate to structuring long-term investment in enduring capital assets such as residential property, where income returns come over the longer run and where implicitly incentivising only short-run capital gains militated against supporting the private rented sector's rejuvenation. In addition, the BES size limits hindered the achievement of scale economies.

The HIT initiative drew on existing investment trust structures and did not meet the full tax transparency needs of gross funds. Moreover, by utilising an existing mechanism it was necessary for the modified HIT form of the investment trust to meet the existing requirements for trusts and also the Stock Exchange's requirements for listing them. These structures, whilst suitable for other trusts, made it difficult for them to work for private rented investment in terms of minimum size, rules on trading and gearing, and the pace of spend required. In the meantime, to ensure value for money in modifying these structures for HITs, capital value rules limited what could be acquired.

When REITs were first mooted (drawing on overseas experience) they appeared to address more of the barriers to City investment in the sector than had the BES and HITs initiatives, and they were explicitly recommended in the Barker report to facilitate investment in new residential vehicles. However, in the course of the long-running consultation on the proposed structures, the powerful lobbying of the commercial property sector led ultimately to a structure which met the needs of the latter far more than the fledgling privately rented corporate sector. In other words, what was originally intended to facilitate the emergence of new residential REITs in fact became a facility for existing property companies to convert to REIT structures. Thus while the subsequent REITs initiative has now introduced tax transparency for indirect investment in the private rented sector this was not, in the end, an initiative aimed solely at private renting because it was aimed at property in general, with the broader intention of creating a more efficient investment market in commercial property and preventing the migration of many taxpaying property funds to offshore tax havens. By introducing REITs in this way, New Labour avoided the potential criticism that it was giving tax breaks solely to private landlords (even though it was only introducing tax transparency). But by avoiding the criticism it did not create a framework conducive to creating brand new residential REITs but rather one that was attractive to existing listed commercial property companies wanting to convert. Despite protestations, the government has been resistant to regular requests from the property industry and others to introduce specific tax changes, such as on stamp duty, to allow residential REITs to get off the ground. It has also been careful to stress the need to ensure that any changes offer value for money to taxpayers.

Thus the use of existing or modified tax structures originally designed for other purposes and industries did not stimulate the long-term growth of new corporate landlords, particularly in the light of the modifications made to secure value for money in tax expenditure Whilst, as we saw in Chapter 2, the regeneration of the private rented sector was a part of the then Conservative government's wider privatisation agenda and New Labour readily embraced the aim of reviving the sector, it was not the key part of either government's housing policies. The failure of BES, HITs and, so far, REITs to work did not risk undermining their wider strategies and did not result in criticism of the government, except at the margin by frustrated lobby groups in the housing and wider property sector. It has probably been seen as unfortunate, at best, within government. Moreover, in introducing the BES to the sector and in designing the HITs and REITs, governments had to take account not only of the wishes of the property industry and the City but the wider issues of introducing tax breaks for private landlords and of value-for-money considerations. Thus in introducing these apparent tax breaks it was necessary to surround them with rules and regulations to secure value for money and also to ensure that they were not used to provide 'upmarket' accommodation. Hence it is, in retrospect, hardly surprising that HITs were not fully tax transparent. There was not only no precedent for this in UK tax arrangements, but had one been introduced it ran the risk of attracting hostile criticism for being uniquely introduced as a way of providing tax breaks for private landlords for whom, as we saw in Chapter 1, there has been long standing antipathy. For the same reasons the initial idea of providing full tax transparency for the private rented sector through REITs then widened out into one for the property industry as a whole, which ensured that it was not uniquely a tax break for the private rented sector. This is ironic given that the journey from BES to REITs via HITs is a journey from tax breaks to full tax transparency, the latter being in principle a much more defendable way of supporting private landlords.

The second lesson concerns the problems faced when grafting a new structure of corporate landlords onto the existing structure of small-scale individual landlords. The conditions were not then in place for this to succeed. HITs and, so far, REITs were attempts to create a new 'structure of housing provision' (Ball, 1981, 1986; Ball & Harloe, 1998). This would have been very different from the existing structure of provision and hence had to be grafted onto the existing dominant structure of small-scale individual landlordism. This existing structure created an environment that did not fit well with the new structure being grafted on to it. Much of the dominant structure used its own 'DIY' resources to manage and do the repairs[1] and appeared to seek capital growth (even more so latterly) as a key element of return as much as (if not more than) income. The dominant provision thus appeared satisfied with low income returns because it ran a low-cost management operation and, so long as rents covered these (low) costs and debt funding, it looked to capital growth to secure investment returns. In so far as the market generated the rents and the capital gains that created this environment, new corporate entrants had to be rent-takers and not rent-setters, unless they could offer a premium or niche product, such as student housing.

Costs of entry for small-scale private landlords were also low and they thrived in this environment. But it is hard to see how new corporate landlords, with higher entry costs (including fund and company set-up costs, due diligence on securing portfolios and the like, and higher transaction costs, including tax, on portfolio acquisition), could so easily have thrived because they were seeking long-term income returns. The companies within this new structure of provision also had to acquire large portfolios in a short space of time. They did not exist during the period of the HITs legislation and new dwellings could not be built fast enough to satisfy the HITs rules. The poor standard of the stock and the poor quality of housing management, allied to the then lack of benchmark information, were all products of the dominant structure, which made it difficult to graft on the new one. This equally applies to the environment within which REITs proposals have, so far, foundered, a point which finds echoes in comments made by senior figures in the Council of Mortgage Lenders and the government's National Housing and Planning Advisory Unit, who argued that small individual landlords have operating costs which no corporate landlords can match whilst also offering an acceptable service to tenants at these low costs (reported in *Estates Gazette*, 2008b; see also Ball, 2004).

The problems in undertaking this 'grafting' were not well understood by those who had lobbied for HITs and also those who lobbied for REITs. It was only when they came to explore specific propositions that these became apparent. Whether the most recent initiatives by the HCA, which we described in Chapter 6, succeed in attracting institutional investment is not yet clear, although the current state of the property market and the levels of demand for private lettings may be making this moment (at the beginning of the second decade of this century) one of the more propitious since the first attempt in 1980 at creating a deregulated market, nearly 30 years ago.

The third lesson from the attempts so far to transform the structure of landlordism is the market context of the wider deregulation of which this was part. The property market cycle after deregulation was much more conducive to small-scale individual landlords than it was to 'corporates'. For example, the initial downturn in the early 1990s led to a growth of 'slump' landlords as owner-occupiers let off property they were unable to sell (Crook & Kemp, 1996b), whilst the subsequent recovery in the market and the much wider availability of cheap credit in the buy-to-let sector created very favourable conditions for speculative purchase of properties for private renting by individuals, mainly with an eye to capital gains. Hence the general property boom of the late 1990s to late 2000s fuelled highly favourable circumstances for the revival of a private rented sector dominated by individual landlords. Deregulation of itself was only a necessary but not a wholly sufficient condition for this. The revival in the early and mid-1990s was steady but not on a large scale. It was the later boom in house prices in the 2000s and the easier availability of cheap loans that created the conditions for the much larger growth in supply. A number of factors made this investment by individuals in physical and not financial assets especially attractive, including the comparatively poorer performance of the equities market and the poor returns from annuities. In particular those looking to annuities and shares for their pensions turned instead to buy-to-let investments. The globalisation of capital markets following their widespread deregulation at the end of the last century and the wider availability of low-interest loans, as those with money to lend sought markets to fund through new forms of structured debt, fuelling the subsequent asset and property bubble (Cable, 2008). This contributed substantially to the growth of private renting in Britain.

Our fourth and final lesson is about the over-reliance on market mechanisms for addressing all problems. Whilst the creation of a more market-oriented approach played a key role in revitalising the sector, some of the assumptions behind the efficacy of markets in producing desirable social as well as private outcomes can be questioned by the evidence. This is particularly the case for the standard of accommodation where our evidence showed that market rents, whilst reflecting tenants' valuation of key attributes such as location and size of accommodation, did not reflect attributes that had long-term impacts on physical standards and the wider neighbourhood consequences of these. Hence the conflict between private and social objectives has been difficult to address within a market framework when grant aid to support better standards has largely been eliminated and local authority staff resources to enforce standards have been stretched (see also House of Commons Committee on Communities and Local Government, 2010).

A broader consensus on private renting?

Despite the desire to modernise private landlordism because of the perceived benefits of doing so, we have seen how the political and market context of the last two decades has instead reinforced the cottage-industry nature of landlordism in Britain. But does this matter? If policy about private renting is to succeed, does it critically require more corporate ownership and City investment? If so, what is needed to make this happen? And is there now more of a consensus than there was at the inception of deregulation, which would potentially enable more long-lasting support to be provided for any emergent City-funded corporate sector?

The need and demand for new dwellings show no signs of abating and estimates show that need has increased in the period since the credit crunch (NHPAU, 2009). The requirement for rented housing is equally undiminished, not the least because mortgage availability following the credit crunch is making it more difficult for young households to buy, whilst the waiting lists for social rented housing are lengthening. The sharp deterioration in Britain's fiscal fortunes following the credit crunch will lead to equally sharp reductions in public capital expenditure on new affordable rented housing over the next decade (HM Treasury, 2009b).

Additional private rented housing will thus be even more important in the future. Rents will continue to rise in line with earnings, providing an attractive investment for institutional investors, whose liabilities are related to earnings growth, at a time when returns from equities and from other property assets have recently been less attractive and more volatile than returns from residential lettings. While demand for assured shorthold tenancies let by individual landlords will continue, new 'build-to-let' investments by those taking a longer-term view could become more important. If the prospects for capital gains are poor and the cost and terms of debt funding for individual landlords are less attractive than in the last decade, fewer buy-to-let investors will enter the market and existing ones may not add to their portfolios. Although there has been some new build since deregulation it is largely limited to niche markets (such as student housing) and city centres, and hence most of the sector's growth has come from transfers of existing stock, mainly from the owner-occupied sector. Encouraging new build for private landlords in the future will thus be crucial if the sector is to help expand overall housing supply. Existing small-scale landlords, focused on buying existing stock, do not have the capacity to engage in new construction, although they may be the customers for newly constructed dwellings.

It is no accident, therefore, that there has been a series of reviews and proposals about the sector from government, trade associations, professional and lobby groups (see for example Shelter, 2002, 2009a,b; BPF, 2006; House of Commons Committee on Communities and Local Government, 2008; Law Commission, 2008; Rugg & Rhodes, 2008; Association of Residential Lettings Agents, 2009; Crisis & National Landlords Association, 2009; Residential Landlords' Association, 2009; Royal Institution of Chartered Surveyors, 2009). Taken together, these reveal that a much broader consensus exists now than for many years, particularly over the three major areas where policy choices will be critical to a successful transformation of landlordism: the role the sector should play, the need for more institutional investment in new building and how this can be secured, and the regulatory environment.

This broader consensus can be seen by comparing and contrasting four milestone reports over the last 30 years. In 1982, before the full deregulation of 1989, evidence to a House of Commons Select Committee revealed distinct differences of opinion about future policy directions (House of Commons Environment Committee, 1982a). Ten years later, shortly after deregulation, a Joseph Rowntree Foundation report identified much more agreement, especially about the role the sector could play (Best *et al.*, 1992). A further decade later, a wide range of tenants and property groups produced a report on the sector's role and regulatory framework. By 2008 the evidence received by a House of Commons Select Committee confirmed the existence of this much broader consensus (Shelter, 2002; House of Commons Committee on Communities and Local Government, 2008).

The role that private renting should play

The private renting sector is now an accepted part of everyday life. Press reports are now much more likely to portray positive images of the sector, indicating how normal it has become. Although private renting is never going to be the dominant tenure again, it is now accepted as having specific and important roles to play.

The specific roles to be played are important. If the sector serves only those with market power it would need minimum regulation, but if wider needs are served, including vulnerable households with little market power, greater regulation may be required. This creates a tension if the degree of regulation to ensure good housing for the vulnerable deters those who would invest to provide high-quality accommodation for the better off. It also requires landlords to have much more confidence in the workings of the Local Housing Allowance scheme.

There is now a general acceptance that the sector will continue to house more than the young and mobile. Shelter, for example, stressed the role the sector plays in housing the vulnerable and that more longer-term accommodation is needed (Shelter, 2007). The British Property Federation saw the sector playing a role in meeting affordable and key-worker housing as well as the needs of those benefiting from the flexibility the sector provides (BPF, 2006).

The 2008 House of Commons report was concerned with improving the conditions of the vulnerable in the worst part of the sector (House of Commons Committee on Communities and Local Government, 2008). The government endorsed this approach in its responses both to this report and to the independent Rugg and Rhodes review (CLG, 2008c, 2009b; Rugg & Rhodes, 2008). It stressed that it wanted a sector providing high-quality accommodation for those who choose not to buy, and a safety net for those who could not access other tenures, striking the right balance between the rights and responsibilities of landlords and tenants. In Scotland, a recent government review of the sector also emphasised the diversity of the sector, wanting it to play a greater role in providing accommodation for homeless households (Scottish Government, 2009).

The need for more institutional investment and corporate landlords

Just as with the broad agreement about the sector's role, so too there is broad agreement on the need for more large-scale corporate landlords with City funding. There are some sceptics. For example, Ball (2004) argued, on *a priori* grounds, that no economies of scale or better risk diversification arose from size. There was therefore no case for deliberately creating large landlords. The Rugg review of the sector was also circumspect about the value of fostering institutional investment and argued for policy to help all good landlords to expand, whatever their size (Rugg & Rhodes, 2008). But most express no such reservations. Shelter, for example, viewed it as a way of getting newly built dwellings into the sector and of providing growth and stability (Shelter, 2002, 2009a). The BPF argued that large landlords can achieve specific objectives that small landlords cannot, including building new supply and driving innovation (BPF, 2006). The 2008 House of Commons Select Committee argued that the prospects for more individual investment were uncertain and that further significant increases in supply required large institutional investors to be attracted back to the sector (House of Commons Committee on Communities and Local Government, 2008).

The New Labour government took a positive stance on institutional investment (CLG, 2009b). The Scottish government was also keen to see a larger and institutionally funded corporate sector and asked the UK government to make taxation changes to encourage institutional investment (Scottish Government, 2009). But new tax and other related measures to achieve this are not yet accepted by the Westminster government, although very widely endorsed by others. We saw in Chapter 6 the kinds of incentives trade and other lobby groups said were needed and three key points are worth reinforcing. First, all professional and housing lobby groups argued that incentives are needed. Crucially this unanimity included a Commons Select Committee and an all-party parliamentary group (House of Commons Committee on Communities and Local Government, 2008; APUDG, 2009). In addition, the housing minister at the time emphasised that the need for more private rented housing required the government to support the introduction of new institutions into the market, including through changes to tax support and incentives (Healey, 2009). Second, many of the arguments were about the fine-tuning needed to get residential REITs off the ground rather than radical surgery. Third, many proposals would benefit all landlords, not just emerging and fledgling REITs. They would help new residential property companies to behave as normal property companies. If they succeed they may in time decide to convert to REITs and thus attract more equity from pension and other gross funds (see a similar argument about HITs in Crook & Kemp (1999)).

In its response to these views, the New Labour government argued that it was keeping all these matters under review, including potential reforms to the REIT regime, but that it was not then clear if the proposals would have the desired effect and offer taxpayers value for money. The Homes and Communities Agency's Private Rented Sector Initiative (see Chapter 6) seemed to be the then government's chosen vehicle for promoting institutional investment in England (CLG, 2009b). However the government also announced that it would further consult on any barriers to investment (HM Treasury, 2009b, 2010).

Regulation and consumer protection

The debate about regulation also shifted significantly. In the past, the state took a command-and-control approach to a large part of the regulatory framework. Despite the change to a more market-based approach to rents and to security of tenure since deregulation, the remainder of the framework retained this command-and-control flavour. This was despite the fact that there have been significant moves towards a more modern form of regulation, with aspects of 'smart' (involving participants), 'better' (more proportionate) and 'risk-based' (focusing where risks are greatest) approaches, for example in the development, respectively, of accreditation schemes, selective licensing and the health and safety rating system (see Chapter 2). This mixture of approaches represented, on the one hand, the legacy of the historical mistrust of landlords and, on the other, the growing non-partisan approaches to the sector (see also Law Commission, 2008).

Command-and-control approaches to standards have problems because they rely on the state having the will and resources to carry out inspections and enforce standards, but our evidence shows that these were rarely available and that local councils faced conflicting priorities so that poor conditions at the bottom end of the sector persisted. In addition, the complexity of regulation, registration, licensing and accreditation systems meant there was much variation, creating often very different requirements and fostering uncertainty and inconsistency for landlords (Jones, 2009). These forms of regulation were primarily framed in terms of legal relationships and ignored the importance of economic and social relationships, particularly important between small landlords and their tenants (Lister, 2007).

In contrast, modern regulation involves participants in its design and delivery on the basis that, if those who are subject to the regulations are involved in their design, self-regulation has a better chance of working than command-and-control. But very few landlords and only about half of all managing agents belong to trade associations or professional bodies. While this makes it difficult to secure standards wholly through self-regulation, partial self-regulation backed by state approval and enforcement now commands much support. Proponents argue that it has a better chance of working than command-and-control and could thus relieve the regulatory burden imposed on landlords. It is also more likely to raise confidence amongst landlords, especially those institutional investors thinking of entering the market for the first time and much concerned to protect their own reputation (Crook & Kemp, 1999; BPF, 2008). If this form of self-regulation leads to greater investment and increases supply it could result in more competition and drive up standards (Law Commission, 2008).

Whilst there were differences between the many organisations which have lobbied and commented on this issue of regulation, there was much in common (see for example Shelter, 2002, 2009a,b; BPF, 2006; Carsberg, 2008; House of Commons Committee on Communities and Local Government, 2008; Law Commission, 2008; Rugg & Rhodes, 2008; Association of Residential Lettings Agents, 2009; Crisis & National Landlords Association, 2009; Jones, 2009; Residential Landlords' Association, 2009; Royal Institution of Chartered Surveyors, 2009).

Most common amongst these authors was an acceptance that there should be a statutory obligation on all landlords to belong to trade or professional bodies (or to use a managing agent in membership of one) that set standards and codes of practice, and that discipline members and provide redress for tenants when members do not comply. Many also argued for a statutory body to act as a 'central regulator' to approve schemes of self-regulation. Others recommended that local councils took on the job of regulator when landlords decided not to join a trade body or use a regulated managing agent. Many proposals fit the concept of better regulation because they enable local councils to concentrate on rooting out the very worst cases of non-compliance rather than with regulating all provision.

Most contested of the proposals was the registration of landlords and their properties and the extent to which they should be licensed. Some were keen to see this implemented, particularly tenants' groups, partly as a means for communicating better with all landlords. Others, however, argued that extending licensing and registration to cover all landlords and properties ran the risk of deterring potential good landlords. All were in favour of the statutory regulation of managing agents, putting them on a par with estate agents.

The New Labour government proposed a national register of private landlords (and their holdings), which they claimed would enable councils to better identify properties, both to deal with substandard ones and to ensure that all landlords get more information about their rights and duties. Landlords persistently in violation of required standards would be removed and existing powers used to take over management of the property. The existing HMO and selective licensing arrangements would continue to operate in parallel with the proposed register (CLG, 2009a). In addition, managing agents would be subject to mandatory regulation by an independent body (CLG, 2009b, 2010b). In Scotland, the Scottish government wanted local councils to make fuller use of their existing register and enforcement powers to tackle the minority of landlords who failed to comply with housing law (Scottish Government, 2009).

Future prospects

Despite the inevitable differences between the views of such a wide range of government, professional, trade and other lobby groups reviewed above, there is quite substantial agreement on many fronts and a much more non-partisan approach to private renting has now emerged. This is not to say that there are no differences at all, but the consensus is much less fragile than in the past and needs to be sustained if a real transformation is to occur.

On the role of the sector there is now quite widespread acceptance that it will continue to house some vulnerable and other low-income households as well as the young and other mobile groups. On the need for creating more corporate landlords with institutional funding, there is substantial agreement that this is desirable, particularly in the changed environment of financial markets after the credit crunch. This will help ensure a continued flow of new investment, especially equity investment, to create a build-to-let market led by those taking a long-term view of their returns and willing to offer tenancies over longer periods. On the appropriate tax and incentive structures, there is significant agreement on the need for these and in particular for the tax structure to be designed to take account of the way mature residential property companies would operate and particularly the need for some initial incentives to enable pioneer investors to take the risks of entering into this still fairly new market. On the issue of regulation, there is broad agreement that no major changes should be made to the legal framework for letting, but a new approach is required to ensure all landlords are made aware of their rights and obligations and that standards are enforced in a proportionate and risk-based manner that does not impose high regulatory burdens on all landlords. There is no dispute that regulation needs to be more effective in driving out poor landlords if the sector as a whole is to thrive.[2]

In the light of these observations, what are the prospects for the future? Earlier in this chapter we identified four lessons from the previous attempts to restructure landlordism in Britain. In the end these reinforced the existing structure of provision due to the lack of supportive politics, the difficulty of adding a new structure of provision, the way the market environment supported short-term investors interested in capital gains and the over-reliance on the market to address the worst conditions. Are prospects different for the next decade?

The political discussion surrounding private renting will need to accept the legitimacy of nurturing the sector on its own merits, and of designing tax and support systems that explicitly reflect the private rented sector's needs and that are not simply adaptations of incentive systems originating in other sectors. It should be easier for government to introduce such changes now than it was in the last two decades for two reasons. First, the need for more investment in private rented housing, particularly 'build-to-let', is now much more widely accepted. Second, there is substantial understanding of the need for incentives across a range of influential bodies. A government introducing such incentives will run much less of a risk of opposition than in the past, arguing that it should not be subsidising (or incentivising) unpopular and poorly performing private landlords. The growing everyday acceptance and experience of private landlords makes this no longer a small and marginal sector. This, combined with the development of a regulatory environment that increasingly embraces smart self-regulation combined with forms of better regulation by the state to police standards and outlaw the worst practices, means that hostility to subsidies and incentives should be less pronounced than in the past, enabling supportive legislation to be more easily introduced. It is important therefore that systems of supporting corporate landlords and systems for rooting out bad landlords go hand in hand. Of course government will still need to address basic questions of value for money in tax and public expenditure but this will be done in a fiscal environment where investment in social rented housing is more likely to be cut than increased. Any fiscal or other incentives (like short-term rent guarantees) may be contingent on landlords offering a mix of long- as well as short-term tenancies and on being members of accreditation schemes and trade bodies that have systems for regulating landlords' conduct and with redress schemes to deal with tenant grievances. Incentives could also be directed towards some form of housing bonds placed by institutions owning rented housing, thus enabling individuals to directly invest in rented housing without requiring them to own it themselves.

Equally important to any successful transformation of the sector is to more carefully graft any new corporate sector onto the existing cottage industry. This requires greater recognition of the long timescale over which a new corporate sector needs to be nurtured. There also needs greater recognition of the different business models (the trading model of individual landlord and the investment model of institutions) in the sector. Unless these are accepted, there is a danger that any new structure will as easily fail as in the past because no adequate account is taken of the way in which new frag-ile corporate structures must be nurtured towards a more mature and thriving existence. Whilst the housing market environment in the second decade of this century suggests there will be a demand for the dwellings that might be provided by institutions at the rents they require to earn long-term income yields, all new 'grafts' require sustained support if they are not to be rejected by the wider body and this suggests that the kind of revenue support currently being discussed by the HCA in its initiative will be necessary for an initial period. If this demonstrates that there is demand at the rents that give good income returns, this will enable the interim support to be removed from the initial investors as other investors then decide to make residential lettings one of their standard asset classes. It also suggests that the taxation changes identified in Chapter 6 to help small companies should also be con-sidered (for example, allowing companies to be able to trade in property as way of maintaining a well-performing portfolio). These will help fledgling residential property companies grow to a size at which they are sufficiently large and profitable to attract equity financing from the major institutions, and at which they will be ready to convert to a REIT to enable such funding to be secured.

The market environment is also likely to be much more conducive to institutional investment than in the last decade. Past evidence suggests that rents will continue to rise in line with earnings and continue to be less vola-tile than capital values. There is likely to be a continuing demand to rent from young earning households, especially given the more restricted avail-ability and more difficult terms of house-purchase mortgages than in the past. Lower capital values are more likely to enable good income returns to be earned on the acquired assets than in the past, whilst the immediate cli-mate at the beginning of this century should allow build-to-let projects to succeed because of lower prices and readier land availability. Insofar as UK monetary policy in the future may be designed to prevent the reoccurrence of asset bubbles like the boom in house prices at the end of the last decade, there is unlikely to be the big increase in new buy-to-let landlords seeking short-term capital gains, but instead a more modest expansion of existing individual landlords, adding to their portfolios and looking at them as long-er-term investments.

Finally the prospects will be further enhanced to the extent that the mar-ket is no longer relied upon solely to address the problems of poor standards in homes occupied by vulnerable and other low-income households. If the policy to remove such property is to succeed, then tough enforcement action will be needed, allied with grants from local councils to make improve-ments profitable or to enable acquisition by local councils or housing asso-ciations where landlords are unable to carry out the work themselves. In a context where an expansion of social rented housing is less likely than in recent years, the use of public funding to secure standards at the bottom end of the private rented sector is crucial to the success of modernising the sector. If not, there is a danger that institutions will fail to enter the sector because of associated reputation risk. It will be ironic if all the proposals to regulate the sector to get rid of the worst conditions fail to achieve this, whilst also adding a regulatory burden on the majority of the sector and without achieving wider benefits.

In our judgement the next few years offer some of the best prospects for the modernisation of the sector for some time. If this happens it will be a slow process and even after two decades institutional landlords will by no means dominate the market, but will sit alongside an increasingly professional and well-managed cottage industry, provided that our four lessons are learned and acted upon.

Notes

1. See Glascock &Turnbull (1994) for a parallel and helpful discussion about the use of 'DIY labour' in the USA.
2. However, the new Conservative government has said that it will not introduce a registration scheme for landlords.

References

All Party Parliamentary Urban Development Group (APUDG) (2009) *Delivering Urban Homes: The Role of the Public and Private Sector*. APUDG, London.

Allen, J. & McDowell, L. (1989) *Landlords and Property*. Cambridge University Press, Cambridge.

Andrew, M. (2006) Housing tenure choices by the young. *Housing Finance*, **7**, 1–13.

Arden, A. (1983) *Manual of Housing Law*. Sweet & Maxwell, London.

Armstrong, H. (1997) Speech by Minister of Housing at the Annual Conference of the Association of Residential Lettings Agents. *Journal of ARLA*, **4**, 5.

Association of Residential Lettings Agents (ARLA) (2009) *ARLA Welcomes the Government's Historic Shift in Thinking on the Private Rented Sector*. Press Notice 13 May.

Austin, I. (2010) *Treasury Deposit Schemes*. House of Commons Written Answer, 5 February. Hansard, London.

Bailey, N. (1999) Deregulating private renting: a decade of change in Scotland. *Journal of Housing and the Built Environment*, **14**, 363–384.

Ball, M. (1981) The development of capitalism in housing provision. *International Journal of Urban and Regional Research*, **5**, 145–177.

Ball, M. (1983) *Housing Policy and Economic Power*. Methuen, London.

Ball, M. (1986) Housing research: time for a theoretical refocus? *Housing Studies*, **1**, 147–165.

Ball, M. (2004) *The Future of Private Renting in the UK*. Social Market Foundation, London.

Ball, M. (2006a) *Markets and Institutions in Real Estate and Construction*. Blackwell, Oxford.

Ball, M. (2006b) *Buy-to-Let Ten Years On*. ARLA, London.

Ball, M. & Glascock, J.L. (2005) *Property Investment Funds for the UK: Potential Impact on the Private Rental Market*. Council of Mortgage Lenders, London.

Ball, M. & Harloe, M. (1998) Uncertainty in European housing markets. In: *European Integration and Housing Policy* (eds M. Kleinmen, W. Matznetter & M. Stephens). Routledge, London.

Ball, M., Lizieri, C. & MacGregor, B.D. (1998) *The Economics of Commercial Property Markets*. Routledge, London.

Banting, K.G. (1979) *Poverty, Politics, and Policy*. Macmillan, London.

Barker, K. (2003) *Review of Housing Supply: Interim Report – Analysis*. The Stationery Office, London.

Barker. K. (2004) *Housing Supply*. HM Treasury, London.

Barnes, Y. (1993) *Beyond Housing Investment Trusts*. Savills, London.

Barnes, Y. (1996) *The Prospects for Large Scale Investment in Residential Property*. Joseph Rowntree Foundation, York.

Benwell Community Development Project (CDP) (1978) *Private Housing and the Working Class*. Benwell CDP, Benwell.

Best, R., Kemp, P.A., Coleman, D., Merrett, S. & Crook, A.D.H. (1992) *The Future of Private Renting*. Joseph Rowntree Foundation, York.

Bibby, P., Craglia, M. & Crook, A.D.H. (2007) A GIS analysis of rent determination in the private rented sector in England. In: *The Private Rented Housing Market: Regulation or Deregulation?* (eds M. Hughes & S. Lowe). Ashgate, Aldershot.

Bill, P., Hackett, P. & Glossop, C. (eds) (2008) *The Future of the Private Rented Sector*. The Smith Institute, London.

Booth, P.A. & Crook, A.D.H. (1986) *Low Cost Home Ownership*. Gower, Aldershot.

Bovaird, E., Harloe, M. & Whitehead, C.M.E. (1985) Private rented housing: its current role. *Journal of Social Policy*, **14**, 1, 1–23.

Bowley, A.L. (1947) *Wages, Earnings and Hours of Work. 1914–1947, United Kingdom*. London and Cambridge Economic Service.

Bowley, M. (1945) *Housing and the State 1919–1944*. Allen & Unwin, London.

British Property Federation (BPF) (2003) *The Barker Review of Housing Supply: BPF Response*. BPF, London.

British Property Federation (BPF) (2006) *Letting in the Future*. Housing Manifesto. BPF, London.

British Property Federation (BPF) (2008) *Relax Investment Rules to Bring More Homes*. Press Notice April, BPF, London.

Business Development Research Consultants Ltd. (BDRC) (2009) *BDRC Landlord Panel Syndicated Research Report*. BDRC, London.

Byrne, D. & Damer, S. (1980) The state, the balance of class forces, and early working class housing legislation. In: *Housing Construction and the State, Political Economy of Housing Workshop*, London, pp. 63–70.

Cable, V. (2009) *The Storm: The World Economic Crisis and What It Means*. Atlantic Books, London.

Cairncross, A.K. (1953) *Home and Foreign Investment: Studies in Capital Accumulation*. University of Cambridge, Cambridge.

Carey, S. (1995) *Private Renting in England 1993/94*. HMSO, London.

Carsberg, B. (2008) *Review of Residential Property: Standards, Regulation, Redress and Competition in the 21st Century*. Royal Institution of Chartered Surveyors, Association of Residential Lettings Agents and the National Association of Estate Agents, London.

Catalano, A. (1999) The essence of Pears. *Estates Gazette* 9th October.

Citizen's Advice Bureau (CAB) (1998) *Unsafe Deposit*. CAB, London.

Cleary, E. J. (1965) *The Building Society Movement*. Elek Books, London.

Cobbold, C. (2007) *What Is the Extent of Buy to Leave Empty?* Paper for CLG Housing and Markets Expert Panel. CLG, London.

Collett, A. & Theakston, I. (1996) Investors HIT residential. *Estates Gazette* 7 December.

Committee on the Rent Acts (Chairman Hugh Francis QC) (1971) *Report*. Cmnd 4609, HMSO, London.

Communities and Local Government (CLG) (2005) *Sustainable Communities: Settled Homes, Changing Lives*. HMSO, London.

Communities and Local Government (2006) *Dealing with 'Problem' Private Rented Housing*. CLG Research Summary 228. CLG, London.

Communities and Local Government (2007a) *Homes for the Future: More Affordable, More Sustainable – Housing Green Paper* Cm 7191. The Stationery Office, London.

Communities and Local Government (2007b) *Evaluating the Impact of HMO and Selective Licensing: The Baseline Before Licensing in April 2006*. CLG, London.

Communities and Local Government (2008a) *CLG Review of Sustainable Communities White Paper*. HMSO, London.

Communities and Local Government (2008b) *English House Condition Survey 2006: Private Landlords Survey*. CLG, London.

Communities and Local Government (2008c) *Government Response to the Communities and Local Government Committee's Report: The Supply of Rented Housing*. Cm 7326. CLG, London.

Communities and Local Government (2009a) *Selective Licensing*. CLG, London.

Communities and Local Government (2009b) *The Private Rented Sector: Professionalism and Quality*. The Government's response to the Rugg Review. CLG, London.

Communities and Local Government (2010a) *Local Powers for Councils to Protect Communities and Improve Standards in the Private Rented Sector*. CLG Press Note, London.

Communities and Local Government (2010b) *The Private Rented Sector: Professionalism and Quality*. CLG, London.

Coopers & Lybrand (1993a) *Fiscal Incentives to Regenerate the Private Rented Sector*. Coopers & Lybrand, London.

Coopers & Lybrand (1993b) *After the Business Expansion Scheme*. Coopers & Lybrand, London.

Coopers & Lybrand (1996) *The Outlook for Housing Investment Trusts*. Coopers & Lybrand, London.

Coopers & Lybrand with Kemp, P.A., Crook, A.D.H. & Hughes, J. (1995) *Private Renting at the Crossroads*. Coopers & Lybrand, London.

Council of Mortage Lenders (CML) (2009a) Press Release, 12 November, accompanying data. CML, London.

Council of Mortgage Lenders (2009b) *Lender Repossession of Residential Property: Protection of Tenants*. CML response to CLG consultation paper. CML, London.

Crisis & National Landlords Association (NLA) (2009) *New Directions for Renting: A New Vision for the Private Rented Sector*. NLA, London.

Crook, A.D.H. (1986a) Privatisation of housing and the impact of the Conservative Government's initiatives on low cost home ownership and private renting between 1979 and 1984 in England and Wales 1. Privatisation policies. *Environment and Planning A*, **18**, 639–659.

Crook, A.D.H. (1986b) Privatisation of housing and the impact of the Conservative Government's initiatives on low cost home ownership and private renting between 1979 and 1984 in England and Wales 4. Private Renting. *Environment and Planning A*, **18**, 1029–1037.

Crook, A.D.H. (1989) Multi-occupied housing: the application of discretionary powers by local authorities. *Policy and Politics*, **17**, 41–58.

Crook, A.D.H. (1991) The regulation and financing of standards in private rented housing. In: *Changing Housing Finance Systems*, Studies in Housing No.3 (ed. M. Satsangi). Centre for Housing Research, University of Glasgow, Glasgow.

Crook, A.D.H. (1992a) Private rented housing and the impact of deregulation. In: *Housing Policy in the 1990s* (eds J. Birchall & M. Gibson). Routledge, London.

Crook, A.D.H. (1992b) The revival of private rented housing: a comparison and commentary on recent proposals. In: *The Future of Private Renting* (eds R. Best, P.A. Kemp, D. Coleman, S. Merrett & A.D.H. Crook). Joseph Rowntree Foundation, York.

Crook, A.D.H. (2000) *The Private Rented Sector and Institutional Investment: Lessons from Overseas*. Submitted to Department of the Environment, Transport and the Regions on behalf of the Joseph Rowntree Foundation in response to public consultation on the Housing Green Paper 'Quality and choice: a decent home for all'. Joseph Rowntree Foundation, York.

Crook, A.D.H. & Bryant, C.L. (1982) *Local Authorities and Private Landlords*. Sheffield Centre for Environmental Research, Sheffield.

Crook, A.D.H. & Hughes, J.E.T. (2001) Market signals and disrepair in privately rented housing. *Journal of Property Research*, **18**, 21–50.

Crook, A.D.H. & Hughes, J.E.T. (2003) *Disrepair in the Private Rented Sector in Scotland: a review of policy options in reserved areas*. Communities Scotland (for the Scottish Executive), Research Report 15, Edinburgh.

Crook, A.D.H. & Kemp, P.A. (1991) Subsidies and private rented housing: lessons from the Business Expansion Scheme. *The Property Journal*, **xvi**, 12–15.

Crook, A.D.H. & Kemp, P.A. (1996a) *Private Landlords in England*. HMSO, London.

Crook, A.D.H. & Kemp, P.A. (1996b) The revival of private rented housing in Britain. *Housing Studies*, **11**, 51–68.

Crook, A.D.H. & Kemp, P.A. (1999) *Financial Institutions and Private Rented Housing*. Joseph Rowntree Foundation, York.

Crook, A.D.H. & Kemp, P.A. (2002) Housing Investment Trusts: a new structure of rental housing provision. *Housing Studies*, **17**, 741–753.

Crook, A.D.H. & Kemp, P.A. with Barnes, Y. & Ward, J. (2002) *Investment Returns in the Private Rented Housing Sector*. British Property Federation, London.

Crook, A.D.H. & Martin, G.J. (1988) Property speculation, local authority policy and the decline of private rented housing in the 1980s. In: *The Private Provision of Rented Housing* (ed. P.A. Kemp). Gower Publications, Aldershot.

Crook, A.D.H. & Moroney, M. (1995) Housing associations, private finance and risk avoidance: the impact on inner cities and urban renewal. *Environment & Planning A*, **27**, 1695–1712.

Crook, A.D.H. & Sharp, C.B. (1989) *Property Dealers, Local Authority Policy and the Repair and Improvement of Unfurnished Private Rented Housing*. Occasional Paper TRP 89. Department of Town and Regional Planning, University of Sheffield, Sheffield.

Crook, A.D.H., Kemp, P.A., Anderson, I. & Bowman, P. (1991a) *The Business Expansion Scheme and Rented Housing*. Joseph Rowntree Foundation, York.

Crook, A.D.H., Kemp, P.A., Anderson, I. & Bowman, P. (1991b) *Tax Incentives and the Revival of Private Renting*. Cloister Press, York.

Crook, A.D.H., Hughes, J.E.T. & Kemp, P.A. (1995) *The Supply of Privately Rented Homes Today and Tomorrow*. Joseph Rowntree Foundation, York.

Crook, A.D.H., Hughes, J.E.T. & Kemp, P.A. (1997) First HITs will face lack of confidence from funders. *Agenda, the Housing Magazine*, **1**, 4–6.

Crook, A.D.H., Henneberry J.M. & Hughes, J.E.T. (1998a) *Repairs and Improvements to Private Rented Dwellings in the 1990s*. Department of the Environment, Transport and the Regions, London.

Crook, A.D.H., Hughes, J.E.T. & Kemp, P.A. (1998b) Housing Investment Trusts and the returns from residential lettings. *Journal of Property Research*, **15**, 229–248.

Crook, A.D.H., Henneberry, J.M., Hughes, J.E.T. & Kemp, P.A. (2000) *Repair and Maintenance by Private Landlords*. Department of the Environment, Transport and the Regions, London.

Crook, A.D.H, Ferrari, E.T. & Kemp, P.A. (2009) *Views and Experiences of Landlords in the Private Rented Sector in Scotland*. Scottish Government, Edinburgh.

Cullingworth, J.B. (1963) *Housing in Transition*. Heinemann, London.

Cullingworth, J.B. (1979) *Essays on Housing Policy*. George Allen & Unwin, London.

Currie,H. (2002) The system of licensing houses in multiple occupation. In: *The Private Rented Sector in a New Century* (eds S. Lowe & D. Hughes). The Policy Press, Bristol.

Damer, S. (1976) *Property Relations and Class Relations in Victorian Glasgow*, Discussion Paper in Social Research No.15. University of Glasgow, Glasgow.

Daunton, M.J. (1977) *Coal Metropolis: Cardiff 1870–1914*. University of Leicester Press, Leicester.

Department for Work and Pensions (DWP) (2002) *Building Choice and Responsibility: A Radical Agenda for Housing Benefit.* DWP, London.

Department for work and Pensions (DWP) (2009) *Supporting People into Work: The Next Stage of Housing Benefit Reform.* The Stationery Office, London.

Department of the Environment (DoE) (1977) *Housing Policy Review, Technical Vol. 3.* HMSO, London.

Department of the Environment (1979) *National Dwelling and Household Survey, 1977.* DoE, London.

Department of the Environment (1987) *Housing: The Government's Proposals.* Cm 214. HMSO, London.

Department of the Environment (1994) *Housing Associations as Managing Agents: The Pilot Schemes.* HMSO, London.

Department of the Environment (1995) *Our Future Homes: Opportunity Choice Responsibility.* Cm 2910. HMSO, London.

Department of the Environment (1996) *Private Sector Renewal: A Strategic Approach.* Circular 17/96. DoE, London.

Department of the Environment, Transport and the Regions (DETR) (2000a) *Quality and Choice: A Decent Home for All – The Housing Green Paper.* DETR, London.

Department of the Environment, Transport and the Regions (2000b) *Quality and Choice: a Decent Home for All, a Housing Policy for England.* DETR, London.

Department of the Environment, Transport and the Regions (2001a) *Developing a Voluntary Accreditation: A Good Practice Guide.* DETR, London.

Department of the Environment, Transport and the Regions (2001b) *Voluntary Accreditation by Private Landlords.* Housing Research Summary 144. DETR, London.

Department of the Environment, Transport and the Regions (2001c) *Private Sector Housing Renewal.* Consultation paper. DETR, London.

Dickens, P. (1978) Social change, housing and the state: some aspects of class fragmentation and incorporation 1915–1946. In: *Urban Change and Conflict* (ed. M. Harloe). Centre for Environmental Studies, London.

Dodd, T. (1990) *Private Renting in 1998.* HMSO, London.

Doling, J. & Davies, M. (1984) *The Public Control of Privately Rented Housing.* Gower, Aldershot.

Donnison, D.V. (1967) *The Government of Housing.* Penguin, Harmondsworth.

Donnison, D.V., Cockburn, C. & Corlett, T. (1961) *Housing Since the Rent Act.* Codicote Press, Welwyn Garden City.

Dorling, D. & Cornford, J. (1995) Who has negative equity? How house price falls in Britain have hit different groups of home buyers. *Housing Studies,* **10**, 151–178.

Down, D., Holmans, A.E. & Small, H. (1994) Trends in the size of the private rented sector in England. *Housing Finance,* **22**, 7–11.

Dyos, H.J. & Reeder, D.A. (1973) Slums and suburbs. In: *The Victorian City, Images and Realities,* Vol 1 (eds H.J. Dyos & M. Wolff), pp. 359–386. Routledge & Kegan Paul, London.

ECOTEC (2008) *Evidence Gathering – Housing in Multiple Occupation and Possible Planning Responses.* CLG, London.

Elliott, B. & McCrone, D. (1975) Landlords in Edinburgh: some preliminary findings. *Sociological Review,* **45**, 553.

Estates Gazette (1995a) Capital ventures to float (7/10).

Estates Gazette (1995b) Auctioneers set to benefit from residential gloom (14/1).

Estates Gazette (1995c) BES properties available for residential investors (28/10).

Estates Gazette (1995d) Trust Homes in on £21m portfolio (24/6).

Estates Gazette (1996a) Johnson Fry net £10m for new type of BES portfolio (14/9).

Estates Gazette (1996b) Pemberstone to raise stake in FRPT (19/10).

Estates Gazette (1997) Pemberstone buys out BES scheme properties (11/12).

Estates Gazette (1998a) City North aims for the market to raise £10m (3/2).

Estates Gazette (1998b) Electra hits houses (25/7).

Estates Gazette (1998c) Pemberstone splashes out (9/5).

Estates Gazette (1998d) Dutch firm sets out on £50m UK investment spree (19/9).

Estates Gazette (1998e) GA benefits as business expands (28/3).

Estates Gazette (2001) ING tipped as favourite to buy at.home portfolio (30/6).

Estates Gazette (2007a) Life as a REIT begins for big property groups (3/1).

Estates Gazette (2007b) Investors snub resi REIT launches (19/5).

Estates Gazette (2007c) Invista sells portfolio after scrapping resi REIT plan. (23/6).

Estates Gazette (2008a) Radical move to revive housing (28/7).

Estates Gazette (2008b) Institutional investors 'not suited' for rental sector (5/2).

Estates Gazette (2009a) Banks may use REITs to offload property debt (18/7).

Estates Gazette (2009b) Global investors race for HCA fund (13/6).

Estates Gazette (2009c) Government amends REIT structure to aid struggling firms (7/7).

Eversley, D. (1975) Landlords' slow goodbye. *New Society*, **31**, 119–121.

Finnis, N. (1977) The private landlord is dead but he won't lie down. *Roof*, **2**, 109–112.

Financial Times (2009) Identical flats seen as way to stimulate sector. 30 July.

Financial Times (2010) British Land to run buy-to-let fund. 13 January.

Forrest, R. & Murie, A. (1988) *Selling the Welfare State*. Routledge, London.

Forrest, R. & Murie, A. (1994) Home ownership recession. *Housing Studies*, **9**, 55–74.

Gibb, K. & Nygaard, C. (2005) The scale and impact of buy-to-let residential investment on local housing markets: evidence from Glasgow, Scotland. *European Journal of Housing Policy*, **5**, 301–326.

Gibb, K., Istephan, N. & Kemp, P.A. (1998) *An Evaluation of GRO Grants for Market Rented Housing*. Scottish Homes, Edinburgh.

Glascock, J.L. & Turnbull, G.K. (1994) On the supply of landlord labour in small real estate rental firms. *Journal of Real Estate Finance and Economics*, **8**, 21–33.

Grainger Trust (2004) *Annual report and accounts*, Grainger Trust PLC, Newcastle.

Grainger Trust (2008) *The English Private Rented Sector in the Twenty First Century: Encouraging Greater Quality and Quantity*. Grainger PLC, London.

Gray, P.G. & Todd, J. (1964) *Privately Rented Accommodation in London*. Central Office of Information, London.

Greater London Authority (GLA) Economics (2008) *Overcoming Barriers to Institutional Investment in Residential Housing*. Working Paper 29. GLA Economics, London.

Green, H. & Hansbro, J. (1995) *Housing in England 1993–1994*. The Stationery Office, London.

Greve, J. (1965) *Private Landlords in England*. Occasional Papers on Social Administration 16. Bell, London.

Hamnett, C. & Randolph, B. (1988) *Cities, Housing and Profit*. Hutchinson, London.

Harloe, M. (1985) *Private Rented Housing in the United States and Europe*. Croom Helm, London.

Healey, J. (2009) Housing after the crunch. Speech by Rt Hon John Healey MP, Minister for Housing and Planning, 9th December. Fabian Society, London.

Heron, J. & Stevens, S. (1999) From deregulation to buy-to-let: developments in the private rented sector. *Housing Finance*, **44**, 27–34.

Hills, J. (1991) *Unravelling Housing Finance*. Clarendon Books, Oxford.

HM Treasury (2003) *Pre-Budget Report*. HMT, London.

HM Treasury (2004) *Promoting More Flexible Investment in Property, a Consultation*. HMT, London.

HM Treasury (2005) *UK Real Estate Investment Trusts: A Discussion Paper*. HMT, London.

HM Treasury (2007) *Pre-Budget Report*. HMT, London.

HM Treasury (2009a) Personal communication to Professors P.A. Kemp and J. Muellbauer from the Chancellor of the Exchequer.

HM Treasury (2009b) *Pre-Budget Report*. HMT, London.

HM Treasury (2010) *Investment in the Private Rented Secto*r. HMT, London.

HM Revenue and Customs (HMRC) (2009) *Guidance on Real Estate Investment Trusts*. HMRC, London.

Holmans, A.E. (1987) *Housing Policy in Britain*. Croom Helm, London.

Holmans, A.E. (1995) Where have all the first time buyers gone? *Housing Finance*, February.

Homes and Communities Agency (HCA) (2009) *Invitation to Submit an Expression of Interest for the Private Rental Sector Initiative*. HCA, London.

House of Commons Committee on Communities and Local Government (2008) *The Supply of Rented Housing*. 8th Report of Session 2007–08. HC 457-I. TSO, London.

House of Commons Committee on Communities and Local Government (2010) *Beyond Decent Homes*. 4th Report of Session 2009–10, HC 60-I. TSO, London.

House of Commons Environment Committee (HCEC) (1982a) Environment Session 1981–1982. *The Private Rented Housing Sector*, Vol. 3 *Memorandum*. HC 40-III. HMSO, London.

House of Commons Environment Committee (1982b) Environment Session 1981–1982. *The Private Rented Housing Sector*, Vol. 1 *Report*. HC 40-I. HMSO, London.

House of Commons Environment Committee (1984) Environment Session 1983–1984. *The Department's Response to the First Report, Session 1982–1983 (HC201)*. HC 221. HMSO, London.

House of Commons Select Committee on Transport, Local Government and the Regions (2001) *Empty Homes*. HC 2401. HMSO, London.

House of Lords Economic Affairs Committee (2009) *Third Report: The Finance Bill 2009*. HL 113-I. TSO, London.

Hughes, D. & Houghton, R. (2007) Accreditation. In: *The Private Rented Market: Regulation or Deregulation?* (eds D. Hughes & S. Lowe). Ashgate, Aldershot.

Hughes, J.E.T. & Madin, J. (1998) An assessment of the long run impact of the Business Expansion Scheme and the prospects for individual investment in privately rented housing in the UK. *Journal of Property Research*, **15**, 35–55.

Hughes, J.E.T. (1999) Happy returns: the individual investors as a source of new capital for rented housing in a time of changing welfare structures. *Housing Studies*, **14**, 507–524.

Inquiry into British Housing (1985) (Chair HRH the Duke of Edinburgh). *Report*, National Federation of Housing Associations, London.

Jackson, A. A. (1973) *Semi-detached London: Suburban Development, Life and Transport 1900–1939*. Allen & Unwin, London.

Jolliffe, A. (2006) Real Estate Investment Trusts: the opportunity for an RSL REIT. *Social Housing*, April, p. 7.

Jones, C. (2007) Private investment in rented housing and the role of REITs. *European Journal of Housing Policy*, **7**, 383–400.

Jones, C. (2009) *Government Review of Regulation and Redress in the UK Housing Market: final report*. Department of Business, Enterprise and Regulatory Reform, and Department of Communities and Local Government, London.

Kavanagh, M. (2009) Paragon targets loan restart. *Financial Times*, 25 November, p. 19.

Kemp, P.A. (1979) *The Changing Ownership Structure of the Privately Rented Sector: a case study of Partick East, 1964 to 1978*, Town and Regional Planning Discussion Paper 17. University of Glasgow. Glasgow.

Kemp, P.A. (1982) Housing landlordism in late nineteenth century Britain. *Environment and Planning A*, **14**, 1437–1447.

Kemp, P.A. (1984) *The Transformation of the Urban Housing Market in Britain C.1885–1939*. DPhil Thesis, University of Sussex, Brighton.

Kemp, P.A. (1987a) The ghost of Rachman. *New Society*, 6 November, pp. 13–15.

Kemp, P.A. (1987b) Some aspects of housing consumption in nineteenth century England and Wales. *Housing Studies*, **2**, 3–16.

Kemp, P.A. (1988a) *The Future of Private Renting*. The University of Salford, Salford.

Kemp, P.A. (1988b) Assured tenancies. In: *The Private Provision of Rented Housing*. (ed. P.A. Kemp). Gower, Aldershot.

Kemp, P.A. (1990) Deregulation, markets and the 1988 Housing Act. *Social Policy and Administration*, **24**, 145–155.

Kemp, P.A. (1997) Ideology, public policy and private rental housing since the war. In: *Directions in Housing Policy* (ed. P. Williams). Paul Chapman Publishing, London.

Kemp, P.A. (2000) Images of council housing. In: *British Social Attitudes 17th Report* (eds R. Jowell *et al.*). Sage, London.

Kemp, P.A. (2004) *Private Renting in Transition*. Chartered Institute of Housing, London.

Kemp, P.A. (2007) Housing benefit in Britain: a troubled history and uncertain future. In: *Housing Allowances in Comparative Perspective* (ed. P.A. Kemp). Policy Press, London.

Kemp, P.A. (2009) The transformation of private renting. In: *Housing Markets and Policy* (eds P. Malpass & R. Rowlands). Routledge, London.

Kemp, P.A. & Keoghan, M. (2001) Movement into and out of the private rented sector in England. *Housing Studies*, **16**, 21–37.

Kemp, P.A. & Rhodes, D. (1994) *Private Landlords in Scotland*. Scottish Homes, Edinburgh.

Kemp, P.A. & Rhodes, D. (1997) The motivations and attitudes to letting of private landlords in Scotland. *Journal of Property Research*, **14**, 117–132.

Kleinman, M., Whitehead, C.M.E. & Scanlon, K. (1996) *The Private Rented Sector*. National Federation of Housing Associations, London.

KPMG (2007) *Taxation of Real Estate Investment Trusts: An Overview of the REIT Regimes in Europe, Asia, the United States and Canada*. KPMG, London.

Lamont, N. (1988a) The business of renting. *Housing Review*, **37**, 195–196.

Lamont, N. (1988b) Second reading debate on 1988 Finance Bill. *House of Commons Hansard*, 15th March. HMSO, London.

Law Commission (2006) *Renting Homes: the final report*. LC312. The Law Commission, London.

Law Commission (2008) *Housing: encouraging responsible renting*. LC312. The Law Commission, London.

Lee, R. & Meyler, H. (2009) Time to turn talk into action. *Estates Gazette* (7/11).

Lipsky, M. (1980) *Street Level Bureaucrats*. Sage Books, New York.

Lister, D. (2007) Controlling letting arrangements in the private rented sector? In: *The Private Rented Housing Market* (eds D. Hughes & S. Lowe). Ashgate, Aldershot.

Maclennan, D. (1978) The 1974 Rent Act – some short run supply effects. *The Economic Journal*, **88**, 331–340.

Maclennan, D. (1985) Urban housing rehabilitation: an encouraging British example. *Policy and Politics*, **13**, 413–419.

Maclennan, D., Gibb, K. & More, A. (1991) *Fairer Subsidies, Faster Growth. Housing, Government and the Economy*. Joseph Rowntree Foundation, York.

Malpass, P. (2000) *Housing Associations and Housing Policy*. Palgrave Macmillan, London.

Malpass, P. & Murie, A. (1999) *Housing Policy and Practice*, 5th edn. Macmillan, Basingstoke.

Marriott, D. (1967) *The Property Boom*. Hamish Hamilton, London.

Mason, C., Harrison, J. & Harrison, R. (1988) *Closing the Equity Gap?* Small Business Research Trust, London.

Melling, J. (1980) Clydeside housing and the evolution of state rent control. In: *Housing, Social Policy and the State* (ed. J. Melling). Croom Helm, London.

Merrett, S. (1979) *State Housing in Britain*. Routledge & Kegan Paul, London.

Merrett, S. (1982) *Owner Occupation in Britain*. Routledge & Kegan Paul, London.

Merrett, S. (1992) *Towards the Renaissance of Private Rental Housing*. Institute for Public Policy Research, London.

Mew, B. (1994) Improving relations and security for investors. In: *Towards a Viable Private Rented Sector* (ed. C.M.E. Whitehead). London School of Economics, London.

Milner Holland Committee (1965) *Report of the Committee of Inquiry into Housing in Greater London*. Cmnd 2605, HMSO, London.

Ministry of Housing and Local Government (MHLG) (1953) *Housing: The Next Steps*. HMSO, London.

Mishra, R. (1984) *The Welfare State in Crisis*. Wheatsheaf Books, Brighton.

Morgan, N. & Daunton, M.J. (1983) Landlords in Glasgow: a study of 1900. *Business History*, **XXV**, 264–286.

Muellbauer, J. (1990) *The Great British Housing Disaster and Economic Policy*. Institute for Public Policy Research, London.

National Housing and Planning Advisory Unit (NHPAU) (2009) *Housing Requirements and the Impact of Recent Economic and Demographic Change*. http://www.communities.gov.uk/nhpau.

Nevitt, A.A. (1966) *Housing Taxation and Subsidies*. Nelson, London.

Offer, A. (1981) *Property and Politics, 1870–1914*. Cambridge University Press, Cambridge.

Office of the Deputy Prime Minister (ODPM) (2002) *An Evaluation of the Pilot Tenancy Deposit Scheme*. ODPM, London.

Office of the Deputy Prime Minister (2003a) *Housing Renewal*. Circular 05/2003. ODPM, London.

Office of the Deputy Prime Minister (2003b) *English House Condition Survey 2001. Survey of private landlords*. ODPM, London.

Office of the Deputy Prime Minister (2005) *Sustainable Communities: homes for all*. Cm 6424, HMSO, London.

Office of the Deputy Prime Minister (2006) *English House Condition Survey 2003. Survey of private landlords*. ODPM, London.

Onslow Committee (1923) *Final Report of the Departmental Committee in the Increase of Rent and Mortgage (Restrictions) Act 1920*. HMSO, London.

Owen, D. (2007) Action needed if Government is to get the resi REITs it wants. *Estates Gazette* 16 June.

Paley, B. (1978) *Attitudes to Letting*. Social Survey Division, Office of Population Censuses and Surveys. HMSO, London.

Pannell, B. & Heron, J. (2001) Goodbye to buy-to-let? *Housing Finance*, **52**, 18–25.

Paragon (2009) *Rent Index*. http://www. paragon-mortgages.co.uk.

Patten, C. (1987) Interview with Mr John Patten, Minister of Housing. *Roof*, **12**, 23–25.

Pearce, B.J. (1983) Private rental housing: prospects and consensus. *Housing Review*, July–August, pp. 117–120.

Peat Marwick (1985) *The Peat Marwick Report on the Business Expansion Scheme: an in depth study*. Peat Marwick, London.

Piven, F.F. (1986) Cities, housing and the rise of 'hypercapitalist' regimes. Paper presented at the *International Housing Conference on City Renewal Through Partnership*, Glasgow, 6–10 July.

Pollard, S. (1969) *The Development of the British Economy 1914–1967*, 2nd edn. Edward Arnold, London.

Property Industry Alliance (PIA) (2008) *UK REITs: Representation by the PIA*. PIA, London.

Piesse, J., Peasnell, K.V. & Ward, C.W.R. (1995) *British Financial Markets and Institutions*. Prentice Hall Europe, Hemel Hempstead.

Price Waterhouse (1989) *Private Renting in England and Wales*. Department of the Environment (DoE) London.

Priemus, H. & Maclennan, D. (1998) The different faces of private rented housing. *Netherlands Journal of Housing and the Built Environment*, **13**, 99–104.

Residential Landlords' Association (RLA) (2009) *Comments on Anticipated Green Paper on Licensing*. Press Release, April. RLA, London.

Rex, J. & Moore, R. (1967) *Race, Community and Conflict: A Study of Sparkbrook*. Oxford University Press, Oxford.

Reynolds, L. & Smith, J. (2009) *The Private Rented Sector in the Recession*. Shelter, London.

Rhodes, D. (1993) *The State of the Private Rental Sector*. Joseph Rowntree Foundation, York.

Rhodes, D. (2007) Buy-to-let landlords. In: *The Private Rented Housing Market: Regulation or Deregulation?* (eds D. Hughes & S. Lowe). Ashgate, Aldershot.

Rhodes, D. & Bevan, M. (1997) *Can the Private Rented Sector House the Homeless?* Centre for Housing Policy, The University of York, York.

Rhodes, D. & Bevan, M. (2003) *Private Landlords and Buy-to-Let*. Centre for Housing Policy, The University of York, York.

Rhodes, D. & Kemp, P.A. (2002) Rents and rates of return in the residential lettings market. In: *The Private Rented Sector in a New Century: Revival or False Dawn?* (eds S. Lowe & D. Hughes). Policy Press, Bristol.

Richardson, H.W. & Aldcroft D.H. (1968) *Building in the British Economy between the Wars*. Macmillan, London.

Ridley, N. (1987) *Conservative Proposals for Housing*. Conservative Party Central Office, London.

Rifkind, M. (1988) *Second Reading Debate on the Housing (Scotland) Bill*. House of Commons, Hansard 9th May, London.

Robertson, J. & Rowe, R. (1993) *Rented Housing after the BES*. Joseph Rowntree Foundation, York.

Robertson, J. & Rowe, R. (1996) *The Outlook for Housing Investment Trusts*. Coopers & Lybrand, London.

Rose, A. (1998) US fund makes a £3m splash. *Estates Gazette* 11 April.

Rose, A. (1999) Bankers Trust swoops on BES portfolio with JV. *Estates Gazette* 29 May.

Roxburgh, H. (2009) HCA chief reveals four step plan to boost private rental sector. *Estates Gazette* 19 September.

Royal Institution of Chartered Surveyors (RICS) (2009) *Housing Policy: Private Rented Sector*. RICS, London.

Rugg, J. (1997) *Closing Doors: Access Schemes and the Recent Housing Benefit Changes*. Joseph Rowntree Foundation, York.

Rugg, J. & Rhodes, D. (2008) *The Private Rented Sector: Its Contribution and Potential*. Centre for Housing Policy, The University of York, York.

Rugg, J., Rhodes, D. & Jones, A. (2002) Studying a niche market: UK students and the private rented sector. *Housing Studies*, **17**, 289–303.

Saul, S.B. (1962) House-building in England, 1890–1914. *Economic History Review, 2nd Series*, **XV**, 119–137.

Scanlon, K. & Whitehead, C.M.E. (2005) *The Profile and Intentions of Buy to Let Investors*. Council of Mortgage Lenders, London.

Schwartz, H.M. (2009) Housing, global finance and American hegemony. In: *The Politics of Housing Booms and Busts* (eds H.M. Schwartz & L. Seabrooke). Palgrave Macmillan, Basingstoke.

Scott, P. (1996) *The Property Masters. A history of the British Commercial Property Sector*. E and FN Spon, London.

Scottish Government (2004) *Mandatory Licensing of Houses in Multiple Occupation – Guidance for Licensing Authorities*. Scottish Government, Edinburgh.

Scottish Government (2006) *Guidance Notes for Local Authority Officers Involved in the Delivery of Private Landlord Registration*. Scottish Government, Edinburgh.

Scottish Government (2007) *Firm Foundations: The Future of Housing in Scotland: A Discussion Document*. Scottish Government, Edinburgh.

Scottish Government (2008) *Repairing: Standard Advice Pack for Landlords*. Scottish Government, Edinburgh.

Scottish Government (2009) *Role of Private Landlords*. Press Notice 24 March, Speech by Minister of Housing Alex Neil.

Shelter (2002) (and the Joseph Rowntree Foundation) *Private Renting: A New Settlement. A Commission on Standards and Supply*. Shelter, London.

Shelter (2007) *Fit for Purpose? Options for the Future of the Private Rented Sector*. Shelter, London.

Shelter (2009a) *Shelter's Response to the CLG Consultation: The Private Rented Sector – Professionalism and Quality*. Shelter, London.

Shelter (2009b) *A License to Rent? How Regulating the Private Rented Sector can Mean a Better Deal for Tenants, Landlords and Taxpayers*. Shelter, London.

Shiller, R.J. (2008) *Subprime Solution*. Princeton University Press, Princeton NJ.

Soley, C. (1991) Labour signals U turn on private landlords policy. Reported in *The Independent* 24 May, London.

Sprigings, N. (2007) *Housing Market Renewal: pathfinders and the buy-to-let housing market*. Report of national evaluation to the housing market renewal programme. CLG, London.

Sprigings, N. (2008) Buy-to-let and the wider housing market. *People, Place and Policy on Line*, **2**, 76–87.

Stafford, B. & Doling, J. (1981) *Rent Control and Rent Regulation in England and Wales 1915–1980*. Occasional Paper No. 2, New Series. Centre for Urban and Regional Studies, University of Birmingham, Birmingham.

Stafford, D.C. (1976) The final economic demise of the private landlord. *Social and Economic Administration*, **10**, 3–14.

Stanley, J. (1982) Evidence of Minister of Housing to the House of Commons Select Committee on the Environment Sessions 1981–1982. *The private rented housing sector*, Vol. *2 Evidence*. HC 40-II. HMSO, London.

Sunday Times (2009) The smart money is on buy-to-let. 10 May.

Swenarton, M. (1981) *Homes for Heroes: the Politics and Architecture of Early State Housing in Britain*. Heineman, London.

Taylor, R. (2008) Buy-to-let mortgage lending and the impact on UK house prices. NHPAU Research Findings 1. http://www.communities.gov.uk/nhpau.

Thomas, A. D. (1986) *Housing and Urban Renewal*. George Allen & Unwin, London.

Thomas, A. & Snape, D. (1995) *In From the Cold. Working with the Private Landlord*. DoE, London.

Thomas, A.D. & Hedges, A. (1986) *The 1985 Physical and Social Survey of HMOs in England and Wales*. HMSO, London.

Thomas, R. (2006) The growth of buy-to-let. *Housing Finance*, **9**, 1–14.

Thomas, W.A. (1978) *The Finance of British History*. Methuen, London.

Todd, J.E. & Foxon, J. (1987) *Recent Lettings in the Private Rented Sector 1982–1984*. HMSO, London.

Todd, J.E., Bone, M.R. & Noble, I. (1982) *The Privately Rented Sector in 1978*. HMSO, London.

Treble, J.H. (1971) Liverpool working class housing 1801–1851. In: *The History of Working Class Housing: A Symposium* (ed. S.D. Chapman). David and Charles, Newton Abbott.

Urban Task Force (1999) *Towards an Urban Renaissance*. Department of Environment, Transport and the Regions, London.

Weber, B. (1960) A new index of house rents for Great Britain, 1874–1913. *Scottish Journal of Political Economy*, **VII**, 232–237.

Whitehead, C.M.E. (1978) Private landlords in London: who stays, who goes? *CES Review*, **4**, 48–52.

Whitehead, C.M.E. (1979) Why owner occupation? *CES Review*, **7**, 37–50.

Whitehead, C.M.E. (1994) Economic flexibility and the private rented sector. *Scottish Journal of Political Economy*, **45**, 361–375.

Whitehead, C.M.E. & Kleinman, M. (1986) *Private Rented Housing in the 1980s and 1990s*. Granta, Cambridge.

Whitehead, C.M.E. & Kleinman, M. (1988) Capital value rents: an evaluation. In: *The Private Provision of Rented Housing* (ed. P.A. Kemp). Gower, Aldershot.

Whitehead, C.M.E., Kleinman, M. & Chattrabhutii, A. (1995) *The Private Rental Housing Market: A Review of Current Trends and Future Prospects*. Council of Mortgage Lenders, London.

Wilding, P. (1973) The Housing and Town Planning Act 1919. *Journal of Social Policy*, **2**, 317–334.

Williams, P. (1976) The role of institutions in the inner London housing market. *Transactions of the Institute of British Geographers*, New Series, **1**, 72–82.

Young, G. (2006) *Speech in Second Reading Debate on Finance Bill 2006*. House of Commons Hansard 24 April. HMSO, London.

Index

Transforming Private Landlords: Housing, markets & public policy, by Tony Crook & Peter
A. Kemp   © 2011 Tony Crook & Peter A. Kemp